HERESIES EXPOSED

HERESIES EXPOSED

A Brief Critical Examination in the Light of the Holy Scriptures of some of the Prevailing Heresies and False Teachings of Today.

Compiled by

WM. C. IRVINE

Editor, THE INDIAN CHRISTIAN

LOIZEAUX BROTHERS

Neptune, New Jersey

First Edition as *Timely Warnings* 1917
Second Edition as *Modern Heresies Exposed* 1919
Third Edition as *Heresies Exposed* 1921

Thirty-seventh Printing, September 1980

Published by LOIZEAUX BROTHERS, Inc.

A Nonprofit Organization, Devoted to the Lord's Work and to the Spread of His Truth

ISBN 0-87213-401-6
PRINTED IN THE UNITED STATES OF AMERICA

Table of Contents

TABLE OF CONTENTS

TABLE OF CONTENTS

AN ALLEGORY

I was walking along the streets of Vanity Fair the other day and had my attention drawn to a huge edifice which was in the course of construction. Apparently there was a strike on, as something had happened greatly to hinder the work. On enquiring what was the trouble, I was told that there was a dispute among the workmen. The men were holding a meeting, and as anyone was admitted, I went inside out of curiosity.

Some had returned to their work, others were divided in opinion as to what was best to be done. It seemed that some were in fear that the building might fall, saying that some of the workmen were tampering with the foundations; the others were laughing them to scorn, vehemently asserting that their friends were but resetting the foundations: which, they said, had never been truly laid.

On further enquiry I found out that the building was called the CHURCH, and that the workmen were divided into two camps which some called "Fundamentalists," and "Modernists." The great fear of the former was that the latter would remove the foundations, and on examining the damage already done I was persuaded that there was much reason for alarm.

I found several of the huge foundation-stones partly out of place. Indeed, one on which I had deciphered the words:—

"The Virgin Birth"

was more or less broken, and almost entirely removed from its place: if moved a little more a great part of the building would be in jeopardy. Another had an inscription which was partly obliterated by the workmen's tools; it read—

" . . spir . tion of . oly Scrip . . re"

A third which appeared to me to be the chief corner-stone was being vigorously attacked with pick and crowbar; it bore the words—

"The Deity of Christ"

I drew the attention of some of those destructive workmen, many of whom appeared to be scholars, to a notice the builder had left nearby. It read:—

**If the FOUNDATIONS be destroyed,
what can the righteous do?**

But they scoffed at me, and muttered something about "Progress" and "Modern Building Methods,' and fell to with greater zeal than ever. I turned away sad in heart, feeling that this beautiful building was doomed.

But as I was about to step out into the street, a young man in shining garments touched me on the shoulder, and gave me a letter from the Builder of the edifice, bidding me read it. I broke the seal and read:

"NEVERTHELESS THE FOUNDATION OF GOD STANDETH SURE" and "I WILL BUILD MY CHURCH; AND THE GATES OF HELL SHALL NOT PREVAIL AGAINST IT."

Much comforted by these words I passed on.

WM. C. IRVINE.

INTRODUCTION

To the TENTH EDITION

BY LOUIS T. TALBOT, D.D.

"If any man shall say unto you, Lo, here is Christ, or there; believe it not. For there shall arise false Christs, and false prophets, and shall show great signs and wonders; insomuch that, if it were possible, they shall deceive the very elect" (Matt. 24: 23, 24).

The great prophecies contained in the Olivet Discourse were uttered by the Lord prior to His crucifixion on Calvary. As He sat on the Mount of Olives, where in the future His feet shall stand in the day of His manifestation, He prophesied concerning the destruction of the magnificent temple building, and His disciples questioned Him, saying, ""Tell us when shall these things be? And what shall be the sign of Thy coming and of the end of the age?" (Matt. 24: 3, R.V., *margin*).

In answer to their questions, the Lord, looking through the years to the consummation of the age, pointed out certain unmistakable signs by which believers were to know when the age was drawing to a close. He saw kingdom rising against kingdom, and nation against nation. He heard the sound of war and rumors of war. He saw pestilence and earthquake, Bolshevism, Communism, anarchy, lawlessness. He saw a time of trouble, the like of which has not yet been known, a time which He called "the great tribulation." He spoke plainly concerning these matters in order that the believers in every age might be fully instructed.

Among these conditions and events the Lord warned His disciples concerning the religious conditions that would prevail in the end time. "False Christs, and false prophets, shall arise," He declared. So great will be their delusions at that time that "if it were possible, they shall deceive the very elect."

The Holy Spirit, coming on the day of Pentecost, heralded through Paul, Peter, James, and John, and the other inspired writers, the same warning, making it known that toward the end of the age the great foundational truths of the gospel will be denied. The word "*Denial*" will characterize the religious condition of Christendom when those closing days become reality. Let us observe several instances wherein this is evidenced.

1.—There will be a denial of God and the Saviour.

> "For there are certain men crept in unawares, who were before of old ordained to this condemnation, ungodly men, turning the grace of our God into lasciviousness, and denying the only Lord God, and our Lord Jesus Christ" (Jude 4).

2.—There will be a denial that Jesus Christ has come in the flesh.

> "And every spirit that confesseth not that Jesus Christ is come in the flesh is not of God: and this is that spirit of antichrist, whereof ye have heard that it should come; and even now already is it in the world" (1 John 4: 3).

3.—There will be a denial of the Lord "that bought them," referring to the *Atonement*.

> "But there were false prophets also among the people, even as there shall be false teachers among you, who privily shall bring in damnable heresies, even denying the Lord that bought them, and bring upon themselves swift destruction" (2 Pet. 2: 1).

These false teachers may possibly acknowledge Jesus as a man, but deny His purchase of mankind, and His redemptive work through the blood, as does the Unitarian philosophy today.

4.—There will be a denial of the power of godliness.

> "This know also, that in the last days perilous times shall come. For men shall be lovers of their own selves, covetous, boasters, proud, blasphemers, disobedient to parents, unthankful, unholy, without natural affection, trucebreakers, false accusers, incontinent, fierce, despisers of those that are good, traitors, heady, highminded, lovers of pleasures more than lovers of God; having a form of godliness, but denying the power therof: from such turn away" (2 Tim. 3: 1-5).

5.—There will be a denial of sound doctrine, and the substitution of *fables*.

"For the time will come when they will not endure sound doctrine; but after their own lusts shall they heap to themselves teachers, having itching ears, and they shall turn away their ears from the truth, and shall be turned unto fables" (2 Tim. 4: 3, 4).

6.—There will be a denial of authority.

"Likewise also these filthy dreamers defile the flesh, despise dominion, and speak evil of dignities" (Jude 8).

Our imagination may be occupied with applying these conditions to China or India, bound by heathenism, but the Scripture reveals that these warnings and descriptions apply to professing Christendom at the end of the age:

"Now the Spirit speaketh expressly, that in the latter times some shall depart from the faith, giving heed to seducing spirits, and doctrines of devils; speaking lies in hypocrisy; having their conscience seared with a hot iron" (1 Tim. 4: 1, 2).

The perilous hour to which the Lord Jesus and the Holy Spirit referred is upon us. There has never been a time in which there was such a tendency to depart from the faith as there is in the present days. *Spiritualism,* or better named, *Spiritism,* founded by the Fox Sisters: *Mormonism,* founded by Joseph Smith; *Russellism,* founded by Pastor Russell; *Theosophy,* founded by Madame Blavatsky; *Seventh-day Adventism,* founded by Ellen G. White; *Christian Science,* founded by Mary Baker Eddy, and *New Thought,* are a few of the deceptive cults that have come in recent years in the name of Christ. Other philosophies, cults and beliefs are: *Unity, Anglo-Israelism, The Oxford Movement* and *Modernism.*

A careful study of these false systems results in the conclusion that there is a master mind behind every one of them, a master mind so well schooled in human nature that he has adopted and projected systems covering the entire field of experience, thought and longing. That master mind is Satan, the deceiver. The purpose and one outstanding aim of Satan is to defeat the plan and purpose of God in the salvation of men. He is thoroughly acquainted with the fact that the only remedy for sin is the atoning work of Christ, and he is aware of the fact that regardless of how beautiful a religious system might be, it is absolutely of no avail as a saving power if the atoning work of Christ is eliminated from its teaching. Therefore, his plan in deluding people is to present to them religions that will acknowledge God, exhort man to be good, kind, and sweet, and couple with those beliefs ceremonies which will appeal to the imagination, but which will avail nothing because of their neglect and absence in recognizing Jesus Christ, the Saviour, and His redemptive work on Calvary. To Paul these things were made known:

> "For such are false apostles, deceitful workers, transforming themselves into the apostles of Christ. And no marvel; for Satan himself is transformed into an angel of light" (2 Cor. 11: 13, 14).

The days in which you and I are living are days in which Christians need to know their Bibles, for the only way by which we may know whether or not a system of teaching is of God is by viewing the system through the lens of Holy Writ—*reading the system in the light of the Bible and not reading the Bible in the light of the system.*

Because of the crying need of Biblical light on these erroneous teachings, I gave a series of addresses in the Church of the Open Door, on *"The Cult Kingdom,"* selecting ten of the most damaging heresies for discussion. When people saw them revealed in the searchlight of God's Word a large number of men and women, held in their grip, were mercifully delivered.

This created a wide-spread interest among God's children, culminating in a demand for the printing of these addresses so that others, caught in the meshes of false doctrine, might also find freedom.

I was about to comply with this request when I discovered a book compiled by William C. Irvine, called "HERESIES EXPOSED." This book completely covers not only the ten cults I exposed, but many others, so instead of publishing my addresses I have arranged with the writer to allow me to print this special edition of his excellent work. By so doing we meet the demand of friends for this material and provide my radio audience with another valuable book.

PREFACE

To the Eighth Edition

Shortly after the seventh edition of *Heresies Exposed* was printed a re-print was called for, and that now being sold out an eighth edition has been printed.

In this edition will be found some new articles. We draw the readers' attention to Dr. W. B. Riley's paper on *Atheism,* Dr. W. H. Pettit's on *Evolution* and the Editor's on *Buchmanism.* Other articles have been touched up, and in order that the cost of the volume should not be increased, the articles *Sinless Perfection* and *The Fatherhood of God and Brotherhood of Man* have been deleted.

In the Preface of our last edition we gave as a definition of heresy: "Some theory tenaciously held, but not in subjection to the authority of Scripture." That definition should be borne in mind by the reader.

The following, culled from *The Witness,* seems to us very apt and to the point:—

Although God rent the veil and thereby abolished the whole system of animal sacrifices, which now became merely "the Jews' religion" (Gal. 1: 13), yet we know that the rent veil was joined up again by the priests, and the Jewish sacrifices were persisted in for more than thirty years. Still from the altar, abandoned, and left "desolate" by Christ, the smoke from the sacrifices of the sin offering rose slowly and forlorn to Heaven. It rose in vain. And still the high priest entered the holiest once each year and sprinkled the blood on the mercy-seat. Yet that blood appealed to God in vain. For already "Christ our Passover is sacrificed for us" (1 Cor. 5: 7). At last God, in righteous anger, blotted out the whole mocking system, at the destruction of Jerusalem by Titus, when the temple was burned, and the Jewish sacrifices were for ever abandoned.

But that joining up of the veil by the Jewish priests, and the consequent excluding of men from God is typical of what has been done since, so many times, in so many ways. ALMOST EVERY HERESY, in its last analysis, does just this, *it interposes a veil between needy man and a waiting God,* which hinders or prevents communion. The historic Roman Church, with its mediatorship of Mary, erects exactly such a veil. And all the vestments and trappings of ceremonialism, all that panders to a sensual religion, these all are man-made obstacles which tend to distract the worshipper, and detract from the One worshipped, and so to hinder that free and spiritual communion of the humblest believer with God Himself to which we are here invited by the Spirit. Ought we not "to obey God rather than man?" (Acts 5: 29).

In Acts 6: 7 we read: "And a great company of *the priests* (our italics) were obedient to the faith."

We submit that the rent veil and later patched up by their fellow-priests, was one of the main reasons (if not the main one) why "a great company of the priests were obedient to the faith." In *Heresies Exposed* we endeavor to show up the various veils which the different cults seek to interpose between the believer and his God. They are but patched veils, but as such they hide the way to God, and keep the worshipper from entering the "holiest" *through the rent veil,* which is his right as taught in Hebrews 10: 19-22.

"Let us hold fast the profession of our faith"—which in the Scriptures of Truth has been once for all delivered to the saints—"without wavering: (for He is faithful that promised)"—Heb. 10: 23.

It is with the hope and prayer that this volume will aid many of our fellow-Christians to hold fast the profession of their faith *without wavering*—despite the many "false teachers" and their teachings, which the Apostle Peter inspired by the Spirit of God warned us would appear among us (2 Peter 2: 1)—that this new edition of *Heresies Exposed* is launched.

WM. C. IRVINE.

Belgaum, India.

AGNOSTICISM

By A. McD. Redwood

" 'The natural attitude of a thinking mind toward the supernatural is that of skepticism'—skepticism, not agnosticism. The skeptic halts at the cross-roads, to take his bearings; but at the sight of a cross-road the agnostic gives up his journey altogether. True skepticism connotes intellectual caution, but agnosticism is intellectual suicide." With these words Sir Robert Anderson opens one of his chapters in his *In Defence,* a book which we commend to everyone who suffers from mental doubts.

What is Agnosticism?

In the words of Professor Alexander Stewart, it is "the name by which those designate their position who do not *deny the existence* of God, the future world, and other doctrines of religion, but declare that we do not, and *cannot, know* anything about these subjects, and should therefore leave them out of account." Agnosticism denies that there is a revelation, and therefore denies the Bible. In effect, the agnostic is neither logical nor philosophical, for, whilst he acknowledges there is a God, he will not allow that God can reveal Himself to the creatures of His own hands. "The Agnostic recognizes the facts of nature and the duties of life: of these he admits we have a knowledge sufficient for all practical purposes, though even here there are deep problems which remain unsolved; but because he cannot solve *all* deep problems with regard to God, he will not admit that we have even a practical knowledge of Him — a knowledge to be gained by inference from the facts of nature and the constitution of man, even if we leave that given by Revelation out of account. Agnosticism is thus essentially inconsistent and untenable whenever it goes beyond the declaration that there is much in relation to God which our intellects cannot apprehend."

Such a half-way position, with atheism on the one side denying the very existence of God, and skepticism on the other side endeavoring to find the way (as Paul says: "If haply they might find Him"), although it be but a feeling one's way in the dark, is surely only possible to those who *refuse* to know and are wilfully blind. One can have much patience with the honest doubter, the man with sincere intellectual difficulties, who is willing to make use of even a rush-light if it will but lead him in the way of Truth. But no amount of argument will avail for the one who deliberately rejects; his agnosticism is with him a "creed," a "creed" of illogical ignorance.

An Appeal

This article is not so much an exposure as an appeal, and that to the former class. Agnosticism has done its own exposing; it stands self-condemned in the eyes of all honest minds who have themselves made honest search and found the Way. Now, our appeal is—Will you search and find? Christianity declares with no equivocal challenge that "God hath spoken unto us by His Son." The Son Himself has said: "I am THE WAY, THE TRUTH and THE LIFE." And He has further laid down His principle, and a truly scientific principle at that, fully in accord with the modern scientific method, by which we may arrive at a clear knowledge of Truth, of Himself. This is given in John 7: 17: "If any man will *do* His will, he shall know of the doctrine, whether it be of God, or whether I speak of Myself." You are in doubt as to whether God can and does reveal Himself to the human heart; you are in doubt as to whether Christ Jesus is the manifestation of God and His love to man? Right! Then there, in the few words quoted above, you will find a method of testing it for yourself. You believe in the existence of God, somehow, somewhere. Act on that belief. *Do* His will and you *shall know*. He has pledged Himself to do His part, if you will do yours. "But," you answer, "what is His will? How shall I find it out?" My answer is this: In nature everywhere we see the evidence of His power and of His workings; but in the Bible we see His will and His love. "But how do I know that?" you ask. Test it. Here is the commandment, the will of God, as given in His Word: "This is the commandment,

That we should *believe* on the name of His Son Jesus Christ," and again, "This is the will of Him that sent Me (the Son), that everyone which seeth the Son (by faith) and believeth on Him, may have everlasting life: and I will raise him up at the last day" (1 John 3: 23; John 6: 40). You don't believe the Bible? Never mind, for the moment; test those words practically; receive Jesus Christ into your heart by an act of simple faith, believing Him to be true to His Word, asking Him to open your eyes that you may see and know Him. Keep asking, sincerely and persistently, and — YOU WILL KNOW! "Really?" Absolutely certain! God does not lie, He is not a gamester, He is God! And He wants you to know and to love HIM, for He knows and loves YOU!

Anybody tried this way before you? Literally thousands, a host innumerable. Here is a sample of one who thus found Christ, taken from J. F. Clarke's booklet, *Does God reveal Himself to men?* It tells of the conversion of H. Musgrave Reade, for twenty years, not merely an agnostic, but an out-and-out atheist, nevertheless an honest thinker, as recorded in his own book, *From Atheism to Christ*:

A Testimony

I read eagerly Strauss' *Life of Christ*, in which he contended that the Gospel account was on a par with the mythology of ancient Greece and Rome, and that Christ was simply a myth, probably taken from the Hindu God Krishna. Then I readily drank in Renan's *Vie de Jésus*, with its beautiful, but soul-destroying picture of Christ, neither divine, nor human, neither the Son of God, nor a truly noble and good man. Fichte, Hegel, Schopenhauer, and a host of German metaphysicians then captivated my fancy, and I was soon in the vain imaginings of idealism, transcendentalism, and pessimism, and thus blossomed into a philosophical deist. Auguste Comte, with his Positivist Philosophy, then attracted my attention; his plausible theory of science and religion gained many adherents, mainly through his attempts to spiritualize freethought into a religion. The Religion of Humanity was the cult, and its devotees were asked to worship an abstraction, that is, to elevate the idea of the whole humanity, past, present, and to come, into a grand being, to be reverenced and worshipped. Professor Huxley aptly termed it Catholicism minus Christianity. These, in turn, gave way to more extreme critics and opponents of Christianity. Rousseau, Voltaire, Volney, Paine, and others, were eagerly sought for, and the tenets of Christianity were insidiously uprooted from my mind. I became what is termed a Freethinker (why a rejecter of Christianity should have the monopoly of this title I have never been able to understand). The transition from this phase was greatly facilitated by a course of studies in the realm of science, in which I was introduced to the works of Buchner, Haeckel, Darwin, Tyndall, Huxley, etc., and imbibed the doctrines of evolution—this completed the work, and left me a materialistic atheist.

While in this state of mind Reade met Charles Bradlaugh, Mrs. Annie Besant, Dr. Edward Aveling, and other prominent atheists, and became himself an anti-Christian propagandist. In 1882 he became Secretary of a branch of the National Secular Society of which Charles Bradlaugh was president, and in 1892 he was one of the seven men who formed the Independent Labor Party. In 1900 he was appointed by his employers to undertake a long journey in America, and in this connection he visited sixty-two of the largest towns and cities in the United States. The various sights witnessed and the many cities through which he passed deeply impressed him, and formed the first link in the chain of evidence of the existence of God. In his own words the memorable journey and its consequence are thus described:—

An Agnostic Convinced

What, then, was the result of this experience to me? Was it by mere accident that I was allowed to undertake this journey? No. I am fully convinced that it was God's merciful providence that ordained this as His method of drawing me to Himself, with the ever-unfolding panorama that came before me as I was travelling over those thousands of miles, coming into contact with all the races of mankind—black, red, yellow and white-skinned people. Now on the wild prairies of the West, then across the wonderful, awe-inspiring canyons of the Colorado, up 14,000 feet on the snow-capped Rockies, across sandy deserts for hundreds of miles, amongst the Red Indians of New Mexico, mixing with the cow-boys of Arizona, into the beautiful scenes of California, then the sights of China-town, with its 50,000 Chinese, and amongst the negroes in their log cabins.

All this had its deep influence upon my mind unconsciously, and it eventually resulted in the revelation of God to me as a Personal Being, knowing and loving the creature He had made. The hour of the revelation drew nigh. I was in the train, slowly climbing the wonderful Rocky Mountains. We had reached an altitude of 10,000 feet. We had left Colorado 90 degrees in the shade, and here we were passing through snow-capped pinnacles, where eagles were sweeping past us as the train slowly labored up the heights. The panorama to a city man brought up amidst the bricks and mortar of Manchester, was overwhelming. Here I beheld a wonder cataclysm of nature. The "Royal Gorge" some three miles deep, lay on one side of the rails over which we were passing, and we were now on the edge of a precipice, and again mounting up to another peak until we reached the highest point. At this altitude the train climbed so slowly that all the passengers left the car, and I was alone. I sat in a reverie gazing at the spectacle, whilst I began instinctively feeling about, so to speak, in my mind for an explanation of these wonders. The first defined thought was, Surely all this is not the result of fortuitous circumstances, blind chance, matter and force or, as we glibly say, "a concourse of fortuitous atoms!" Something else than the atomic theory must account for all these wonders. Could "evolution" explain it all? Evolution can give a plausible case to us whilst we are studying nature in our chamber amongst our books, but the immediate contact with nature herself, in all her rugged beauty, speaks to us of the existence of a higher power than ourselves. Insensibly I found my mind was undergoing a change; an irresistible feeling of wonder, awe, and reverence crept into my thoughts. I had ever been an honest seeker after truth, and the thought suddenly flashed into my mind—Might I, after all, have been mistaken? I felt I must face the question. I fell on my knees, and cried, "O God, if Thou dost exist, reveal Thyself." I asked for *light* and it came like a flood! The whole car seemed full of light. It was the veil torn off my mind by the Spirit of God. I felt that I was in the presence of God, and I capitulated without a struggle. I who had resisted so long His gracious pleadings, who had rebelled against His authority so many years, was at last brought into submission. I arose from my knees filled with joy, saying, "GOD IS!" There had come to me "that Light which lighteth every man that cometh into the world" (John 1: 9). There could be no "association of ideas," as some would say, to account for this, for as I fell on my knees I had in my hand one of Ingersoll's books which I had been reading. The *sudden* change simply meant that the Spirit of God had come into my life, in spite of my resistance, without my seeking, and without the help of man or books, and I knew that I beheld the glory of *God* and His wondrous works! Oh, what a revelation and a revolution of ideas, what joy and peace to know the unfathomable love of God! Was I dreaming, or ill with the fever? Nay, neither; I never felt better in health than at that moment. ***It was my first realization of the Personal Presence of God.***

But although the great discovery had been made, months passed before he came into possession of the new life.

An Agnostic Converted

On his return to England, a Bible was at length purchased and carefully studied, and the joyful news comprehended that there is a new life or salvation to be had through trusting Christ

The new life brought with it, not only great joy and peace, but an earnest desire to spread the good news to others. Having tasted that the Lord was good I yearned to let other blind souls know this great joy, but I soon found out to my surprise that they did not want to know about this "good thing of God." They did not wish to be disturbed, they were quite comfortable in their sin and blindness. I marvelled greatly that they could spurn such love, that the blessed news of Christ's love to sinful men would meet with such a cold response: but I remembered my own sad case, how blind and perverse I had been for twenty years.

Moreover, innumerable witnesses could be produced, not only from amongst those who have written, but from those whom we know.

We have seen changes wrought in the lives of individuals that nothing short of divine power could effect — changes certainly not the result of the cherishing of high ideals, intellectual culture, mesmeric influences, or sentiment. We have seen these changes effected in individuals possessing minds incapable of appreciating the glories of classical literature, or even, to a great extent, the sublimity of nature. We have seen these desirable effects wrought in those with weakened will power, and with records of broken resolutions; and the explanations given by the individual have always been that these results have been consequent upon the committal of themselves and their lives into the hands of Jesus Christ, who has become real to them, and who manifests His saving and keeping power in their lives.

There can be but one explanation—an actual power. If these results are effected—(and they are), to deny them is simply to deny facts—an adequate cause is essential. That cause is God in Christ, revealing Himself through the Bible by the Holy Spirit. Truly, agnosticism is inconsistent and inadequate.

ANNIHILATION AND CONDITIONAL IMMORTALITY

By A. McD. Redwood and Wm. C. Irvine

Doctrine Set Forth

One of the dangerous doctrines rampant today is that known as the "non-eternity of punishment." One writer tritely calls it a "hydra-headed monstrosity" because of the many forms and guises under which it appears. Two of these form the subject of this article.

What is the generally accepted meaning of the word "annihilation"? Annihilation is the act of reducing to nothing; used by theologians it is the extinction or cessation of being.

At the outset it would be well to note that even *matter* cannot be annihilated; how unthinkable then is the annihilation of *spirit!* "Conditional Immortality" when used by the Annihilationist and his kind, means that *life beyond the grave* is conditional on accepting Christ, and thus finding life in Him here and now, *i. e.,* prior to death. If the one is in possession of salvation (*i. e.,* life in Christ through the new birth), at the resurrection he rises to "put on" immortality, never more to be subject to death. This "putting on" is a result of faith in Christ. If not in possession of salvation, then at some period either before or after the resurrection (Annihilationists differ among themselves on this point) that soul, *i. e.,* the whole being, *ceases to exist, is annihilated,* is exterminated. In other words, immortality or eternal life or endless existence (*they all mean the same thing,* say they) are conditional upon salvation—apart from salvation there is only extinction of being. Such is the doctrine.

Basic Words

Upon what is the teaching based? As we look over the doctrine as given here, we note some leading words, around which every thought gathers. These are "immortality" (or its equivalents), "eternal life," "endless existence," and "death." It is upon the *particular meaning* the Destructionist attaches to these words, *that his proofs for this teaching rest.* And it is very unfortunate that many sincere, orthodox believers fall into the trap of using these words in a wrong sense, and thus play into the hands of the others.

Practically all the arguments put forward by the Destructionists have their true source in the *assumption* that "immortality," "eternal life" and "endless existence" are *synonymous terms,* and interchangeable, and these assumptions are supported by their definition of "eternal," "destruction," "loss," "punishment," and "death." Their general line of reasoning runs as follows, with certain individual variations:—

Immortality and eternal life are the same; both mean endless existence. Life is the *opposite* of death, and eternal life the opposite of eternal death. It follows then that if eternal life (or immortality) means eternal existence, death means *non-existence,* and is eternal or endless, from which none can escape save those who are regenerated in Christ through salvation.

But is this correct? That is the vital question. Let us examine briefly.

We affirm that these three phrases are *not the same* in meaning, and are not interchangeable.

Definitions Examined

(*a*) "Immortality" is *not* "eternal life" *nor* "endless existence" (although we must of necessity have endless existence to have either of the others!). In the New Testament the true word for "immortality," *athanasia,* occurs only three times— 1 Cor. 15: 53 and 54; 1 Tim. 6: 16. There is another word, *aphtharsia,** twice translated in the A. V. as "immortality," but its correct meaning is "incorruption," and is not the same as "immortality;" we therefore refuse to consider it. Now if "immortality" means the same as "eternal life" or "endless existence," then it ought to make good sense if we substitute either of them for "immortality" in the passages where it occurs. Here is the result:—

"For this corruption must put on incorruption, and this *mortal* must put on (substituting) 'eternal life' or '*endless*

---

* The passages where *aphtharsia* occurs are Rom. 2: 7; 1 Cor. 15: 42, 50, 53, 54; Eph. 6: 24; 2 Tim. 1: 10; Titus 2: 7.

existence.' So when . . . this *mortal* shall have put on '*eternal life*' or '*endless existence,*' then shall be brought to pass . . ." (1 Cor. 15: 53, 54).

Doing the same with the other passage in Timothy: "Who only hath '*eternal life*' or '*endless existence*'."

These passages, as above changed, do *not* tell the truth. As given by Paul, they *do* speak the truth.

By keeping strictly to Scripture alone, no one can fail to see that "immortal" is the opposite of "mortal," and if "mortal" means "*subject to death*" (and no one will deny that) then "immortal" means "*not* subject to death"—nothing more, nothing less. When the Destructionist then uses the phrase "conditional immortality" to mean "conditional eternal life" or "conditional endless existence," he is culpable of using phrases and words *in a wrong sense,* and the phrase "conditional immortality" is made to stand for a lie.

(*b*) "Eternal life" does *not* mean "eternal existence" (although one must have the latter to have the former). Leaving out the adjectives, it is still true that "life" does not mean "existence." If it does, then chairs, tables, stones and houses have life because they exist! Space forbids us going into the subject fully, but we make the statement here which we challenge anyone to disprove, that life is a *condition* of existence—perhaps the highest and best—but a *condition* of existence it is, yet *not synonymous* with existence. A simple test is to substitute "existence" for "life" or "eternal life" where these occur in Scripture. Take one example: 1 John 5: 12 says, "He that hath the Son hath life, and he that hath not the Son hath not life." Substitute the words and we get: "He that hath the Son hath *existen*ce, and he that hath not the Son hath not *existence*"*!* Bear in mind the verse speaks of the *present,* not of the future—HATH. Both the natural life of man and eternal life in Christ are not the same as existence or endless existence—they tell us of the *state* or *condition* of existence.

(*c*) "Death" does *not* mean "cessation of existence," or "extermination," or "annihilation." Who can deny that life is the opposite of death? Now, what is life? So far as we were able to go, it was seen to be a *condition* of existence. "It necessarily follows that death, the opposite of life, is not, and *cannot be, non-existence.*" Death is a condition of existence—a condition the *opposite* of life. We affirm that the fundamental idea underlying death is *separation*—the soul and spirit separated from the body—and never by any logical reasoning means cessation of existence. If we allow the Destructionist to hoodwink us in declaring that life is existence, then of course death is non-existence. But such is not the case. Life is a *condition* of existence, death is *another condition* of existence—the opposite of life. Life means unity—a united body, soul and spirit; death means the opposite—a *disunity,* a separation of spirit, soul and body, another *kind* of existence. The same applies to spiritual or eternal life. Eternal life is a life united to God in Christ by the new birth. Eternal death, or spiritual death, is an eternal existence apart from God.

(*d*) "Destruction" as used in Scripture does not mean "annihilation," "extinction," as the following passages clearly prove: Hosea 13: 9; John 2: 19; Matt. 27: 20; and see 2 Pet. 3: 6, 9, where the word "perish" is used. In Scofield's Reference Bible, Dr. Scofield gives the following note on 1 Cor. 5: 5: "'Greek *olethros,* used elsewhere, 1 Tim. 5: 3; 2 Thes. 1: 9; 1 Tim. 6: 9, never means annihilation."

Scripture and the Resurrection

Let us go back once again then and ask: "What is the meaning of Immortality?" The answer is, "Not subject to death." Is there anyone who possesses that state or condition? No; not a single soul in this present life; but the believer, and the believer only, will possess it after he is raised up to meet Christ at His coming. As the apostle says, he will then "put on immortality," he will never more be subject to death. This is true of the believer only—to that extent immortality is conditional.

But that in no conceivable manner countenances the error of the Destructionist. For the Scripture clearly states that *all* will be raised (John 5: 28, 29)—not all at one event but in stages, first those who form the Church (1 Thess. 4: 16, 17), then those who have laid down their lives for the testimony of Christ in the Tribulation period (Rev. 6: 9-11), and finally those who have rejected Christ and who are appointed for the "resurrection of damnation" (Rev. 20: 12-15). And not only will all be raised, but each will go to "his own company"—none to *cessation of existence.* Those who *cannot* "put on immortality" will be subject to the "second death," which, as clearly taught in Luke 16, is conscious *existence* apart from God, a state and condition of existence diametrically the opposite to the state and condition of existence of those who are enjoying life with God and Christ in heaven.

The *duration* of the punishment of the wicked is proved to be eternal by the fact that the same words which are used to describe the *glory* of the saved, and *blessings* of the saved, the *priesthood* of Christ, and the *existence* of God, are also used to describe the *duration* of the punishment; and these words have the same meaning in every case (*R. McMurdo*).

It has been stated that *annihilation* is endless punishment as it entails being shut out of heaven eternally. But, as Spurgeon has pithily said, "Annihilation would be *ended* punishment, not *endless!*"

Many other proofs could be set forth, did space allow, to show the same result; but sufficient has been given to prove that the Destructionist, by attaching his own meaning (*and that an exceedingly erroneous meaning*) to certain words, makes an otherwise harmless phrase stand for unscriptural and therefore dangerous doctrine.

Let us beware of his pernicious doctrine and be quite clear always of *the definitions of important words.*

Dr. James M. Gray gives the following Scriptures as teaching that death is not annihilation, but continued existence in a state of conscious eternal punishment: Matt. 3: 12; 5: 29, 30; 8: 12; 12: 32; 13: 42; 18: 8, 9; 25: 46; 26: 24; Mark 3: 29; 8: 36; 9: 43-48; Luke 12: 4, 5; 16: 19-31; John 3: 36; 5: 29; 1 Thess. 1: 10; 2 Thess. 1: 8, 9; 1 Tim. 6: 9; Heb. 6: 2; 10: 26-31; 2 Pet. 2: 3-10, 17; 3: 7; Rev. 14: 10, 11; 19: 20; 20: 10, 16; 21: 8.

ATHEISM, THE ENEMY OF CIVILIZATION

By Dr. W. B. Riley

The subject, "Atheism, the Enemy of Civilization," is an affront, but it states a fact. Infidelity is uniformly egotistical and readily imagines it is the friend of all that is good. It shall be our purpose to show that historically the exact opposite is true. It is as perfectly the enemy of man and the foe of civilization as it is the opponent of God. The sacred Scriptures are in this matter, as in all others, the last word (Ps. 14: 1), "The fool hath said in his heart, There is no God. They are corrupt, they have done abominable works, there is none that doeth good." History has provided thousands of illustrations of this divinely inspired assertion.

Atheism is the Enemy of Science

This statement runs counter to the boasted claim of infidelity. Unbelievers have ever been enamored of the notion that they are scholarly and even scientific. Their boasts in this matter are to be found upon every page emanating from their pens, and heard in every hall where one of their representatives secures an audience; but in spite of all that, we propose to state clearly and prove abundantly the exact opposite.

The discoveries of science clearly indicate the existence of God. If it be true as Professor Leuba, of Bryn Mawr, contends, that the majority of teachers of science in America are infidels, that is only proof of their superficiality and incompetence. It is not science that has made them so, but rather "a pseudo-science"—evolution; and a false science always makes for unbelief, while a true one eventuates in faith. The outstanding experts in the established sciences of mathematics and astronomy have been outstanding believers, while the representatives of the Darwin speculation have just as unanimously been atheists, agnostics and skeptics of all sorts.

In the very nature of the case, a study of the works of God impresses one with His personality, power, wisdom, infinity, and from the least speck of material existence to the infinity of the universe, all unite in declaring both His greatness and His glory.

Man used to talk of monads and imagined that they were the smallest particle of matter; such language is now out of date. The monad, so it is claimed, is a world of molecules. The ancient philosopher Giordano Bruno conversed of these as eternal, and declared each of them a microcosm or mirror of the Deity. Leibnitz regarded the monads as non-spatial units, each one representing the same universe, but presenting that universe from a different point of view, and each attaining its activities through the will of God. There was a time when biology thought of a monad as a simple single-celled organism; that time is past. A molecule was discovered; it was so small that men declared it the smallest part of a substance that could exist separately and still retain its composition and proportion; the smallest combination of atoms that would form a given chemical compound. But alas for the recent deliverances and the instability of so-called science! We are now told that each molecule contains 740 electrons, and no man knows what will be the next deliverance upon this subject. It is evident, however, that the complexity of the simplest things is past the imagination of man. When you rise in the scale of existences and consequently advance in the study of science, you come across the most mysterious secrets in the natural world—secrets so illusive that as yet the mind of the modern man has utterly failed to uncover them. But a few days since the Associated Press carried "For Science Service" an article proving the discovery of heatless light. This suggestion is based on the fact that low forms of life have been found to generate heatless light. The bacteria and fungi that cause rotten wood to glow in the dark, and the mysterious firefly that can, with a wilful or automatic motion in his body, emit a heatless light out of all proportion to the best that man's devices have ever approached; these bugs and bacteria becoming, as the article stated, at once the admiration and despair of scientists, but clearly indicating the acceptance of a mind infinitely above that of man. Man's invention of light involves a slow combustion and always generates heat; not so with the light of the bacteria and the bug; and to date that secret is with God.

God's work, in its simplest form, exceeds the understanding of man, and our amazement grows as we acquire additional knowledge.

The Psalmist said of his body, "I am fearfully and wonderfully made: marvellous are Thy works. My substance was not hid from Thee, when I was made in secret, and curiously wrought in the lowest parts of the earth. Thine eyes did see my substance, yet being unperfect; and in Thy Book all my members were written, which in continuance were fashioned, when as yet there was none of them" (Ps. 139: 14-16).

In order to impress this truth one needs only to study physiology a little.

I don't know that I shall even attempt to talk to you about the intricacies and efficiencies of the human eye. I will leave to others the detailed description of its lenses, the intricacies of its muscles, the delicacy and efficiency of its nerves. The eye constantly baffles the imagination and justifies Darwin's statement, "To suppose that the eye with all its illusive contrivances for adjusting the focuses to different distances and admitting different amounts of light, could be formed by natural means, fails in the highest degree. But when it is all analyzed and the mind comes as near comprehending it as the human mind can, one simply stands amazed at the minutest evidences of the Divine, in the eye, and the proposition of an infinity fixed greater credit to the same."

But the eye is not alone. Let some physicist tell you of the 600 muscles in the human body, the one thousand miles of blood-vessels in the human body, the 550 main arteries of the human body, or let him place before you the fact that 1,500,000 sweat-glands spread out on the surface of the same, or that the lungs are composed of 7,700,000 cells, or that in the 70 years of human life the heart has struck 2,500,000,000 beats and has lifted by its throbs a load of 500,000 tons of blood; and if this does not bewilder you, then let him add that the "nervous system, controlled by the brain, has three trillion nerve cells, while the blood itself is made up of thirty million white corpuscles and one hundred trillion native red ones," and you will be ready to throw up your hands in despair in comprehension of your physical self. And yet, with such an intricate machine, completed perfectly, set in operation, apart from accidents and incidents of danger, known to function from 70 years, the natural limit of a person's life, to 969 years, the longest on record, and who will say that there was no intelligent designer for this competent machine?

But if the study of physiology does not suffice to impress one with all the wisdom and power of an infinite God, then let him lift his face to the heavens above and the stars will speak; and when he has been told that the moon is 240,000 miles removed from the earth and that the sun is more than 90,000,000 miles distant, he will begin to think in terms of space, and then he learns that the sun is, in science, more than a million times as large as our earth.

It is only unused light that leads to spiritual darkness. The naturalist who does not find God in the universe has utterly failed to correctly interpret anything in it, from its greatest central sun to its most insignificant bacteria. To go back to the text, Paul tells us exactly how the process is accomplished. "The invisible things of Him (namely, His wisdom, power, beauty, and grace), from the creation of the world are clearly seen, being understood by the things that are made, even His eternal power and Godhead." And then he tells us how it came about that they failed to so connect the two as to create in their own hearts faith; and he indicts them with moral deficiency, saying:

"When they knew God, they glorified Him not as God, neither were thankful; but became vain in their imaginations, and their foolish heart was darkened. Professing themselves to be wise, they became fools, and changed the glory of the incorruptible God into an image made like to corruptible man, and to birds, and four-footed beasts, and creeping things" (Rom. 1: 21-23).

It would be difficult, indeed, to see in all literature any more accurate description of the degenerating effects of Darwinism than the apostle here pens. For inanity, could anything surpass the combination of infidelity and the acquisition of learning?

Only men whose imaginations are wild and whose foolish hearts are darkened and whose egotism has puffed them up, could ever come to the conclusion of atheism. The portrait shown is impressed in the following words:

"There is no God, the fool in secret said;
  There is no God that rules o'er earth or sky.
Tear off the band that binds the wretch's head,
  That God may burst upon his faithless eye!

"Is there no God?—The stars in myriads spread,
  If he looks up, the blasphemy deny;
While his own features, in the mirror read,
  Reflect the image of Divinity.

"Is there no God?—The stream that silver flows,
  The air he breathes, the ground he treads, the trees,
The flowers, the grass, the sands, each wind that blows,
  All speak of God; throughout, one voice agrees,
And, eloquent, His dread existence shows;
  Blind to thyself, ah! see Him, fool, in these!"

It is only false science that leads to the bestial philosophy of infidelity, Darwinism has never done anything else. Its history of 3,000 years since the days of the Greek philosophers and down to its most modern revival, first by Erasmus Darwin, and later by his grandson, Charles, has accomplished no better ends. Never, in the history of man, has it made one colossal character or eventuated in a single outstanding discoverer of nature's secrets. The established sciences were found out and proved to the satisfaction of the public by believing men. The histories of these individuals are an open page. They were not only men of God, but many of them ministers; men in touch with God, and consequently capable of interpreting the work of God. In the universities the professed scientists of this present day are not scientists. What have they discovered? What contribution have they given to men by their knowledge? Certainly you do not count "The Hall of the Age of Man," by Henry Fairfield Osborne, a contribution, since it is evidently a hypocritical pretense.

Certainly you do not call Charles Darwin a contributor to modern science. His speculation has only succeeded in exciting an endless controversy. Why should you name Conklin or Davenport scientists? All that they have ever done was to mouth over what other men have said; neither has made any discovery! Neither can you add Millikan, since his published discoveries are not yet proved, nor have they received anything like assured acceptance. These men are either open unbelievers or largely advocates of the mechanical theory.

Galileo was an ardent Christian believer; Copernicus, while a Papist, had an unshaken confidence in God and His Word, and was brought up in the house of a priest. Kepler was a ministerial student of such scientific tendencies as to triumph over the priest, and the works of Sir Isaac Newton show that he combined in one man a search for nature's secrets and the discovery of the secrets of revelation; and lastly, Mendel, the devoted monk, who, while about his pastoral duties, checked up many facts and discovered more of the laws of nature than all his boasted scientific brethren combined. Now let it be forever understood that Atheism is the enemy of science, and Faith its father and friend.

God-deniers are not delightful souls! Go where you will throughout the world, when you find them you will not want to abide with them, and it would be difficult for God Himself to brook them.

Atheism is the Enemy of Society

The first murder that stained the earth with human blood was wrought by a man who refused to recognize the sacrificial atonement as a type of the saving Christ. And when the flood came and wiped the earth with the besom of destruction, it was that it might rid it also of skeptics and atheists—men who had forgotten and denied God.

There has been a stir recently in the circles of education and religion over the wave of suicide sweeping our colleges, and outstanding men have been discussing methods of abating this blot upon civilization. The solution of the problem is not far to seek. When the schools stop teaching an atheistic philosophy, the fruits thereof will not be so openly found, and those fruits are despair, degradation and death.

God-deniers are usually men of reprobate morals. You will seldom find a man who combines in one and the same person the philosophy of atheism and a course of upright moral conduct. "The American Association for the Advancement of Atheism" declares that they "will undertake to abrogate all laws for enforcing Christian morals." Later they add they wish to better civilization by "operating as a wrecking company."

That is what atheism has ever been—an enemy of Christian morals, "a wrecking company," indeed! Had others charged them with this, they would, undoubtedly, have repudiated the charge; but now that they have asserted their purpose, they can hardly complain. Intelligent and thoughtful men will remind them that they are running true to form. The history they make will of necessity be of a sort which atheism has known through all the centuries.

The love of sin is the individual's lowest estate. There are many unfortunate men and weak women who fall into sin, but who positively loathe the same. The adversary's trap takes them; his pitfalls catch them, but they uniformly grieve over their weakness, regret their folly, and plead with God for recovering favor. But Paul says in this text that they come to the point where they not only give themselves up to uncleanness through lust, where they not only change the truth of God into a lie, worshipping the creature rather than the Creator, where they not only offend against God, but even against nature itself, being filled with all unrighteousness, but where they actually have pleasure in them that do evil.

That is the character of infidels! "The American Association for the Advancement of Atheism" deliberately publish their pleasure in them that do evil, and express the hope that "one representative from their camp may undo the work of a score of missionaries," and that "a few thousand dollars spent in the circulation" of their infamous literature may "offset millions spent by the churches."

The drunkard is not the lowest man; the man who takes pleasure in making other drunkards, is lower still. The harlot is not the lowest of women, but the woman who takes pleasure in teaching her sister harlotry is taking the last plunge toward the pit. The grieved doubter is not necessarily damned, but the man who destroys the faith of his friends and the professor whose teaching wrecks the confidence of students—such are allies of Satan himself!

Atheism Is the Enemy of the State

Civilization has not been the product of atheism. We challenge "The American Association for the Advancement of Atheism," or any other advocate of this God-denying, soul-destroying doctrine, to show one instance in which their philosophy has built a State, or a single instance in which they have made anything but an evil contribution to the same. In view of this fact is it not amazing to find many school-men—men set in positions of opportunity and responsibility—stealthily poisoning the minds of the young? "The American Association for the Advancement of Atheism" is quoted in the following:

"Dr. Irwin Erdman, of Columbia University, teaches his students that 'man is a mere accident,' that 'immortality is a sheer illusion,' and that 'there is practically no evidence for the existence of God.'

"Everett Dean Martin, Director of Cooper Union in New York City, has the largest class in philosophy in the world. He teaches his students that 'religion is primarily a defense mechanism,' subjective in its organism.

"Professor John B. Watson, of Johns Hopkins, teaches that 'freedom of the will has been knocked into a cocked hat,' and that 'soul-consciousness, God, and immortality, are merely mistakes of the older psychology'."

All across this continent text-books are filled with their vicious work, going under the name of Science, which is being compelled to carry the straining burden of such statements, and society already feeling the consequences of the same, is but reaping the first-fruits of a bitterer harvest that is sure to come.

Witness France and her plunge into atheism and the reign of terror that followed; or, take Russia and her present debauch of infidelity, and the natural disgrace coming in consequence.

Civilization has ever been the product of religion, and false religion will produce poor civilization. Heathen countries have illustrated this; yet even their religion is helpful, and the wildest superstition has proven more beneficial than the most balanced atheism that ever voiced itself. If you want to know what the condition of any state or nation is, find out what its religion is, and you can readily determine; it is as unerring as the electric needle!

The world has suffered much from religion; Paul charged the people of Athens with being "too religious." Yet perhaps it can be said with absolute candor that none of these are so detrimental to society, so harmful to the state and so destructive to national life, as atheism or "no religion." Christianity has produced the highest known civilization.

There is not an ennobling influence known to humanity that is not the emphasized product of Christianity. There is not a desirable institution existing with any peoples that has not been fostered and favored by the Christian faith. There is not a philosophy that tends to the social, political and spiritual uplift of mankind that may not be found better phrased in the Bible than unbelieving men have ever expressed the same. The Christian faith, with its one and true God and its wondrous and true Book, has brought to the world more light and has given to living men more happiness than all the philosophies of unbelieving men combined; and the crime of the ages is not the murder of individuals, now characterizing and cursing modern society, but it is the sinister, devilish, damnable doctrine, now lurking in the halls of every university in the land and of all civilized lands, and seeking by smooth speech and in the name of "Science," falsely so-called, to destroy the faith of men in God and in His Son, Jesus Christ, and in His revealed Will, the Scriptures!

BAPTISMAL REGENERATION

By J. H. Todd

In some sections of the Church it is taught that baptism as a sacrament saves, or that those who are baptized by certain ones who have the right to baptize are "born again" and became "members of Christ." It is believed that certain power or authority is vested in the Church and in the clergy so as to make it a saving ordinance.

The word "regeneration" is found in two places only in the New Testament, namely, Matthew 19: 28, and Titus 3: 5.

Meaning of Regeneration

The truth, however, of the new birth, or of being born again, or born of God, is dealt with in several passages, particularly in John 3 and in the First Epistle of John.

In His interview with Nicodemus, Christ said, "Except a man be born of water and of the Spirit he cannot enter into the kingdom of God" (John 3: 5). If by the "water" He meant baptism, it means then that not a single soul can be saved unless baptized! That would at once shut out the thief, who was crucified at the same time as Christ Himself, and all others who might in the hour of death turn to Him in faith. It would exclude all infants dying in infancy, who had not been baptized, from any part in God's Kingdom.*

It is inconceivable that if He had meant baptism He would not have baptized, for we are told in John 4: 2 that Christ Himself baptized not. And yet to many a one He said, "Thy faith has saved thee." And if He had meant baptism, why did He not teach that at other times instead of giving only this pronouncement?

*It would also exclude all Quakers and most belonging to the Salvation Army, beside all others who mistakenly do not practise the rite of baptism.—Ed.

We do not accept, however, that that was what He meant. The rest of the chapter is an answer to such a position, and the teaching of Scripture elsewhere on the subject of the new birth is so plain that it shows clearly what He did mean. The word "again" (ver. 3) means "from above," in accord with the statement in John 1: 12, 13, "who were born —*of God.*"

In the First Epistle of John "born of God" occurs four times (3: 9; 4: 7; 5: 1 and 4). John 1: 12, 13 shows that everyone who receives Christ or who believes in His name is born of God, and so becomes a child of God. In chapter 3, Christ shows that this birth is by the Spirit of God in contrast with the natural birth; and in reply to questions by Nicodemus, He explains how this is brought about, in vers. 13-16; it is by believing on Christ as the Son of God lifted up on the cross that eternal life is received.

In 1 John 5: 1 it is stated that, "Whosoever believeth that Jesus is the Christ is born of God," and in that epistle where the new birth is often referred to, and the evidences of it are so clearly given, the subject of "baptism" is never mentioned.

Eternal life is the free gift of God (Rom. 6: 23; John 10: 28). Salvation is of grace solely, and is received by faith and faith alone (Eph. 2: 8, 9). "He that believeth on the Son of God *hath* eternal life" (John 6: 47).

Significance of New Birth

What is the significance of the words, "Except a man be born of water and of the Spirit" (John 3: 5)? The only way that we can learn *that* is by referring to other passages of the Word of God which can give light upon the statement. Water is frequently used as a figure of the Word of God, and also of the Spirit of God. Such passages as Psalm 119: 3; John 15: 3; and Ephesians 5: 26, exemplify its use of the word and connect it with cleansing from defilement. In 1 Pet. 1: 23 we are taught that the Word of God is the direct agent used in the new birth, as also in James 1: 18.

In the verse in 1 Peter we are taught that we are born again by the Word of God, as of incorruptible seed, in the way that seed brings forth life. The *Word* is the incorruptible *seed* which produces the new life in the believer. In James 1: 18 we are begotten by the word of truth, and in ver. 21

the exhortation is to receive the engrafted word which is able to save your souls. In John 6: 63 we have the words of Christ Himself: "The words that I speak unto you are spirit and are life." It is therefore by believing or receiving the Word of God that the life of God is imparted to the believer, as we are told in 2 Peter 1: 4, that we become "partakers of the Divine nature" by the promises of God.

The words in John 3: 5, "of water and of the Spirit," might be read "of water, *even* of the Spirit," and be a perfectly correct translation. And such a rendering would be fully in accord with the teaching in that Gospel regarding the Spirit, for in chapters 4 and 7 water is used as a figure of the Spirit. That would mean that Christ was showing Nicodemus that the new birth was entirely a spiritual one, and this agrees with the words in ver. 8 where the Spirit is likened to the wind; as well as the thought of contrast with fleshly birth in ver. 6.

Not through Baptism

Not only does the truth about the new birth absolutely contradict any thought of baptism being the condition upon which it is received, but the teaching about baptism also refutes such a position. There is not a single instance of the baptism of a child in the New Testament, and in every instance of baptism mentioned in the Acts those who were baptized were said to have believed. The order throughout that book is hearing the Word, believing it, and being baptized. Reference to the following passages will bear this out: Acts 2: 41; 8: 12, 13, 38; 9: 18; 10: 47, 48; 16: 15, 33; 18: 8; 19: 5. The believer's identification with Christ in baptism places him on resurrection ground as having passed out from under sin and death through the waters that speak of death and burial.

In 1 Peter 3: 20, 21 where baptism is said to save, being the antitype to the figure of the flood in Noah's time, it is connected with resurrection, and so brings out the truth noticed in the passages just referred to. The words, "The answer of a good conscience toward God," forbid all reference to infants or irresponsible persons, for they plainly indicate a personal faith in response to truth received.

Baptismal regeneration is doubtless one of the fruits of

the Judaism of the early years of the Church, which taught that the Church of God was simply a continuance of the Old Testament economy, and failed to see that God was doing an absolutely new thing in "calling out" an assembly to be the Body of Christ. Baptism has been looked upon as taking the place of circumcision. If it had, why did not the apostles say so when met in council in Acts 15—for that would at once have been a decisive answer to those enforcing circumcision as a necessity for Gentiles. Besides, we have the meaning of circumcision for the believer brought out in Col. 2: 11. At the same time almost, Nicolaitanism or Clerisy came into being, by which the separate class of the clergy was given a place and a power in utter violation of the Scriptures. This, along with the position which the Church abrogated to itself with the rise of the Papacy, meant the assumption of special spiritual authority which was really an invasion of the Divine prerogative. Baptismal regeneration is a denial of the Word of God which requires a personal faith in Christ to be saved.

Judaistic Origin

[We add to the above the following quotation from an article by Dr. W. Graham Scroggie in *The Evangelical Quarterly, October,* 1929. Baptismal Regeneration belongs to Rome and unfortunately found its way into the Church of England Prayer Book, though Evangelicals in that Church by their practice of presenting the gospel and inviting those in their congregations who have been sprinkled in infancy to accept Christ, and by preaching regeneration by faith alone, show themselves superior to the teaching of their own Prayer Book.—*Editor.*]

Dr. Scroggie says:—

The Romanists acknowledge that the ground of justification is the work of Christ accomplished for men by His death. But they do not consider that that work is by itself, sufficient, for by the imposition of such rites as Penance and Absolution they supplement it, and so invalidate its adequacy.

But it is when we come to the human aspect of the question that we see how contrary to Scripture is the teaching of Rome.

It teaches that the merits of Christ are given to infants and adults in Baptism, and that Baptism takes away original sin both as to its guilt and existence, so that the person thus baptized is restored to the purity which he possessed before the fall.

This is the pernicious doctrine of Baptismal Regeneration, a doctrine which, alas, is not the monopoly of Rome. While the exercise of *faith*, and the action of the *Spirit* in the regeneration of the soul are not wholly excluded, yet they are so completely subordinated to the Virtue of Baptism and the "intention" of the priest, as to be incidental rather than essential.

In this way does Rome [and all holding this theory—*Ed.*] deny that fundamental truth of the New Testament and watchword of the Reformation, that *justification is by faith in Christ alone.*

Protestants believe that by the life and death and resurrection of our Lord Jesus Christ, a *complete salvation was provided; sufficient for all sinners, however many, and for every sinner, however great.*

BRITISH - ISRAELISM

By Wm. C. Irvine

World Federation's Advertisement

On the fourteenth of July, 1930, the British-Israel World Federation inserted a whole-page advertisement in *The Times of India* outlining their teaching, appealing, amongst others, to Indians for their support. It closes with these words:—

"This appeal is also to you, O Brethren,— who are yourselves Indians, but are verily also the sons of Jacob," etc.* Such an appeal, at that juncture (1930), was certain to fall on deaf ears! One might as well today (1935) appeal to the Germans!

Amongst many other statements of the kind, the following was printed in capitals:—

"The Anglo-Saxon Nation and company of Nations, and the United States branch of the same people, constitute the national basis of the Kingdom of God in the Earth."

Now surely such an advertisement, advising that an agent was expected to be sent out to tour India, strongly emphasized the fact that these British-Israelites were very much alive and very much in earnest. In a trenchant article on British-Israelism,† Pastor D. M. Panton, Editor of *The Dawn*, commenced by saying:—

Very holy people can hold very serious error; therefore it behooves us to be cautious in our judgments of persons; but

---

*Is Mr. A. H. Forbes responsible for this Appeal? In his pamphlet, *British Israel under New Searchlights*, in which he criticizes *British Israel Truth* after exposing their line of argument (see later in the article), Mr. Forbes says: "Before taking leave of the book, let me make an alternative suggestion: May not the Hindus of India be the 'lost tribes?' " If agreed, Mr. Forbes must smile!

†*The Indian Christian*, Oct., 1927.

also, error can be disastrous to life and character; therefore, it behoves us to be equally cautious of our creed. It follows that the servant of God is sometimes forced to the almost impossible task of analyzing error without cruelty to the loving and lovable hearts that hold it. British-Israelism is a signal example. It is held by earnest and devout souls who would die for their Lord. It is honestly supposed to prove afresh the inerrancy of the infallible Book. It numbers some honored evangelical names among its adherents. Happily, however, this is a controversy over doctrines, not persons; and we decline as strongly to condemn the man as to mask the error. For British-Israelism is a much more dangerous error than the Church of Christ has yet realized. In a jungle of bewildering verbiage over obscure prophecies concerning Israel, a fundamental overthrow of New Testament revelation (not observable at the first glance) has too long been veiled from sight, in which the truths critically needed for a world on the eve of judgment are cleverly neutralized or denied.

A Superficial Resemblance

British-Israel writers endeavor to make a great deal out of the similitude between the present position of Great Britain among the nations, and that which is prophesied should be that of Israel—as understood by most other teachers *during the Millennium.* That there are such resemblances we do not contest, but what is often overlooked is the fact that such resemblances, in the nature of the case, *must* inevitably be there. In a lesser or greater degree such could be traced at the time of the zenith of Rome's power, and also that of Greece or Spain—why then should these resemblances be thought to be a proof that the Anglo-Saxon race is the lost ten tribes of Israel? But where failure comes in is, that in order to sustain this superficial and artificial likeness, certain prophecies have to be dropped! As one example out of many, take Rom. 11: 13-25. This passage declares *Israel* (not *Judah* only!) to be *"broken off"* during this dispensation, and that *"blindness* in part is happened to *Israel,* until the fulness of the Gentiles be come in." This entirely, in our judgment, *disproves* the whole theory of Anglo-Israelism. Also see Hosea 1: 4-6. Other Scriptures have to be misplaced, from their dispensational point of view, —*e. g.,* prophecies regarding the Tribulation and the Millennium have to be applied to the Anglo-Saxons *now!* All the prophecies connected with Israel's *restoration to the land* are ignored, misplaced or evaded, as well as the fact that their greatness, multiplication, dominion and wealth are to *follow* their *reconciliation and restoration to Palestine.*

As a confirmation of our statement that dispensationally British-Israelism is untenable we again quote D. M. Panton:—

Dispensationally Untenable

Anglo-Saxons, even if they be Israelites, are either saints or sinners: if saints, then they are Israelites no longer, but belong to the "holy nation," the Church, in which there is neither Jew nor Greek; if sinners, then they are doubly under broken law—both the Law of Eden and the Law of Sinai—and therefore doubly under curse. Nationalism—all favored-nation claims before Jehovah—within the Church and under grace, is a complete subversion of Church truth: for it re-erects the barriers of the flesh which the Cross has thrown down: it makes national prosperity and worldly greatness instead of righteousness and truth, the hallmarks of God's spiritual favor—an error negatived even by the Law itself: it ignores, and so implicitly denies, the individual regeneration and sanctity without which no man shall see the Lord: and it concentrates the blessing of God on the British Empire becoming the mistress of the world. No spiritual truth is more radical, more elementary, than that "the flesh profiteth *nothing*" (John 6:63); and therefore no error could be more radical, more fundamental, than to attribute to blood, not grace, to the flesh, not the Spirit, any standing whatsoever before God.

These are weighty words, and expose one of the greatest dangers of this system. The late David Baron, a profound Hebrew and Biblical scholar and teacher, clearly recognized this. He wrote:—

Racial Pride Inflated

It fosters national pride and nationalizes God's blessings in this dispensation, which is individual and elective in its character. It diverts man's attention from the one thing needful, and from the only means by which he can find acceptance with God. This it does by teaching that a nation composed of millions of practical unbelievers in Christ, and ripe for apostasy, in virtue of a certain fanciful identity between the mixed race composing that nation and a people carried into captivity two thousand five hundred years ago, is in the enjoyment of God's special blessing and will enjoy it on the same grounds for ever, thus laying another foundation for acceptance with God beside that which He has laid, even Christ Jesus.

As an exhibition of this national pride, we select another passage from the advertisement in *The Times of India*:—

After the French Revolution, when the thinking of the world had been stabilized by the faith of Britain, and the peace of the world had been re-established by the arms of Britain, the stream of atheistic propaganda ran underground for a while but emerged again in Marxian philosophy in Germany!

Further, British-Israelism seeks to trace the line of British monarchs back to David. In their advertisement in *The Times of India,* they state:—

During this time, specially in the reigns of David—the founder of the reigning House of Britain—and of Solomon, his son and successor, Israel dominated the world situation.

Also: In the next and ultimate stage all nations will constitute the Kingdom of God. To this Kingdom ultimately, and many of us believe, soon, the Lord Jesus Christ will come. There He will find the British Royal House directly descended from the throne of David operating in accordance with the oath to that effect of the Lord Almighty.

Scripture Misinterpreted

With regard to misapplied prophecy take the following culled from a leaflet entitled *"Proved!"* issued by their North of England Council, and sold by the Covenant Publishing Co., Ltd., Book Depot, which publishes and sells so much of their literature:—

Israel had to colonize barren lands and "establish the earth," causing the desert to blossom as the rose (Isa. 27:6; 35:1). This is an achievement which the Anglo-Saxons have accomplished with signal success.

Isaiah 27 is a distinctly millennial chapter. The phrase, "In that day"—which either relates to the Tribulation, or to Christ's Coming as Israel's Deliverer—is found in vers. 1, 2, 12, 13. In ver. 12 it says: "And ye shall be gathered *one by one,* O ye children of Israel." *When* was that true of the

British? It *will be* of Israel, as Scripture proclaims (Jer. 3: 14; 31: 8).

Isaiah 35: 1 tells us that *the land of Palestine* will be rejuvenated *when* the Jewish nation is converted at the coming of Christ (Ezek. 34: 4-35). Why separate verse 1 from the rest of Isaiah 35? It is also a typically millennial chapter (see vers. 5, 6, 8, 9, 10). Wherein has any of this been fulfilled as far as Britain is concerned? Do Anglo-Israelites believe the *British Nation* will ever live in Palestine?

The same pamphlet tells us:—

> Israel had to be exceedingly wealthy, and "lend unto many nations," but borrow from none (Deut. 8: 18; 28: 12). The Anglo-Saxons are the richest community in the world. They lend to all and borrow from none.

"The Anglo-Saxons borrow from none!" Is their tremendous War debt yet owing, forgotten? Did the writer also forget to read Deuteronomy 8: 19, 20? Are not the Anglo-Saxons forgetting God? Are the British-Israelites so deaf that they cannot hear the "bleating of the sheep" and "the lowing of the cattle?" And do not Britishers (apart from Government, which is not indicated in these Scriptures) owe vast sums all over the world? How extravagant and contrary to fact to say they "borrow from none!"

Such are some of their clumsy attempts in conjuring with the Word of God and History in a vain endeavor to reconcile them with their theories concerning the "lost ten tribes" and Great Britain. Their misapplication and misinterpretation of the Scriptures has become a byword. Mr. David Baron characterized some of the interpretations of this school of teachers as "bordering on blasphemy." We give a few extracts from his article published in the sixth edition of his book:—

> 1. The glorious Messianic prophecy of the stone cut without hands which smote the image of Nebuchadnezzar (Dan. 2) is applied to the British people; and the British Empire, which is one of the Gentile world-kingdoms, is made to be identical with the Kingdom of God.
>
> 2. Messiah's Throne of Righteousness and Peace is made out to be identical with the throne of England, and the Eng-

lish peoples are "saints of the Most High," to whom all the kingdoms of the world shall be given.*

3. The smoke which ascends from the "blazing furnaces and steam engines" of London is identified with the Shechinah Glory, the visible symbol of God's presence with His people.†

4. Edward Hine, author of the forty-seven "Identifications," is the promised Deliverer who should come out of Zion.§

The British-Israel people make much of the New Covenant. The fallacy of this teaching, as applied by them, is laid bare by Mr. G. Goodman in the following words:—

The New Covenant

The whole British-Israel theory, if Dr. Mountain is its true exponent, hangs upon this, that the British people have accepted the Christian Faith, and come under the New Covenant, which would mean that they are born again. Alas, it is impossible to think it.

To enter, by personal surrender to Christ, into the blessings of the New Covenant is not the privilege of Israel only, it is free to all men (Eph. 3: 6).

To suggest that while nationally (hardened and veiled) and individually (as lawbreakers) under the curse, Israel is now enjoying the Covenant blessings of Abraham nationally, would be contradictory. To allege that Israel has accepted the Christian Faith is falsehood.

Why, then, all this stir to show that we Anglo-Saxons are Israel? It can only bring us under the curse of a broken law and a disobedient people.

Why go about advocating in England that which can only encourage men to hope in the flesh? Let us rather warn of the wrath due to sin, and point to Christ the Lamb of God and call to faith in Him.

British-Israelism is a false and dangerous theory, that can only lead men to hope in the flesh, to expect "national" blessing, while they continue in personal rejection of Christ and disobedience to God.

**The Lost Ten Tribes*, by Rev. Joseph Wild, D.D. A book containing twenty discourses, which abounds in statements and interpretations as wild and unscriptural as this taken from Discourse XVIII.

†From an article in *The Banner of Israel.*

§When preparing to re-write my little book I was told by a friend that I need not take much notice of the works of Edward Hine. On enquiry, however, I found that his writings are still largely advertised and circulated, and many of the more modern Anglo-Israelite writers profess to draw instruction and inspiration from them (*David Baron*).

Lost Ten Tribes

So much has been written regarding the exodus from the Ten-tribe Kingdom to Judah, showing how probably many more had joined themselves to Judah than were taken into captivity; and also how after the Captivity the former distinction of Ephraim and Judah, or Israel and Judah, was dropped, that we hardly think it necessary more than to refer to this important line of evidence against the British-Israelite theory. Mr. Baron says:—

The names "Jew" and "Israelite" became synonymous terms from about the time of the Captivity. It is one of the absurd fallacies of Anglo-Israelism to presuppose that the term "Jew" stands for a bodily descendant of "Judah." *It stands for all those from among the sons of Jacob who acknowledged themselves, or were considered, subjects of the theocratic kingdom of Judah,* which they expected to be established by the promised "Son of David." Anglo-Israelism teaches that members of the Ten Tribes are never called "Jews," and that "Jews" are not "Israelites;" but both assertions are false. In the New Testament the same people who are called "Jews" one hundred and seventy-four times are also called "Israel" no fewer than seventy-five times (*cf.* such statements as given in Acts 21: 39; 22: 3; Rom. 11: 1; 2 Cor. 11: 22; Phil. 3: 5; Rom. 9: 4, 5).

From the time of the return of the first remnant after the Babylonian exile, sacred historians, prophets, apostles, and the Lord Himself, regarded the "Jews" whether in the land or in "Dispersion," as representatives of "all Israel," *and the only people in the line of the covenants and the promises which God made with the fathers.* (*Cf.* the use of "Judah" and "Israel" in the following: Ezra 6: 17; 8: 35; Zech. 1: 19; 10: 6; 8: 13, etc.).

Mr. C. E. Putnam writes:—

Notice that Paul says, "mine own nation at Jerusalem," "our religion," "the promise made of God unto *our fathers,*" and "*our twelve tribes* instantly serving God day and night." The lost tribes could not be thus spoken of, and it is very evident indeed that St. Paul taught and believed that the Jews of "*mine own nation at Jerusalem*" constituted "*our twelve tribes*" of whom it is said, "the promise was made of God unto our fathers."

Shall we accept man's theories, or shall we believe God's inspired Word? Which? Oh, which?

The above is also finely answered in Mr. Goodman's booklet:—

If we are the ten tribes, our kings are not those to whom the promises were made. The royal tribe was Judah, which is not one of the ten tribes. British-Israelites have talked a great deal about the genealogy of our present royal house. If our kings are to fulfil the national promises, none of the ten tribes can produce such a king. To see the ten tribes with a king from another tribe, would be an anomaly and untrue to history.

Perhaps among the many vulnerable parts in the British-Israel armor, the *historical* to some will prove most convincing.

History Falsifies

Facts are dead against them. Their misreading of history has been exposed most convincingly in a booklet entitled *British-Israel Under New Searchlights,* by Avery H. Forbes, M.A., which *The Christian* (London) termed *"unanswerable."* In his preface of the second edition he says:—

One well-known British-Israel author told me that, when asked by the "Covenant" publishing people to tackle my pamphlet, he refused, saying, "Mr. Forbes is right in his history, and you are wrong." He informed me, however, where my mistake lay; namely, in not recognizing that the British were *Ephraim*—which tribe was promised blessings and privileges above the others. How he ascertained that we were Ephraim, he did not say. I replied that, if we are Ephraim, so also are those Scandinavians who are descended from the same ancestors (unless he held that a man's grandfathers were not descended from his forefathers!) To this reply I have received no answer.

The great historical difficulty the British-Israel people are up against is to bridge over a gap of more than 1,000 years—roughly from 700 B. C., when the ten tribes were in captivity in Assyria, to the fifth century A. D., when the Jutes and Angles first appeared in history. This yawning gulf is precariously bridged by British-Israelism with the aid of the Scythians, whom they assert to be identical with the "lost ten tribes." Herodotus, writing about 400 B. C., says the Scythians were then located in Southern Russia. We will now let Mr. Forbes speak:—

There is thus not a scrap of definite evidence to connect the Scythians with the ten tribes, or the Scandinavians with the Scythians. . . . Of the Scythian nation, placed by Herodotus northwest of the Black Sea, it is asked in *B. I. Truth*, "Could this be the Israelites which had been lost to sight in Asia?" (p. 116). Two pages further on we read: "The emphatic point is this, that the particular Scythian people, whose prowess is set forth by the Greek historian, Herodotus, entered Europe at the very epoch, by the self-same route, and from the identical district of Asia, at, by, and from which journeyed the Israelites of *Esdras*" (p. 118). On the next page we read: "The difficulty is not to trace any possible connection between the Scythians and the Israelites but to conceive how the two people could be anything but one and the same" (p. 119). Therefore Herodotus' description of the Scythian nation "*is a picture of lost Israel*" (p. 119). "Scythia then . . . *was the home* of the ancestors of the English" (p. 123). "So the chain stands complete" (p. 124). "If Scripture then suggests that Israel is in Britain, history emphatically supports this suggestion" (p. 128).

What is at first a bare possibility, is turned into a surmise; a surmise soon becomes a likelihood; the likelihood becomes an extreme probability and ends by becoming a dogmatic certainty!! This is not exactly the way in which responsible historians write authentic history!

Mr. Forbes traces the history of the British nation, writing of the ancient Britons, the Huns, the Danes and Saxons, proving that the British-Israel theory is here up against what he calls "a stone wall." And here is the stone wall:—

Here we are up against a stone wall. That the Normans did not all come to England with the Conqueror—or after the conquest either—is patent to everyone who opens an English or a French history. Now the present people of Norway, Sweden, and Denmark, and a large section of Germans, Sicilians, Italians, Russians, Icelanders and Greenlanders are descended from those same Danes, Norsemen, Angles and Saxons, as certainly as we are descended from the Anglo-Saxons, etc. Are the modern Danes, Norwegians, Swedes, Saxon-Germans, etc., etc., therefore to be included amongst the British-Israelites? And if not, where are we to draw the line?

Such are some of the claims, teachings, fallacies and fables of British-Israelism. Let the reader beware lest patriotism should blind his or her eyes by the teaching of this School, whose persuasive and eloquent words have beguiled so many. Well has the late, beloved Dr. F. B. Meyer said:

"British-Israelism is not capable of argument, it is a kind of infatuation."

Professor Neubauer, librarian of the Bodleian Library and Reader in Rabbinic Literature at Oxford till 1900, sums up his studies in a series of illuminating articles on the subject in the first volume of *The Jewish Quarterly Review* with the words,

"Nowhere!" A Scholar's Answer

Where are the ten tribes? We can only answer, Nowhere. Neither in Africa, nor in India, China, Persia, Kurdistan, the Caucasus, or Bokhara. We have said that a great part of them remained in Palestine, partly mixing with Samaritans, and partly amalgamating with those who returned from the captivity of Babylon. With them many came also from the cities of the Medes, and many, no doubt, adhered to the Jewish religion which was continued in Mesopotamia during the period of the Second Temple.

BUCHMANISM OR THE OXFORD GROUP MOVEMENT

By Wm. C. Irvine

This Movement is being hailed by some as a "twentieth century Pentecost," whilst by others it is denounced as a grave menace. Here in India, as in other lands, it has its enthusiastic champions who are pressing its claims upon Christian communities. It is our intention to lay before our readers what eminent Evangelical Leaders have to say of the Movement. Whilst not quoting the writings or sayings of those who favor it, for this is being done by others, we frankly admit that large numbers have nought but praise for it, and amongst them are a *few* well-known Evangelicals.

We first quote extracts giving the judgment of some evangelical leaders, commencing with a weighty declaration from one of the centres of the Movement:—

This letter signed by Oxford clergymen appeared in *The Record* and *The Guardian*, June 24, 1932, and reads:—

Sir, in view of the articles which have appeared recently in *The Record* on the subject of the Rev. Frank Buchman's "Group Movement" we, who have had the opportunity of watching its development in Oxford, feel it our duty to issue a word of caution to your readers.

While thankfully recognizing the fearless zeal of the leaders and the fact that many lives have been changed by the Group, we find ourselves unable to approve some of their principal doctrines which have led to disastrous consequences in several cases known to us.

Then follow three paragraphs on their teaching concerning Guidance, Sharing and Loyalty to the Group. They close by saying:—

In our opinion they dangerously over-emphasize the importance and authority of subjective experience in spiritual things; with the result that in their public meetings, as also in their private testimonies, little is heard about the objective facts of the Gospel or the work of Christ for us.

Then follow their signatures:

J. S. Bezzant, Fellow and Chaplain of Exeter College C. M. Chavasse, Master of St. Peter's Hall and Rector of St. Peter-le-Bailey; L. B. Cross, Fellow and Chaplain of Jesus College, Oxford; C. M. Gough, Rector of St. Ebbes; Bryan S. W. Green, Oxford Pastorate; D. E. W. Harrison, Chaplain of Wycliffe Hall; E. W. Mowll, Rector of St. Aldate's; D. B. Porter, Tutor of Wycliffe Hall; H. E. H. Probyn, Vicar of St. Andrew's; E. C. Ratcliff, Fellow and Chaplain of Queen's College; W. F. Scott, Chaplain of St. Peter's Hall; D. K. Stather Hunt, Vicar of Grandpoint.

Dr. W. B. Riley, Editor of *The Pilot,* writes:

Unitarian ministers are heartily commending it; Modernist ministers are opening their pulpits to it; and those churches which have been to a state of spiritual death by hypnotizing D.D.s and Ph.D.s are hailing the apostles of this "another gospel" with joy.

Pastor H. A. Ironside, Moody Memorial Church, Chicago, and Editor of *The Moody Church News,* in a sermon, sums up a long discourse by saying:

The moment I find there is no emphasis upon the blood of Jesus, there is nothing in it for me.

President Hibben of Princeton says:

As long as I am President of the University, there is no place for Buchmanism in Princeton.—Quoted in *The Oxford Group Movement—Some Evaluations.*

Dr. Basil J. C. Atkinson, M.A., Ph.D., of Cambridge University, writes:

Another point about this Movement, as I have seen it, is that it is disruptive. Wherever it appears it breaks the harmony and unity of true Christian workers.—Quoted in *The Oxford Group Movement—Some Evaluations.*

(*Rev.*) *H. T. Commons,* pastor of the First Baptist Church, Atlantic City, N. J., who was "actively associated with the Group for over three years" and knew all the leaders of the Group "intimately," says:

After three years on the "inside" I finally severed my connection with the Group out of loyalty to my Lord, for I realized that it is actually far removed from real N. T. Christianity.

Dr. Lewis Sperry Chafer in an editorial in *Serving and Waiting*, says:

Doubtless the leaders of the so-called "Oxford Movement," or "The First Century Christian Fellowship," would be shocked to be told that their teaching is no nearer a comprehending of Christianity than is Christian Science . . . each system, behind its outward claims, offered the most violent contradictions to pure first century Christianity.

(*Rev.*) *Wright Hay*, the Secretary of the Bible League, Great Britain, writes:

The Movement is anti-Christian because it is non-Biblical.

We do not claim that the quotations above *prove* that the Oxford Group Movement is *all* wrong, or *all* of the Devil; but we do submit that they are sufficient to make devout Christians "furiously to think" and to pause before casting in their lot with this Movement.

"Sharing"

Perhaps the thought of "sharing" one's religious experiences with others, in which *confessing one's sins* takes the most prominent part, is that which distinguishes this Movement more than any other individual practice. This *sin-sharing* is fundamental to the Movement, hence we will first glance at what well-known evangelical leaders have to say about it. As a matter of fact, that which is now spoken of as "sharing experiences," was first called "sin-sharing." Changing its name has not altered its character.

We first quote from *J. C. Brown's* book *The Oxford Group Movement* (pp. 46, 47):

Another dangerous doctrine which they hold is summed up in one of their favorite words, "Confession." Quoting from the text, "Confess your faults one to another" (Jas. 5: 16), they practise a full and often indiscriminate confession of sins to strangers in public and private, and so do much harm by this entirely unscriptural habit.

Mr. Brown then proceeds to show how the Scriptures teach us to confess our sins to God (Ps. 32: 5; Ps. 51 and 1 John 1: 9), and rightly adds that sins committed against an individual are to be confessed to that individual (Matt. 5: 23, 24), and those, and only those, against a community to be publicly confessed—as with Achan (Josh. 7: 19).

To illustrate the danger, he says:

> A godly friend of mine when writing . . . said: "I honestly believe that there is a subtle attraction about talking about one's sins, which is wholly unhelpful to spiritual growth. The movement is sex-obsessed (as Chavasse points out), and there is a danger of one's horror of immorality being lessened by too much talk on this subject. One's sense of shame gets easily dulled.

The writers of *The Oxford Group Movement—Some Evaluations* say:

> As shepherds of souls we are bound to heed the warning of psychology—that to share may mean for some the stimulation of latent exhibitionist perversion; and to listen, the subtle indulgence of sex curiosity.

A further voice raised in warning as to this danger may be cited. In *The Oxford Letter* already quoted above, we read:

> They urge the need of "*deep sharing,*" or open confession within the Group, as a means of release from sin and cementing the fellowship of the Group. This is especially dangerous when *the sharing of sexual sin is encouraged.*

Dr. W. B. Riley in *The Pilot* (Jan., 1935) says:

> The text that reads, "Be ye not partakers of other men's sins" is said to be literally translated, "Be ye not sin-sharers"—the inspired prohibition of the very practice in which Oxfordites take both pride and pleasure.

But, it may be asked, is the sharing of *sexual* sin encouraged or permitted? Alas, testimony to this effect is only too prevalent. *Pastor H. A. Ironside* in *The Moody Church News* tells us:

When I was in Boston, I found a good deal of scandal had been occasioned by mixed companies holding these parties and confessing their sins, many of which were of such a character that Scripture says, "It is a shame even to speak of those things which are done of them in secret" (Eph. 5: 12). Yet they confessed these things openly, men before women, and women before men. You can understand that the result was anything but helpful. Where do you find anything in the Word of God that suggests this kind of confession of sin?

Surely the teaching of Scripture that all unconfessed sin must be dealt with at the judgment-seat of Christ (if the saint who has sinned refuses to confess now), and will be there *manifested,* should be, and if we only believed would be, a sufficient incentive to confess our faults one to another (see Rom. 14: 10-12; 1 Cor. 4: 5; 2 Cor. 5: 10; 1 Tim. 5: 24).

The Editor of *The Evangelical Christian* (Feb., 1933) truly says:

If it were a sharing and a confession of Christ as a Saviour of sinners—that would be great. But the bringing in of the confessional into the Protestant Church is something that we repudiate and reject. Auricular confession is contrary to the teaching of Scripture, and has been a curse to the Catholic Church.

Dr. S. M. Zwemer, in *The Missionary Review of the World,* raising a warning note against this practice of sharing, writes:

Its use without careful definition is to be deprecated for four reasons. (1) It is not Scriptural; (2) it is subject to many and very loose interpretations; (3) its careless use shifts the very basis and aim of Christian missions; and (4) the idea of sharing our human thought and experience is not the central idea of evangelism.

Guidance

Much stress is rightly laid on the subject of Guidance. Every Christian should be a Spirit-led man or woman: "For as many as are led by the Spirit of God, they are the sons of God" (Rom. 8: 14). The devout soul longs for an ever-increasing experience in the leadings of the Spirit; but many Christians, alas, apparently do not even expect to be led by the Spirit. To such the "leadings" of the members of the Group seem to speak of a deep spiritual life to which they are entire strangers. It captivates them.

When we commenced to cull the opinions of leading evangelicals on this subject, we were almost dumbfounded to find that they with one accord lift a warning voice regarding the *method* whereby Oxford Group members obtain their guidance, and indicate a specific *danger.* Is this a plot to discredit the Movement? The characters of the writers forbid the thought. Did they lay their heads together and agree to an attack? The time at which they wrote, the distance they live from one another, their different interests, and, again, their characters, emphatically answer in the negative.

Surely, then, their united testimony should cause anyone to pause before throwing in their lot with the Movement, and surely every man and woman reading these warnings will realize the tremendous responsibility of influencing young Christians to place themselves under such teaching! The italics in the following extracts are ours. We commence with a word about the leader, Dr. F. N. D. Buchman:—

What is Dr. Buchman's manner of living? Taking "Life-Changers" again as our authority, we find he begins each day by spending an hour or more in complete silence of soul and body while he gets guidance for that day. On this "spiritual silence" he lays especial emphasis, and puts it in a more important place than even reading the Bible and prayer. He teaches his votaries to wait upon God with paper and pencil in hand each morning in this relaxed and inert condition, and to write down whatever guidance they get. This, however, is just *the very condition* required by *Spiritist mediums* to enable them to receive *impressions* from evil spirits and, as D. M. Panton in *The King's Herald,* August 15, 1929, wisely remarks, is simply Planchette, and it is a path which, by abandoning the Scripture-instructed judgment (which God always demands) for the purely occult and the psychic, has again and again led over the precipice. The soul that reduces itself to an automaton may at any moment be set spinning by *a demon*—(From *The Oxford Group Movement,* by *J. C. Brown*).

We next take the opinion of one of England's foremost physicians, one who writes most graciously of the Groups, A. Rendle Short, M.D., B.S., B.Sc., F.R.C.S.:—

We have heard of some strange and amusing results following this well-meant but *dangerous* method of seeking to know the Lord's mind.

Our next witness, the well-known churchman, *C. M. Chavasse,* M.A., Master of St. Peter's Hall, Oxford, who, living at that centre of the Movement, has studied it since its appearance in 1926 in that city. His words are weighty:—

It is the *method* of seeking Divine guidance practised by the Oxford Group Movement that we do not like. The attaining to a *state of quiescence* in which one may "listen in" to God is —on the showing of Group writings—more important than definite prayer.

If it could be proved that God is the *only* Spirit that transmits "luminous thoughts" to "listeners," the method of seeking Divine guidance which the Groups favor would be absolutely safe. But do the communications which come to *Spiritualists* in their trances proceed from God? We think not. And how can people who are so woefully and wilfully ignorant of doctrine, as the average Grouper is, rightly discriminate between the communication which is from God and that which is *not from God?—From Some Evaluations,* p. 10.

Dr. Rowland V. Bingham, Editor of *The Evangelical Christian,* shall give the next testimony. He writes:—

There are some in the Oxford Movement who were converted before they touched it, who do state that guidance should come through the Scriptures, by the aid and the illuminating of the Holy Spirit; that God has already spoken to His children. This is the great secret of guidance. We do not object to their taking a pad and pencil to write down any thoughts of guidance which come to them. But to take the thoughts especially *generated in a mental vacuum* as Divine guidance would throw one open to all the suggestions of *another* who knows how to come as an angel of light and whose illumination would lead to *disaster.*—From *Evangelical Christian,* Feb., 1933.

Harold T. Commons, pastor of the First Baptist Church, Atlantic City, whose long active association with the Movement lends much weight to his words, writes:—

Finally their idea of "guidance" is false to the Scripture. . . . But the practice of the Groups in sitting down with paper and pencil in hand and letting the mind go *absolutely blank,* and then writing down whatever flashes across the mind as God's

orders for the day, is beyond anything promised or sanctioned in Scripture. Indeed this *"passivity" of mind* is a very *perilous condition* to be in, for it is precisely at such moments that *Satan gains control* and does his devilish work.—From *Buchmanism,* by H. T. Commons, p. 5.

Will the reader pause, and consider for a moment the united testimony of these men, most of them known, loved and revered for their works' sake world-wide; all of whom, seeing the danger,—oh, how grave!—lift a warning note to save their brethren from the peril of coming under the influence of evil spirits, that so evidently threatens them.

As an illustration as to where this method of obtaining guidance may lead to we give the astounding conversation—which so far as we know has never been challenged—that Mr. J. C. Brown held with one of their men missionaries (p. 38 in his book):—

"For what reason did Christ die?"
"To tell you the truth, I don't know myself."
"Has the Group any list of sins?"
"No, we have no list of sins."
"Would you call adultery and murder sins?"
"Only if God told you they were."
"What would you do if you had a strong desire to commit adultery with another man's wife, or to murder some one?"
"I would go to God and get guidance about it."
"You mean that you would pray to God and ask Him to show you whether it was right or wrong?"
"No, I should not pray about it. I would just wait for God to give me guidance about it."
"And how would God give you this guidance?"
"I should get a strong impression what I should do."
"And if this strong impression was that you should murder that man, would you do it?"
"I should!"

We close with a strong statement made by *C. M. Chavasse,* quoted in *The Witness,* which any one thinking of throwing in their lot with this Movement should surely know:—

At Oxford the Groups are established as *a cult,* strongly organized, with a headquarters, and a band of full-time workers . . . and their intolerance and exclusiveness is a strong and

distressing feature. The leaders of the Groups . . . will brook *no criticism*, and rule it out as *unguided*.

The *collective guidance* of the Group has become the accepted test of the guidance of each of its members. And it is well to remember that behind the many local Groups there is the *Inner Group* with its head, which—I dare to affirm with deliberation and knowledge—can fairly be *compared to the hierarchy of the Roman Church and an infallible Pope*. And the extreme importance placed on the Group as the Body, has tended to obscure the *centrality of Christ* as the Head.

Blood Atonement

If you are not sure of any teaching, enquire what is its attitude to the doctrine of the Blood Atonement—that is the acid test today! First let us see what a few of the leading cults teach, and then turn to Buchmanism:—

Christian Science: "The blood of Jesus Christ was of no more avail, when it was shed upon the cursed tree, than when it was flowing through His veins in daily life."—From *The Spirit of Truth and the Spirit of Error*.

Spiritism: "The whole doctrine of original sin, the Fall, the vicarious atonement, the placation of the Almighty by blood—all this is abhorrent to me. The spirit-guides do not insist upon these aspects of religion."—*Sir Conan Doyle*. Quoted from address by Dr. A. C. Dixon.

Theosophy: "We believe neither in vicarious atonement, nor in the possibility of the remission of the smallest sin by any God," etc., from *Key of Theosophy*, p. 135.

Christadelphianism: "The death of Christ was not to appease the wrath of offended Deity, but to express the love of the Father in a necessary sacrifice for sin," etc.

Russellism (now *Jehovah's Witnesses*): "One unforfeited life could redeem one forfeited life and no more."—*The Spirit of Truth and the Spirit of Error*.

Modernism: "The 'slaughter-house religion' belongs to the dark ages."—*Ibid*.

Mormonism: "Christ's atonement has to do only with the sins of Adam."—*Ibid.*

Seventh-Day Adventism: "The blood of Christ, pleaded in behalf of penitent believers, secured their pardon and acceptance with the Father, yet their sins still remained upon the books of record."—From *The Great Controversy*.

In the above quotations it is evident that whereas some scorn, others deny or belittle, none fully recognize the Scriptural doctrine of the Atonement in its alone sufficiency to deal with, entirely atone for and blot out all remembrance of sins committed against a holy God—(See Matt. 26: 28; Rom. 3: 24, 25; Eph. 1: 7; Col. 1: 20; Heb. 9: 12-14; 10: 14, 17, 18; 1 Pet. 1: 18, 19; 1 John 1: 7 and Rev. 1: 5).

We wish it clearly understood that we do *not* charge the Oxford Group Movement with *denying* the Blood Atonement, or, for the matter of that, any other great fundamental doctrine. That would never do, it would divorce the sympathy of the very people they are seeking to influence. Our object is to show this Movement's *attitude* to this basic doctrine of Christianity. Do they emphasize it? Do they teach it? Or do they evade it? We now call on some of our witnesses to give evidence:—

There is a "doctrine of the Cross" in Group literature, but it is not "the doctrine of the Cross" as evangelicals know it—(Rev.) G. N. M. Collins, B.D., in *The Evangelical Quarterly*, April, 1933.

I had a three hours' talk with Mr. Buchman, seeking to get at what he really believed himself. . . . Never once during those three hours did Dr. Buchman mention the blood of Christ. I have attended meetings in connection with the Movement in which men who imagined that they had received help through the Movement have given their testimony. Not one of them, in my hearing, made any mention of the blood of Christ—R. Wright Hay, Secy., Bible League, Great Britain, *The Oxford Group Movement—Some Evaluations.*

In all the meetings of the Groups I have ever attended or heard about, there has never been any mention of the blood of Christ in its expiatory character.—Quoted by Dr. Bingham, Editor of *The Evangelical Christian*, as the testimony of one who "was actively associated with the Movement, taking part in their house parties, knowing all their leaders."

A Christian business man had a long talk on doctrine with Dr. Buchman, who professed to believe in every fundamental doctrine. However, he says, Dr. Buchman explained, *he never touched any doctrine in any of his meetings, as he did not want to upset or offend anyone.*—*The Sunday School Times,* Dec. 23, 1933.

God in His Word puts all the emphasis upon the BLOOD, that precious blood. The writer has not found that blessed word in the Oxford Group Movement literature.—Editor, *Our Hope.*

In reply to my question how the experience of the living Christ, of which one heard so much in the public meetings, was related to the atonement, of which one heard so little, Mr. Shoemaker stated that the experience presupposed the fact of the atonement. Immediately, however, he added the startling imperative, *"But don't talk about the atonement to the unsaved! That would be like trying to explain the binomial theorem to a young child."* In other words, according to the Group, one can become a true Christian without ever having heard of the Cross of Christ; later on there will be time enough to study the meaning of His death.—Ned Bernard Stonehouse, Th.D., in "Christianity To-day."

"When the Oxford Movement begins to preach salvation by the blood of our Lord, then we will have more to say on the subject."—Editor, *The China Fundamentalist.*

We submit that our witnesses abundantly prove that so far as the Oxford Group Movement is concerned their attitude towards the doctrine of the Atonement is one of *evasion,* and that they entirely fail to emphasize the true significance of the Cross of Christ.

Life Changing

Few, if any, who have seen aught of this Movement, or have read about it, will question their claim to be Life-changers. The question is not: Are lives changed? but rather: What does this change signify? Is it Reformation or Regeneration? A work of man, or a work of God?

The Editor of the *Sunday School Times,* Philadelphia, once asked Dr. Buchman whether he believed it was necessary for a man to be born again. "Of course I do," came the quick reply: "I believe a man ought to be born again every day." Certainly *that* is not the teaching of Scripture, and completely negatives the words of our Lord in the third chapter of John.

That the Movement's changing of lives is not synonymous with conversion is surely proved by the author of "For Sinners Only"—Mr. A. J. Russell—who admits that the Movement is ashamed of the old terms "conviction of sin" and "conversion" and tells us plainly: "Frank (Buchman) declines to accept the division of the world into two classes—the saved and the unsaved"—W. J. Grieb, B.A., in *Biblical Recorder*, December 1, 1932.

There is a scriptural change of life known as the New Birth, a passing from death to life, conversion, becoming a "new creation" wrought by the inworking of the Holy Spirit through the preaching of the gospel. Would that this were the Life-Changing of the Oxford Group Movement. We will again turn to our witnesses and seek to learn what these well-known evangelical leaders have to say on this subject.

Dr. Gaebelein in an Editorial in his magazine *Our Hope* says:—

> If the Buchmanite Movement speaks of "revitalizing Christianity," what does it mean by it? Is it leading back to the great Gospel foundation? Is it unfolding afresh the marvels of John 3:16? How much does the Oxford Group Movement make of the cross of Christ, the blood of Christ? Does it declare the blessed finished work of Christ on the cross? Does it exalt and glorify Christ, the risen Saviour, the Priest and Advocate in God's presence? How much has it to say of the glorious goal, the return of the Lord? If Christianity is to be revitalized then that process of revitalization can only be brought about by preaching Christ.

How extraordinary that a Movement out to *revitalize* Christianity should falter in its teaching on the new birth!

Mr. Harold T. Commons, Pastor of the First Baptist Church, Atlantic City, in his booklet, tells us:—

> The "changed lives" of the Group are nothing more than moral conversions, in no sense corresponding to the New Birth of the New Testament, which designates the passing of a soul from death to life by the acceptance of Christ's atoning work on the cross. Anything that omits God's one remedy for sin (1 John 1:7) leaves the human soul still guilty before God.

regardless of how many moral conversions the person may have gone through.

(*Note*: Frank Buchman's Five 'C's' for the sinner supposedly cover the whole ground. They are: Conviction, Contrition, Confession, Conversion and Continuance. Every one of those is possible on a purely moral basis—know you are a sinner, feel sorry for your sins, confess them, turn away from them and continue on the new way. But if, in addition to all this, there is no faith in the blood of Christ and no acceptance of the Lord Jesus Christ as personal Substitute and Saviour, then the guilt of sin still remains and the soul is unsaved).

From *The S. S. Times* (Philadelphia) of Jan. 13, 1934, we cull the following:—

On page 7 in *Life Changers* we read: "There is no need, as there was no need in the days of Jesus, to present a complete and dogmatic theology to the mind of the seeker. Love of God is still the first commandment. Love of God and love of man are still the only essentials. *It may be true or it may not be true that God repented of His creation; that Christ came upon earth to make atonement between God and man, and that because of the sufferings of Christ God is now willing to accept our hearty repentance for our sins.* These teachings may be true or untrue, but their acceptance is not essential to the great and wonderful experience of conversion." It is rather shocking to the Christian to be told that "it may not be true" that Christ came to make atonement between God and man.

A generation or so ago had a minister uttered such words as we have italicized, he would have been unfrocked. Today many are not even shocked when they read them!

Mr. J. C. Brown in his book, *The Oxford Group Movement*, tells us:—

An evangelist in South Africa, writing . . . says: "Their great slogan is 'life-changers,' and there seems to be evidence with some of a real change of life. Some of them seem aglow with joy and happiness, and they are on fire to tell others what has happened to them. . . . When you ask them how the 'life change' has come about, is it based on the Atonement . . . they are strangely silent. One man was asked whether the new birth, which he said had taken place in him, was based on the redemptive work of Jesus, and he answered that he did not believe in the Atonement. And yet he talked of a 'life change!' "

Worldliness

The Scriptures are so clear in their teaching concerning the Christian's relationship with the world, that beyond a quotation or two very little needs to be said on the matter.

"If ye were of the world, the world would love his own: but because ye are not of the world, but I have chosen you out of the world, therefore the world hateth you" (John 15: 19).

"But God forbid that I should glory, save in the cross of our Lord Jesus Christ, by whom (R. V., 'which') the world is crucified unto me, and I unto the world" (Gal. 6: 14).

"Know ye not that the friendship of the world is enmity with God? Whosoever therefore will be a friend of the world is the enemy of God" (James 4: 4).

Bearing these passages in mind, let us read what our witnesses have to say on this point:—

Dr. R. V. Bingham, Editor of *The Evangelical Christian*:

If Christ the crucified ever comes into our life we shall find that the cross He brings will crucify us unto the world. The Oxford Group Movement follows the fashions, the foibles and follies of the world. At their opening meeting the dress and the undress of the world were clearly in evidence, and that not upon the visitors and the guests, but on the part of those who were supposed to be with the Movement.—*Some Evaluations.*

Mr. J. C. Brown:

The great majority of groups are Christian in name, you can gamble, dance, go to theatres and cinemas, be a Roman Catholic, or believe almost anything, and go in for almost any worldly amusement, and nothing is said as long as you are loyal to Dr. Buchman and the Group.—*The Oxford Group Movement,* p. 52.

Mr. W. Wilcox:

Worldliness is not only condoned among its ordinary members, but among those who have been sent forth as its missioners. Again, in our reading of its literature, it appears that non-Christians may join a group even though the non-Christian faith be not abandoned.—*The Bible League Monthly.*

(Rev.) Charles Fisher, M.A.:

Here is a religious movement which has managed to do away with "the offence of the cross." Ardent advocates of this movement find it possible to go to the dance and the theatre and to indulge in betting just as much as before they were "changed." One reads of a man taking his partner aside from the dance, and leading her to the Lord, and then going back to join the rest of the worldly throng. "We have not so learned Christ!" There may have been a "change," but there has been no "New Birth," for when that takes place, "Old things pass away; lo, *all things become new*."

Dr. A. C. Gaebelein, Editor of *Our Hope*:

The Editor spent the second evening of the new year in the great ballroom of the Waldorf-Astoria Hotel in New York City. It was not an evening for dancing, but it was a *religious meeting.* It was the opening service of the famous "Oxford Group Movement" or, as it is also known, "Buchmanism." There were over 2,000 people present. We never saw such gorgeous gowns as worn by a number of young women. It was a riot of color, and the arms and backs were bare. Then there were costly furs and diamonds and pearls displayed. The gentlemen came in evening dress. Many appeared in clerical dress. Three Bishops, called "Right Reverends," were on the reception committee, among them the Right Reverend Francis McConnell, the well-known modernistic Methodist Bishop. On the platform sat, among them a number of the evening-gowned ladies with bare arms and backs, the sponsors of the movement and the foreign delegates, some fifty of them, including great scholars, clerics, titled Englishmen, and a former Lady-in-Waiting on the Empress of Germany. A religious meeting! *But there was no prayer offered.* Dr. Sam Shoemaker of New York started this religious meeting without prayer. Nor was a verse of Scripture mentioned by the many speakers except one. The first speaker made an appeal to the wealthy to help the unemployed in the city, and he quoted, "What ye have done to the least of My brethren, ye have done unto Me." No other speaker mentioned the Word of God. The persons called upon to speak spoke of what the movement had done for them. They mentioned Jesus Christ having changed their lives. But not once was He called "Lord," nor did we hear Him mentioned as "The Son of God." Not once was the Cross and the Blood mentioned. Several spoke of the adventure they found in the movement or fellowship. While there was no prayer there was a great deal of mirth and laughter. Most of the speakers tried to say something funny, and there was a constant applause. We went home saddened, for God's Spirit was not in that meeting.

We think it entirely unnecessary to make further comment.

We have brought before our readers the considered judgment of these Evangelical Christian Leaders concerning this Movement. Some condemn it *in toto,* others not so severely, but all at least caution Christians against joining it.

Summing up

With regard to the subject of *Sharing, or Confession of one's sins,* the danger of the open confession of sex sins has been stressed, and warnings concerning the "subtle indulgence of sex curiosity" emphasized, as well as the fear of bringing the Confessional into reformed churches.

The terrible danger of seeking *Divine Guidance as practised by the Groups* has been unanimously exposed and condemned. The fear of thus enabling Satan to gain control is declared to be very real.

These honored servants of God testify that all teaching concerning the *Blood-Atonement* is either evaded, scorned or denied. Their united testimony on this point alone should be sufficient to deter any who know they are redeemed by the precious blood of Jesus Christ, from having fellowship with the Movement.

The question of *Life-Changing* has also been dealt with. All our witnesses agree that lives are changed, but the superficiality of the work seen by eye-witnesses is repeatedly stated —the Life-Changing of the Groups is usually merely a matter of reformation and not regeneration.

Then the Movement's utter *Worldliness,* as witnessed by the absence in its teaching and practice of Separation, is proved to the hilt. Not only is this manifested by the wearing of ultra-fashionable clothing, but tobacco, cards, dancing and even gambling are indulged in by some of its members— unrebuked!

We close this somewhat long examination of this world-wide Movement with the Resolution recorded by Fundamentalists in America.

At the Sixteenth Annual Convention of the World's Christian Fundamentals Association, in Chicago, June 26 to July 2, 1933, the following weighty Resolution was issued, as taken from *The Sunday School Times,* for July 22. 1933:—

The Convention recognizes with sorrow the increasing prevalence of false religious cults and movements, and especially that known as the Oxford Group Movement, or First Century Fellowship, or Buchmanism. The Convention believes that this Movement, while calling itself Christian, and while including in its adherents some who are undoubtedly Christians, nevertheless is a subtle and dangerous denial of the evangelical Christian faith, in which Modernists are as welcome as Fundamentalists, and varying shades of belief or unbelief unite on common and unscriptural ground. The Convention believes that the Movement substitutes human and natural psychological laws for the supernatural working of the Holy Spirit and the new birth, and that it puts experience ahead of doctrine, denying the necessity of true belief as essential to Christian life. The Convention therefore urges all true believers to recognize the unscriptural character of this Group Movement, and to refrain from having fellowship with it.

Surely the testimonies of these godly men placed before our readers cannot be brushed lightly aside!

From its attitude to the Bible and its treatment of doctrine—especially that of the Blood Atonement: its unblushing worldliness: its broadness of membership, irrespective of the new birth: its superficial work of "changing lives": and its silence with regard to the Coming of our Lord, we believe this Movement may be truly called

The Twentieth Century Modernist Gospel.

CHRISTADELPHIANISM*

BY A. J. POLLOCK

CHRISTADELPHIANISM makes a great show of appealing to Scripture. Every lover of the truth will be well content to judge this system by such an unerring standard. No seeker after light need fear the result. If it be of God, Scripture will surely be its amplest vindication; if not of God, its fullest exposure.

Nor is it mere details we shall have to consider. There is not one important fundamental doctrine upon which Christendom has for ages been agreed that is not by this system denied.

The book from which we cull extracts to show what they (Christadelphians) distinctly hold, and which was sent to the writer by a Christadelphian to convince him of their tenets, consists of thirty-six propositions, with about five hundred Scripture quotations. The number of Scripture quotations only proves their infatuation, for Scripture is their exposure, as we shall see. Read by the careless or ignorant, they may succeed in misleading, but once let the truth be clearly stated by Scripture, it will soon be apparent how great is the deception.

Unitarian in Belief

1. Christadelphians believe that the Lord Jesus Christ was not divine, but *merely* a man—thus aiming a fatal blow at the whole scheme of redemption. Let us quote their own words:—

"Jesus Christ, the Son of God, is not the 'Second Person' of an eternal Trinity of Gods, but the manifestation of the ONE ETERNAL CREATOR, who is 'above all and through all' (Eph. 4: 6) and 'out of

---

* [This article is abridged from A. J. Pollock's able pamphlet, *Christadelphianism, briefly tested by Scripture.* The writer is well qualified for his task and exposes this system to its very heart.—*Editor.*]

whom are all things'* (Rom. 11: 36). This Creator is Spirit, dwelling corporeally† and personally in heaven, yet in His Spirit-effluence filling immensity. By this Spirit-effluence He begot Jesus, who was therefore HIS SON: by the same power He anointed him and dwelt in him, and spoke to Israel through him (Heb. 1: 1). Jesus Christ, therefore, in the days of his weakness, had two sides—one DEITY; the other MAN; but not as construed by Trinitarians, which make Jesus the Son Incarnate. The man was the son whose existence dates from the birth of Jesus; the Deity dwelling in him was the Father, who without beginning of days, is eternally pre-existent. There were not two or three eternal persons before 'the man Christ Jesus,' but only ONE—God the Father, whose relation to the Son was afterwards exemplified in the event related by Luke (chap. 1: 35), by which was established what Paul styles the 'mystery of godliness;' 'God manifested‡ in the flesh, justified in the Spirit, seen of angels, preached unto the Gentiles, believed on in the world, received up to Glory' (1 Tim. 3: 16)."

In this proposition is stated, as clearly as words are able, that the Lord Jesus is not God the Son. No one believes in "an eternal Trinity of Gods," but Christendom believes in God the Father, God the Son, God the Holy Ghost—ONE GOD. Christendom believes in a Triune God, not in a plurality of Gods. This can be proved most clearly from Scripture. Yet we are told in this proposition that there are not two or three eternal Persons, that Jesus is not the Son Incarnate, that He is only God's Son as begotten into this world, whose existence dates only from His birth, that DEITY is not *essential* to the Person of the Lord Jesus, but "the Deity dwelling in Him was the Father."

The whole proposition is entirely false. Let Scripture, to which they so confidently appeal, answer them. The Christadelphians assert that the Lord Jesus had no existence previous to His incarnation. The Lord's own words are:—

"BEFORE Abraham was I AM" (John 8: 58).

*"Of Him . . . are all things," is the correct quotation.

†How strangely careless yet deceptive is this piece of writing! The Creator is *Spirit*. How, then, can He dwell corporeally in heaven?

‡Should read "manifest," but we quote exactly.

Again observe carefully the words of the Lord Jesus Himself:—

"And now, O Father, glorify Thou Me with Thine own self, with the glory which I had with Thee *before the world was*" (John 17: 5).

"Of whom as concerning the flesh Christ came, who is over all, *God blessed for ever*" (Rom. 9: 5).

"But unto the Son He (God) saith, Thy throne, O GOD, is for ever and ever" (Heb. 1: 8).

"In the beginning was the Word, and the Word was with God, and the Word was God. The same was in the beginning with God. All things were made by Him, and without Him was not anything made that was made" (John 1: 1-3).

"And the Word was made flesh, and dwelt among us (and we [the Apostles] beheld His glory, the glory of the Only Begotten of the Father), full of grace and truth" (John 1: 14).

Could refutation of Christadelphian teaching be more convincing and clear?

In denying the essential Deity of the Son, the fountain of Christadelphian teaching is poisoned at its source. What wonder then, that the stream emanating from such a source is baneful and poisonous! To proceed further:—

Atonement Caricatured

2. Christadelphians deny the atoning value of the death of Christ, and thus would take from us, if they could, the Saviour. They say:—

The death of Christ was not to express the wrath of offended Deity, but to express the love of the Father in a necessary sacrifice for sin, that the law of sin and death which came into force by the first Adam might be nullified in the second in a full discharge of its claims through a temporary surrender to its power; after which immortality by resurrection might be acquired, in harmony with the Law of obedience. Thus sin is taken away, and righteousness established.

Here the death of the Lord Jesus is looked at as the expression of the Father's love. Doubtless it is the expression of God's love, and who would wish to question that? But mark, reader, the righteousness of God demanding satisfaction for sin is entirely ignored. The death of Christ, they say, was not to appease the wrath of God. Surely holiness and righteousness had their claims, and if God's love is to be righteously shown to sinners in the offer of forgiveness of sins and salvation, there must be satisfaction rendered to God's holiness and righteous claims against sin. In the book quoted from, Christ is not referred to as Saviour, nor the precious blood as that which alone can cleanse from sin, and the confession of Jesus as Lord is altogether ignored. How inexpressibly sad!

Spirit Impersonal

3. If Christadelphianism denies the divine personality of God the Son, we are quite prepared that they should deny the divine personality of the Holy Ghost. They teach that:—

> The Spirit is not a personal God distinct from the Father, but the radiant, invisible power or energy of the Father, filling universal space, and forming the medium of His omniscient perceptions and the instrument of His omnipotent behests, whether in creation or inspiration; the distinction between the Father and the Spirit being not that they are two persons, but that the Father is Spirit in focus so intense as to be glowing substance inconceivable, and the Spirit, the Father's power, in space-filling diffusion, forming with the Father a unity in the stupendous scheme of creation, which is in revolution around the Supreme source of All Power.

Thus in grand, swelling, empty words they deny the personality of the Spirit of God.

On the contrary, Scripture repeatedly refers to the Holy Ghost as a Person.

"Howbeit when *He,* the Spirit of truth, is come, *He* will guide you into all truth: for *He* shall not speak of Himself; but whatsoever *He* shall hear, that shall *He* speak: and *He* will show you things to come" (John 16: 13). [See also Matt. 28: 19; John 14: 16, 17, 26; 15: 26—*Ed.*]

Satan's Personality Denied

> The Devil is not (as is commonly supposed) a personal supernatural agent of evil, and that in fact, *there is no such* BEING *in existence.* The Devil is a *scriptural manifestation of sin in the flesh* in its several phases of manifestation—subjective, individual, aggregate, social and political, in history, current experience, and prophecy; after the style of metaphor which speaks of wisdom as a woman, riches as *mammon* and *Satan as the God of this world,* sin, as a master, etc.

The purpose of Satan is well served if people can be persuaded that he does not exist. We do not fear what does not exist. Can subtlety go further?*

Christadelphians, not content with denying heaven to the believer, refuse to believe in a hell or eternal punishment at all. They settle it in very few words. They say: "It also follows of necessity, that the popular theory of hell and 'eternal torments' is a fiction."

Hell Denied

As Christadelphians deny heaven to be the believer's portion, and deny the very existence of hell, they are forced to propound what they call "conditional immortality" to cover their retreat.

Enough has been shown to prove that this system is anti-Christian and Satanic. We can understand that, once having started with a wrong premise as to the Person of God the Son, error after error was needed wherewith to bolster up this daring attack on Christianity.

It may be contended that amidst this mass of error the Christadelphians at least are sound as to their acknowledgment of God the Father. Even this contention Scripture takes from them, and they are left most completely under the curse of Scripture. They deny the Divine Personality of the Son. Scripture tells us in this connection that:—

> "Whosoever denieth the Son, the same hath not the Father" (1 John 2: 23).
>
> "For many deceivers are entered into the world, who confess not that Jesus Christ is come in the flesh. This is a deceiver and an antichrist . . . Whosoever transgresseth, and abideth not in the doctrine of Christ *hath not God*. . . . If there come any unto you and bring not this doctrine, receive him not into your house, neither bid him God-speed; for he that biddeth him God-speed is partaker of his evil deeds" (2 John 7, 9, 10, 11).

Without God, without the Father, without the Son, without the Holy Ghost, without atonement, without a hope of heaven, how truly terrible their condition is! Theirs is indeed a system of error without one redeeming feature.

---

*Christ asserts that He saw Satan, Luke 10: 18, Scripture says He spake with Satan, Matt. 4: 4, 7, 10, and that Satan is finally cast into the lake of fire. Rev. 20: 10.—*Ed.*

CHRISTIAN SCIENCE

By A. McD. Redwood

Mrs. Eddy

Mrs. Mary Baker G. Eddy, the foundress of "Christian Science," now dead, was an ex-spiritualistic medium. Her book, *Science and Health*, is accepted by her followers as *the* text-book of the cult, and portions of it are read at their services. Of it she wrote in 1901:—

> I should blush to write of *Science and Health with the Key to the Scriptures*, as I have, were it of human origin, and I apart from God, its author; but as I was only a scribe echoing the harmonies of heaven in Divine Metaphysics, I cannot be super-modest of the Christian Science text-book.

From these words one would naturally expect that the teachings of "Christian Science" would harmonize with those of the Bible, of which it is supposed to be the key! Let us compare the teachings.

"The principle of Divine Metaphysics is God" (*Science and Health*, p. 5).

Concerning the Trinity

"Life, Truth and Love constitute the triune God, or triple Divine principle" (*ibid.* p. 277).

"The theory of three persons in one God (that is a personal trinity or tri-unity) suggests heathen gods" (*ibid.* p. 152).

Thus "Christian Science" denies a Personal Trinity. Now while the actual doctrine of the Trinity is nowhere explicitly taught in so many words in Scripture, the whole of Scripture testifies to the fact. The very first verse in the Bible reads: "In the beginning God" (*Elohim*—a uni-plural noun, suggesting the Trinity, and used in the Old Testament about 2,500 times, see note in *Scofield's Reference Bible*) "created the heavens and the earth." The initial rite of the Christian religion, baptism, proclaims a Personal Trinity:

"Go ye . . . baptizing them in the name of the Father, and of the Son, and of the Holy Ghost" (Matt. 28: 19).

The plain fact is that "Christian Science" denies the God of the Bible. Take such extracts as the following, picked out at random, and let the reader ask himself—Is this a God who can save me from my sins, who can change my life from unrighteousness to righteousness?

Concerning God

Question.—What is intelligence?

Answer.—Intelligence is omniscience and omnipotence. It is the primal and eternal quality of infinite Mind, of the triune Principle—Life, Truth, and Love—named God (*Science and Health*, 1916, p. 469).

Question.—What is mind?

Answer.—Mind is God (*ibid.* p. 469).

God, the Divine Principle of man, and man in God's likeness are inseparable, harmonious, and eternal . . . God and man are not the same, but in the order of Science, God and man co-exist and are eternal (*ibid.* p. 470).

The Divine Mind is the Soul of man, and gives man dominion over all things (*ibid.* p. 307).

God, without the image and likeness of Himself, would be a nonentity, or Mind unexpressed. He would be without a witness or proof of His own nature. . . . If God Who is Life, were parted for a moment from His reflection, man, during that moment there would be no divinity reflected. The Ego would be unexpressed and the Father would be childless—no Father (*ibid. pp.* 303, 306).

The Jewish tribal Jehovah was a man-projected God, liable to wrath, repentance, and human changeableness (*ibid.* p. 120).

Space forbids us subjecting these statements to the critical "gruelling" they deserve, but to any reasonable mind, capable of reading the Word of God without wresting it, such extracts—of which there are hundreds more as un-"scientific," and even less intelligible—cannot fail to demonstrate the utter variance between "Christian Science" and the Bible. The God of the Bible and the God of "Christian Science" are absolutely different, and we cannot love and worship both at the one time, unless we deny our reason and do despite to the Word of the Living God.

After having said so much that is false about Deity, it is not surprising that Mrs. Eddy is found to be equally false regarding the Person and Work of Jesus Christ. We do not fear contradiction in stating the fact that, on practically every vital point relating to the doctrine of the Person and Work of Christ, "Christian Science" is as far removed from the Bible teaching as East is from West.

Concerning Jesus Christ

The following rigmarole is one out of hundreds found in the book:—

The invisible Christ was imperceptible to the so-called personal sense, whereas Jesus appeared as a bodily existence. This dual personality of the unseen and seen, the spiritual and material, the eternal Christ and the corporeal Jesus manifest in the flesh, continued until the Master's ascension, when the human, material concept, or Jesus, disappeared, while the spiritual self, or Christ, continues to exist in the eternal order of Divine Science, taking away the sins of the world, as the Christ has always done, even before the human Jesus was incarnate to mortal eyes (*ibid.* p. 334).

Commenting on the above, one writer characterizes it as "blasphemous absurdities" — and every sensible Christian who knows his Bible will just about agree with the verdict!

Concerning Atonement

Jesus never ransomed man by paying the debt that sin incurs, whosoever sins must suffer (Vol. II, pp. 143, 144).

Jesus bore our infirmities; he knew the error of mortal belief, and "with his stripes (the rejection of error)* we are healed" (*ibid.* p. 20).

Final deliverance from error, whereby we rejoice in immortality . . . is not reached . . . by pinning one's faith without works to another's vicarious effort (*ibid.* p. 22).

The atonement requires constant self-immolation on the sinner's part. That God's wrath should be vented upon His beloved Son, is divinely unnatural. Such a theory is man-made. The atonement is a hard problem in theology, but its

---

*The words in brackets are Mrs. Eddy's own explanation of what "His stripes" mean! Could she have said anything more foolish?

scientific explanation is that suffering is an error of sinful sense which Truth destroys, and that eventually both sin and suffering will fall at the feet of everlasting Love (*ibid.* p. 23).

Does erudite theology regard the crucifixion of Jesus chiefly as providing a ready pardon for all sinners who ask for it and are willing to be forgiven? . . . *Then we must differ* (*ibid.* p. 24)—our italics.

The efficacy of the crucifixion lay in the practical affection and goodness it demonstrated for mankind (*ibid.* p. 24).

With this doctrine of hopelessness, compare the words in 1 Tim. 2: 5, 6—"For there is one God, and one Mediator between God and men, the Man Christ Jesus; who *gave Himself a ransom for all,* to be testified in due time."

Christian Terms Misused

Many other subjects could be taken up, such as Prayer, the Holy Spirit, Heaven, Hell, Satan, Angels, etc., in all of which "Christian Science" will stand convicted of error and even blasphemy. In a previous edition of this book we showed in a paragraph that "Christian Science" did not believe, as an example, in prayer, and one of their members called us in question on the point—referring to the so-called "creed" given at the end of *Science and Health,* where belief in the Bible, in God, in Christ, etc., is stated. The effective answer to such a contention is the fact that, whilst they *use* the *terms* of the Bible and of Christians, the meaning they attach to those terms is utterly different from the meaning given to them by the Bible. Whilst, on the surface, therefore, their "creed" is so phrased as to *appear* more or less correct and scriptural, in truth it is completely at variance with the Bible! *Their* meaning of God, Christ, prayer, atonement, forgiveness, etc., has nothing in common with the true Biblical teaching. This point is exceedingly important, and reveals the demoniacal source to which it pertains.

Four Basic Propositions

In the 1903 edition of *Science and Health,* p. 113, are given Mrs. Eddy's *four basic propositions.* They are, in her own words:—

First, God is all in all.
Second, God is good, good is mind.

Third, spirit being all, nothing is matter.
Fourth, life, God, omnipotent, good, deny death, evil, sin, disease—
Disease, sin, evil, death, deny good, omnipotent, God, life.

Commenting on this a writer in *The Fundamentals* has well said:

Unconscious of the absurdity of the thing, she placidly tells us, that since these statements may be *read backward* as well as *forward*, this is a proof that they are true! "The Divine Metaphysics . . . prove the rule by inversion." So far as their value goes, these four propositions might just as well be read perpendicularly or obliquely. And by the same method of argument, it would be easy to prove angels, cherubim and seraphim, are butterflies, lizards, guinea-pigs and horses.

Mind Cures

The great attraction of this cult is doubtless the mind cures it is said to have wrought. Nor do we question that many have been cured. But it has again and again been stated that the system never has cured any diseases save those which have been cured by "mental therapeutics." Mrs. Eddy herself had to resort to the dentist!

Dr. A. J. Gordon, of Boston, throws out this warning concerning the teachings of Mrs. Eddy:

If the body is only a phantom and the flesh only a shadow, it is logically certain that by-and-by some very practical sinners will take refuge under this system, and insist that the sins of the body and the transgressions of the flesh are harmless, since they are only the phantom of a phantom, and the shadow of a shadow.

The late Dr. I. M. Haldeman, Pastor of the First Baptist Church, New York, summed up this pernicious cult as follows:

Christian Science has one supreme aim. Its aim is to take away Jesus Christ as the alone Saviour of men. It denies His actual birth, repudiates Him as the Christ, makes Him to be as full of errors as other mortals, rejects the Atonement of the Cross, says He never died, never was buried and never rose, does not exalt His name above every name, refuses to bow to Him as Lord and God, teaches that He does not sit upon the infinite throne, and that He is not in heaven at all. In short, it turns His body into an apparition, His blood to nothingness, His cross to a myth, His death to a fiction, His burial to a mockery, and Himself to a personality that was never real and no longer exists.

Christian Science is a Peril of Perils

It is a peril to Christianity.—It is a peril because it puts on the robes of Christian profession and hides its real antagonism under the plea of a higher and more spiritual concept. It is a peril to Christianity, because it repeats the name of Christ, wards off suspicion, and then, slowly but systematically, seeks to deny Him. It is a peril to Christianity, because it quotes the Bible as its authority, professes to be its best interpreter, and then, in the dark, seeks little by little to wrench it loose from the place of faith and absolute confidence. It is a peril to the Christian, because it talks of God and the Father and, step by step, leads the Christian to think that God is not a person, and the Fatherhood but a name. It is a peril to the Christian, because while it talks to him of Christ, it leads him softly and insensibly away from Christ, or quite beyond Him, where he is his own saviour, and his own Christ, and his own very God. It is a peril to the Christian, because it leads him eventually to deny the Lord who bought him, and thus brings him dangerously near that threshold where swift destruction falls on all who finally deny Him. It is a peril to the unsaved, because it stupefies him on the edge of a precipice, closes his eyes to mortal danger, cries peace where there is no peace, and allows him to plunge headlong into a hopeless and unredeemable eternity.

Ivan Panin tells how he was sent for by a Canadian major who was dangerously ill in hospital. A friend of the major's claimed to have been healed, and urged him to try "Science." He was inclined to do so, but asked Mr. Panin, "What do you advise?" and was a little surprised to get the reply, "I would advise you to try 'Christian Science' if you are prepared to *pay the price.*" *"Price!"* he exclaimed, "what is money in comparison with health, or life itself?" "I did not mean the price in money," replied Panin; "but you would have to give up the Lord Jesus as your Saviour, for, 'Science' denies sin, evil, Satan, sickness, as realities, and hence has no atoning blood or redeeming grace or assurance of salvation." He decided to trust in Jehovah-Jesus rather than in Christian "science falsely so-called" (1 Tim. 6: 20), and lived to tell of being saved by grace (*The Witness*, July, 1928).

Pandita Ramabhai said:

Ramabhai's Testimony

On my arrival in New York, I was told that a new religion was being taught in New York, and that it had won many disciples. I found that the name of the new religion was Christian Science; and when I asked what its teaching was, I recognized it as the same philosophy that had been taught among my people for four thousand years. It has wrecked millions of lives and caused immeasurable suffering and sorrow in my land. It is a religion that knows no compassion or sympathy. It means just this—the philosophy of nothingness. You are to view the whole world as nothing but a falsehood.

"Beware lest any man spoil you through philosophy and vain deceit, after the tradition of men, after the rudiments of the world, and not after Christ" (Col. 2: 8).

THE COONEYITES

or Go-Preachers and their doctrines

By W. M. R.

(Abridged)

Origin

The originator of this new cult was a Mr. William Weir Irvine,* a Scotchman, who went to Ireland about fifty years ago as a preacher in connection with the Faith Mission. He subsequently left them and started an independent Mission on his own lines at a town called Nenagh, Co. Tipperary, where he found a few hearty people who had been but recently converted. These he succeeded in gathering round himself and they became the nucleus of this new sect.

He commenced by holding missions in school-houses and Methodist churches, which had in good faith been placed at his disposal; and in course of time, a number of young men and women professed conversion to his views and followed him from place to place.

The condition of church life in the south of Ireland at that time was such that there were young Christians who were languishing for lack of spiritual food, and were grieving over the want of ardor in the gospel among them. Such were attracted to these preachings, and mistook the vigorous denunciations and excitable preaching of the missioner

---

*Mr. John Long has written us that he was the man who obtained for William Irvine "the first opening for a mission in Nenagh, August, 1897." That "William Irvine is the name of the original leader of the Go-Preachers. Irvine Weir was one of the first staff of preachers who emigrated to America; these two names seem to have got mixed up." He declares that the movement dates from 1897.

for spiritual power and holy zeal. Ultimately, many of them were induced to unite with him.

Irvine then commenced a virulent attack on Methodists and Methodism, and publicly anathematized all churches and their ministers. This led to the withdrawal of all permission to use any of their property for his meetings.

It was about this time that Edward Cooney gave up his secular employment and threw in his lot with Irvine, and became what he termed a "Tramp-Preacher," hence came the new name, "Cooneyites," or "Tramp-Preachers," as they are sometimes called. They are called "Go-Preachers," in that they go out two by two, without money, purse, or scrip, and literally tramp from place to place, claiming to obey the word of Christ to His disciples in Matthew 10: 7: "As ye go, preach;" hence the name "Go-preachers."

Cooney

Cooney was possessed of a strong personality, combined with a fiery zeal, which suited well this militant sect. Fresh attacks of greater vehemence were now launched against all sects and denominations, and their converts warned against them and forbidden to have any connection with them.

Further developments shortly took place. If any of them had money they were exhorted to give it up, and literally carry out the teachings of the Lord Jesus in Luke 9: 1-5 and Matthew 10: 5-42, and this they called "The Jesus Way." Any form of outward respectability in dress was pronounced worldly, and contrary to "The Jesus Way," for He lived and worked as a poor Man.

Only those who follow "The Jesus Way" are regarded by them as Christians, and every profession of conversion through other instrumentality than their own is regarded as Satanic, and their work that of "False Prophets" and "Hirelings." Conversion to "The Jesus Way" or "The Lowly Way," as it is variously called, is, according to them, indispensable for salvation, and this can only be evidenced by their following it; and any divergence of thought from this teaching is denounced as "earthly, sensual, and devilish."

They usually move about in couples, composed of young men or young women. They seem to be very shy of large cities and towns, preferring the country districts, where they seem to gain easier access to souls, and find less opposition to the propagation of their pretentious dogmas and doctrines, which damage spiritually all who lend an ear to them.

Methods and Practices

Their first practice is to visit some place and seek out those that are "worthy," as they deem it; which, in reality means those who are prepared to listen to them and to receive them. They state they have come to preach the gospel in the real "Jesus Way," and that they belong to no sect. If they are refused, they will browbeat, insult, and endeavor to frighten the timid, and end by literally "shaking off the dust of their shoes against them."

If they are received, they very soon bewilder their hosts with their perverted and plausible application of Scripture, and, alas, sometimes eventually gain their adherence, unless they are well grounded in the gospel, and possessed of a well-balanced mind.

For the sake of securing one proselyte they have been known to preach every night for two or three months. Their method of making converts is as follows: At the close of their preaching, an appeal is made to any who realize that they are not right, that they should turn to the Lord in true repentance, and signify the same by raising their hand. Those who do so are accounted as born again, or as having turned from "the wrong way" to the "Jesus Way," or "The Testimony of Jesus," as it is variously styled.

Their converts must be baptized by immersion, and renounce their former religious connections, and, when as is sometimes the case, parents are opposed to their teaching and methods, their children have been known to forsake parents and home and all filial obligation, under the baneful influence of these preachers.

Their aim is to establish churches in every place where they are received. These are presided over by "bishops," men who have strictly conformed to their tenets. They maintain that the only way to worship God is that the meeting must be held in the house of some "saint," for every other kind of religious meeting is "the false way." They meet together privately every Sunday (generally in the house of a "bishop") and "break bread," as was the custom of the early Church. They hold prayer-meetings during the week, and in all these gatherings both men and women take part. They urge a strict attendance at all these meetings, and nothing but extreme sickness must be allowed to keep them away.

Attitude Towards Others

They boldly state that there are no true servants of Christ in any of the churches, and that there are no true Christians except those who are converted in their meetings. They claim that they only are the true servants of Christ, inasmuch as they only have complied with the Lord's command to sell all they have and preach the gospel without money and without price.

"The Jesus Way"

We may now enquire what is this preaching of "The True Jesus Way," of which the Cooneyites claim to hold the monopoly, and without which (and a Cooneyite to preach it) no one can be saved.

When they are asked, all they seem able to tell us is that "The True Jesus Way" is laid down in Matthew 10 and Luke 9 and 10. From these Scriptures they constantly quote, laying particular emphasis on "Go preach," and provide "neither gold nor silver, nor brass in your purses, nor scrip for your journey" (*cf.* Luke 22: 35, 36).

Their Doctrines

It is very difficult for anyone not initiated into their sect to get an official outline of their doctrines, for they purposely refrain from printing books or tracts for public circulation. There is an undoubted object in this practice. We have been given to understand that latterly something has been printed which only those amongst themselves are allowed to see. They are likewise careful to ban all other books and tracts, for they declare that no one can benefit from the reading of such literature. They can go so far as to declare that the Bible is a "dead book" unless it is "made to live" through the mouth of one of their preachers. This again savors of the pretensions of Rome.

Here we have the very surest test, even if it be the very oldest. To be wrong here is to be wrong everywhere.

Their Christology

The Go-Preachers profess to believe in the Deity of Christ, but utterances, such as "Jesus overcame His own flesh," clearly show that they believe that the Lord Jesus Christ had sinful flesh in Him that needed to be overcome! How incompatible this is with Luke 1: 35: "That Holy Thing that shall be born of thee shall be called the Son of God," and "In Him is no sin" (1 John 3: 5)! No one that believed Him to be God the Son, could speak of His "having to overcome the flesh in Him."

"The Jesus Way" of the Cooneyites, accordingly, has no room for the precious atoning blood of Christ as the ground of salvation.

On Atonement

One of them remarked the other day to a friend of the writer, who was pressing the necessity of the precious blood of Christ as the ground of salvation: "How can the blood of a dead man save anyone!" Underlying the statement is an assault upon both the Deity and the atoning work of Christ. A correspondent writes: "Of all the time I was with them, I only once recollect one of their preachers mentioning the blood."

They assert the work of Christ is *not* finished, and that in the face of John 17: 4, when He said, "I have finished the work which Thou gavest Me to do:" and also of that memorable peace-giving and victorious cry of the dying Saviour on the cross—"It is finished" (John 19: 30). In support of this strange contention they quote, and again wholly misapply, Acts 1: 1: "Of all that Jesus *began* both to do and teach." The Cooneyites thus claim to be carrying on the work of Christ which He only began but did not finish! They have even gone the length of blasphemously pronouncing one of their preachers to be "Jesus Christ come in flesh!"

They ignore also the sovereign work of the Holy Spirit in the souls of men. While they admit the term "new birth," and prefer the term "regeneration" to "conversion," yet with them it is simply "turning from the wrong way" to "the Jesus Way." They claim there cannot be new birth without human agency, and that, in their opinion, means a Cooneyite preacher!

From the foregoing and well-attested evidence, it is clearly to be seen that Cooneyism neither offers a Saviour nor salvation, but rather goes far to show that neither is needed.

Review and Warning

If it were necessary for Christ "to overcome His own flesh," as they affirm it was, then His was a sinful condition, and as such, He would need salvation Himself.

If again, there is no atoning value in His precious blood, as they teach, then there is for the sinner no possible means of cleansing, justification or redemption — all of which, the Scriptures tell us, are dependent upon, and are received through, faith in His blood. (See Rom. 3: 24, 25; Acts 10: 43; 1 John 1: 7).

We have no other object in writing the foregoing than to warn the unwary, and seek to help some to "recover themselves out of the snare of the devil, who are taken captive by him at his will" (2 Tim. 2: 26).

[Hearing a "Go-Preacher" state that none but those that heard the gospel through one of *their* preachers could be saved, a man in the crowd asked this pertinent question: "Say, sir, how could my friend who was born *stone deaf* then get saved?" The preacher was dumbfounded, and had no answer.—*Editor.*]

EVOLUTION

By Wm. H. Pettit, M.B., Ch.B.

This pamphlet* is an appeal to reason and common sense. It is not written specially for scientific experts and hence technical terms have been as far as possible avoided. The student or scientist who desires a more detailed and technical treatment of these problems is referred to larger treatises, of which there are a considerable number.

Our purpose is to reach intelligent and thoughtful men and women. We propose to examine the theory of evolution in the light of scientific facts. We ask for an open mind, a careful consideration of the evidence on both sides, and an honest verdict.

Le Conte defines Evolution as "(1) continuous progressive change; (2) according to certain laws; (3) by means of resident forces." The evolutionist assumes that hundreds of millions of years ago one or more tiny, one-celled, living organisms appeared on the earth. Bacteria and amœbae are regarded as examples of these earliest life-forms, which are supposed to have possessed such marvellous powers of development that after long ages they gave rise to all the varied forms of plant and animal life we find around us in the world today.

Atheistic evolutionists see in the wonders of Nature no evidence of a Divine Creator. They believe that the first living cells evolved from sand or mud or slime. They look upon the glories and beauties of Nature and ask us to believe that dead matter gave birth to them all.

Theistic Evolution teaches that Evolution is God's method of Creation. Theistic evolutionists believe that God created in the beginning simple forms of plant and animal life, such

---

*Condensed by the kind permission of the author.

as bacteria and amœbae, and endowed them with the capacity to develop into men.

Some, however, do not possess sufficient credulity to enable them to believe that all the mental, moral and spiritual attributes of man are inherent in an amœba or a typhoid fever germ. These admit that man is a special creation, but regard all other plants and animals as the product of Evolution.

We have, then, three main groups of evolutionists, each holding tenaciously a theory which, if true, proves the other two to be false.

Professor G. M. Price has well said:

> I am perfectly confident that any competent person who will take the time to traverse the evidence now available on this side will reach the same conclusion that I have reached—namely, that the theory of Organic Evolution was a very plausible theory for the times of comparative ignorance of the real facts of heredity and variation, and of the facts of geology which prevailed during the latter part of the nineteenth century; but that this theory is now entirely out of date, and hopelessly inadequate for us, in view of the facts of geology and of experimental breeding as we now know them.

The words of Sir. J. W. Dawson, the great geologist, concerning the widespread acceptance of this unsupported hypothesis are as true today as when they were first written:

> It is one of the strangest phenomena of humanity; it is utterly destitute of proof.

Now let us examine these "proofs" of this "known fact" of evolution which "has been so indubitably established by scientific investigation that it should require no defence."

1. The first "proof" offered is the existence of many different animals which can be arranged in order of increasing complexity: amœbae, jelly-fish, fishes, amphibia, reptiles, birds, mammals and man. Now let us for the sake of clearness concentrate our attention on one section of the series, the step from reptiles to birds. There are two possible explanations of the appearance of the first birds. One is that they are a special creation brought into being by a God of infinite wisdom and power. This is the teaching of Genesis. The only alternative is the evolutionary hypothesis that birds evolved from

reptiles. If the Genesis record is true, we shall find in Nature numbers of reptiles multiplying "after their kind" and numbers of birds multiplying "after their kind," but we shall find no transitional forms between the two groups. This is exactly the position as Biology reveals it. And the study of fossils confirms the fact that such has always been the case since the first appearance of reptiles and birds. If evolution were true, we should of necessity have millions of intermediate forms, part reptile and part bird. The fossils in the rocks would likewise contain ample evidence of these transitional stages. But, as a matter of fact, not one such intermediate form can be produced.

The same inexorable logic of facts can be applied to every step of the supposed evolution from amœba to man. The indispensable transitional forms are entirely lacking.

The "proof" of the theory of evolution based upon the classification of animals is weighed in the balances of *Palaeontology* (the science of fossils), and found wanting.

2. The second "proof" offered is the evidence of *embryology*. At a certain stage in the development of the human embryo several linear arches appear in the region of the neck. The evolutionists used to claim that these arches, resembling in appearance the developing gills of a fish, afforded definite proof that man had evolved from the fish! Unfortunately for the evolutionist, further study has proved that in man these arches develop into the upper and lower jaws, the neck, the tongue and the larynx. They take no part in forming the true breathing apparatus, and hence differ entirely from the branchial arches of the fish. As Prof. G. M. Price says:—

> Any fancied resemblance between these structures and the gill-slits of elasmobranch fishes is merely the product of a highly inventive imagination.

Even so ardent a Darwinian as Sir Arthur Keith is compelled to admit the breakdown of this line of "proof." He says in *The Human Body*, p. 95:—

> Now that the appearances of the embryo at all stages are known, the general feeling is one of disappointment; the human embryo at no stage is anthropoid in its appearance.

We may well ask how any honest scientist can continue to speak of this line of evidence as "proof" that man has ascended from the lowest forms of life *via* the anthropoid apes.

The human embryo, in the earliest stages of its development, may to our imperfect methods of observation look somewhat like the embryo of a fish, a bird, or an ape. But it never develops into any of these lower forms of life. The resemblance is only superficial. There is really just as great a gulf between the different embryos as there is between the various adult forms into which they develop.

3. The third "proof" offered is *atavism,* which means the reappearance in an individual of a character belonging to remote ancestors. It is an interesting phenomenon to the student of heredity, but provides no evidence of evolution. If we had really descended from ape-like creatures, we might expect to find some of the characteristics of these ancestors appearing now and then among human beings. But, as a matter of fact, no such evidence is forthcoming. This "proof" reminds us that within the last few years a scientist solemnly suggested that the present jazz craze was an evolutionary development of the rhythmic movements of the jelly-fish.

4. The fourth "proof" presented is the presence of *vestigial* organs or structures. The wing-bone of the kiwi may be taken as an illustration. This is regarded as evidence that the kiwi is a descendant of a winged bird. Perhaps it is. But this is no proof that the kiwi evolved from a tuatara lizard or will some day grow into a squirrel! Evolutionists claim that the vermiform appendix of man is a vestige of the elongated caecum of herbivorous animals, and hence it is suggested that we have descended from herbivora, such as the sheep! Judging by the sheep-like manner in which one evolutionist follows another in quoting such fantastic "proofs" of his theory one might be pardoned for entertaining the suggestion! Then, again, we are told that the human coccyx, the lowest section of the backbone, is a vestigial tail, which indicates man's descent from the ape. But the coccyx, far from being a useless vestige, serves as the attachment of the important muscles of the floor of the pelvis. The absurd suggestion that it is a vestigial tail shows how hard pushed the

evolutionist must be for "proofs" of his theory. It would be just as reasonable to suggest that the human nose was a vestigial trunk and that this was a clear proof that we were once elephants!

There was a time when the thyroid and other ductless glands were thus classed as useless relics of the past. Now we know they are essential to life and health. It is dangerous to assume that organs are useless simply because of our present lack of knowledge of their functions, and it is unscientific to claim that evolution is the explanation of facts which we cannot understand. Sir Arthur Keith well says: "As our knowledge of the body has increased, the list of useless organs has decreased" (*The Human Body*, p. 236); and E. S. Goodrich declares: "He would be a rash man indeed who would now assert that any part of the human body is useless" (*Evolution*, p. 68).

5. The fifth "proof" of evolution is the *geological evidence*. It was pointed out in connection with the first "proof" of evolution that it was easy to arrange animals in order of increasing complexity, but quite impossible to find any proof that one group had evolved from another. Just in the same way it is easy to arrange the fossils found in the layers of the earth's crust in a regular succession, beginning with the simplest and ending with the most complex. But it is impossible to prove that any group of fossils has descended from any other group. This is clearly shown by the writings of Professor G. M. Price and Lt.-Col. Davies, M.A., F.G.S., F.R.S.E., F.R.A.I. The latter declares:

> It would puzzle any geologist to produce the least shred of evidence for evolution which could stand the test of rigid examination by a capable critic. . . . I would guarantee to get up on a platform with any number of evolutionists as opponents, and riddle their supposed "scientific" case throughout, by putting one fundamental question after another which they would be powerless to answer satisfactorily; although failure to answer any one of those questions would be fatal to all idea of "demonstrating" the truth of Descent (*The Bible and Modern Science*, p. 11).

He further states:

No Proof in Fossils

> Science is powerless to establish descent apart from history. It is an important fact, therefore . . . that fossil series, as such, can never prove anything for evolution. No fossil series, however perfect, can ever prove descent. I have now studied the subject for many years, and I know that there is not a single fossil series which I could not at once pull to pieces as a "proof" of descent.
>
> As a result of this inherent weakness of all fossil series, the best palaeontologists (even when convinced evolutionists) are generally the most cautious of all people in accepting such series as proving descent. Let us take an instance in point: Perhaps no fossil series has ever created a greater impression, or been quoted more often as proving descent, than the famous "ancestry of the horse." Probably everyone has heard of it. In some form or another it appears in countless books, as demonstrative evidence of the evolution of the horse. Yet—and note this—while lesser people are accepting that series with such complete confidence, one of the greatest of modern palaeontologists, Charles Deperet, rejects it altogether! He tells us that: "The supposed pedigree of the Equidae is a deceitful delusion which . . . in no way enlightens us on the palaeontological origin of the horse" (*Transformations of the Animal World*, p. 105). Similarly another eminent palaeontologist, our own Dr. F. A. Bather, when referring to this same supposed ancestry of the horse, showed how little it had stood the test of expert criticism, and remarked that: "Descent, then, is not a corollary of succession" (Address before British Association; see Advancement of Science, 1920: *Geology*, p. 6).
>
> Nor can we doubt that the remarks of the two palaeontologists quoted above are fully justified, for yet another eminent palaeontologist, Sir. J. W. Dawson (who was not an evolutionist), put the whole thing into the simplest terms 30 years ago, when he pointed out that the inherent weakness of all fossil series was surely seen when the modern horse was traced back, by two equally persuasive fossil series, to two entirely different origins! (See his *Modern Ideas of Evolution*, p. 119). In Europe, the horse has been traced back to Paloeotherium, in America to Eohippus. Both series still have their advocates; and the advocates are seldom even agreed about the animals to put into each series. I have compared many supposed ancestries of the horse, and know that the only animal common to all is the modern horse itself. (*The Bible and Modern Science*, pp. 45-47).

It is, of course, perfectly true that modern books on palaeontology (the science of fossil remains) are mostly written by evolutionists who endeavor to arrange and interpret the fossils in accordance with their theory. Prof. W. B. Scott has described the result of these efforts. Writing on "The Palaeontological Record," in *Darwin and Modern Science*, p. 189, he says:

> The ludicrous discrepancies which often appear between the phylogenetic "trees" of various writers have led many zoologists to ignore palaeontology altogether as unworthy of serious attention. . . . What one writer postulates as almost axiomatic, another will reject as impossible and absurd.

In view of the verdict of this authority in Palaeontology how can any evolutionist honestly contend that geology offers any support to his theory?

6. The sixth "proof" offered consists of the facts of *artificial selection.* We will widen this line of evidence to include the facts of "natural selection" also. Darwin believed that all Nature was the scene of a continual "struggle for existence," the result being "the survival of the fittest" and "the elimination of the unfit." He assumed that when certain members of a species developed variations of form, color, size, strength, etc., which proved helpful in this struggle, these favored members would survive, mate and multiply. Nature would thus "select" the most favorable variations, and these would survive while the others died out.

Darwin *assumed* that such a process might continue till the succession of variations produced a new species.

He realized, however, the complete lack of the necessary biological evidence to support his theory. He said (*Life and Letters,* Vol. III., p. 25):—

> There are two or three millions of species on earth—sufficient field, one might think, for observation. But it must be said today that, in spite of all the efforts of trained observers, not one change of a species into another is on record.

Darwin, however, confidently anticipated that further research would furnish the evidence required. But it has not done so. Professor Bateson, one of the most eminent biologists of recent years, and an evolutionist, gave in 1922 a masterly summary of the scientific researches of the previous half-century. He showed that these patient efforts had discovered no evidence of evolution. Each new avenue, entered so confidently, had proved a blind alley. He says:—

> We cannot see how the differentiation into species came about. Variations of many kinds . . . we daily witness, but *no origin of species*. . . . That particular and essential bit of the theory of evolution which is concerned with the origin and nature of species remains utterly mysterious.

The most remarkable fact in the situation is that Professor Bateson and many other eminent scientists are still unable to see or unwilling to admit the perfect correspondence between the facts of Nature and the teaching of Genesis. They still hold that evolution is the only rational explanation of the teeming life around us! They believe in evolution as a universal law, while admitting that they cannot find one instance of its operation! Such is the credulity of the natural mind, even the most gifted and the most learned, when it is closed to the truths of Divine revelation.

By artificial selection remarkable variations can be obtained. Fantail and pouter pigeons, and many other varieties have thus been produced. But they are still pigeons. They never evolve into eagles or into canaries. Nor do they cease to lay eggs; they never evolve into mammals. Moreover, when the directing care of man is withdrawn they quickly revert to the original type, the blue pigeon of the woods. The facts of selection, natural and artificial, furnish no shred of evidence for evolution. They confirm the truth of Genesis that every living thing multiplies "after its kind."

Let no one assume, however, that we believe in the infallibility of the present classification of "species." Far from it. Lt.-Col. Davies says:—

> The dog may . . . be descended from the wolf, and both may have a common origin with the jackal and the fox. The whole cat tribe—from our domestic pet to the lion and the tiger—may also have both a recent and a common origin. The only effect of such admissions would be not to destroy the credit of Scripture, but to reduce the number of animals that Noah would have to take into the ark. (*The Bible and Modern Science*, p. 53).

Professor G. M. Price says:—

> There are now in existence some 40 or 50 species of cats, of the family of the Felidae. . . . But there is no doubt in my mind that they have sprung from a common ancestry. There are some seven species of the Equidae, or horse, and they likewise are probably all of one common ancestry. . . . If these facts and these concessions . . . are of any comfort to the orthodox evolutionists, they are welcome to make the most of them. To my mind, the followers of Darwin and of Mendel . . . are merely the hewers of wood and the drawers of water for those of our day who are now gaining a more accurate insight into that marvellous record of the origin of our present plants and animals, which is the very quintessence of modern scientific discovery, discoveries which so wonderfully confirm the record in the Christian's Bible (*The Phantom of Organic Evolution*, pp. 97, 98).

As true science, dealing with facts and not with theories, learns more of the wonders of Nature, we may find that the different "kinds" of Genesis 1 correspond much more closely with the "genera" than with the "species" of modern biological classification. Certainly all our present knowledge goes to confirm the teaching of Genesis 1, that each type multiplies "after its kind." Mendel's experiments afford no evidence of evolution. They show that variations are due to the sorting of existing factors and not to the formation of *new* ones. Prof. Bateson says:—

> The essence of the Mendelian principle is . . . that the parent cannot pass on to the offspring an element, and, consequently, the corresponding property, which it does not itself possess (*Scientific American Sup.*, 3 January, 1914).

It would be impossible to exaggerate the importance of this fact that actual experiments prove that the parent cannot pass on what it does not itself possess. The amazing thing is that men who know this can still reject Genesis, which teaches the same truth, and accept evolution, which assumes that an amœba or a microbe can produce a man!

Two great facts must always be clearly distinguished. Within the type or "kind" we see a marvellous capacity for variation. Between one type and another there is a great gulf fixed.

Two other "proofs" of evolution are frequently referred to, and will therefore be mentioned at this point.

7. *Homologies,* i.e., similarities of structure in different groups of animals, are often referred to as "proofs" of evolution. The hand of a man, the wing of a bat and the paddle of a whale all show a similar skeletal structure. The keenest advocate of evolution would acknowledge the absurdity of inferring from this fact that the whale evolved from the bat or the man from the whale. He tries to escape from this position by suggesting that they must have arisen from "a common ancestor." We have already seen that the parent can pass on nothing which it does not itself possess. Fancy, then, an amœba or a jelly-fish, which possesses no skeleton, evolving into a bat or a man or a whale! And this is solemnly suggested in the name of "science"! "Hath not God made foolish the wisdom of this world?" (1 Cor. 1: 20).

8. The last "proof" is that derived from the chemical reactions of the blood-serum of animals and men. The subject is highly technical, and students who desire a detailed treatment of it are referred to *The Bankruptcy of Evolution* (Appendix) and to a booklet entitled *Evolution and the Blood Precipitation Test,* by Arthur I. Brown, M.D., C.M., F.R.C.S.E. The latter is probably the ablest treatise obtainable on this question, and exposes the utter fallacy of the whole argument.

Only a few points can be referred to here. In the first place, different series of tests with blood-serum give widely different and contradictory results. For instance, in one of Nuttall's series of tests an exactly similar reaction is given by a whale, a tiger, a baboon, an antelope, and a man! Does the evolutionist ask us to believe that this test proves man to be equally related to each of these?

It would be just as reasonable to claim common descent for the rat, the sheep, the crocodile, the canary, and man, because the bones of each yield calcium!

The proportion of common salt in blood is the same as that in sea-water. Does the evolutionist infer that blood has evolved from sea-water?

Serious and sometimes fatal reactions occur when one man's blood is injected into another man. Does this prove that one of them is not a member of the human race?

Again, the blood-serum of rabbits may be injected into human beings who are "bleeders" with beneficial results. But ox-serum produces a dangerous reaction. Yet, according to the theory of evolution, man is far more closely related to the ox than to the rabbit.

We have now reviewed each of the main lines of "proof" adduced by evolutionists. Not one will bear the searchlight of scientific facts. Not one can maintain its ground under cross-examination.

Failure of "Proofs"

According to this theory, animal life began in one or more tiny one-celled organisms such as the amœbae. It is assumed that these amœbae possessed power to develop into more and more complex organisms, till after hundreds of millions of years they evolved into men! Now evolution is stated to be the *universal law* controlling the development of every living thing. Therefore it must have been operating in *all* of the amœbae for hundreds of millions of years. For amœbae grow only from amœbae—not from sand or slime. Why then is it possible to take a drop of water from any stagnant pool, place it under the microscope and find the amœbae still existing as tiny one-celled organisms, just as they began hundreds of millions of years ago? An amœba which remains unchanged generation after generation for hundreds of millions of years refutes completely the theory of evolution.

The Amoeba Disproves the Theory

In the light of these facts Evolution is seen in its true light—a pretentious superstructure built upon an imaginary foundation. For this false philosophy we are asked to surrender the glorious certainties of a Divine revelation attested by the Lord of Glory! The pathos and tragedy of the present situation is that so many are doing it. The Word of God, nineteen centuries ago, declared that it would be so: "They shall turn away their ears from the truth, and shall be turned unto fables" (2 Tim. 4: 4). The Scriptures of truth, which today men deny and set aside, have accurately foretold all the outstanding features of the present apostasy. The perfect correspondence between these first century prophecies and twentieth century conditions is one of the hall marks of Divine inspiration, confirming our faith in the Bible as "the Word of God which liveth and abideth for ever" (1 Pet. 1: 23).

Let us now turn to the evidence brought forward to "prove" the ape ancestry of man. Four "missing links" are introduced to us.

Four Missing Links

1. *Pithecanthropus erectus,* or the Trinil Ape-Man. This "ape-man" is reconstructed from a piece of a skull found in Java in 1891. Near it a thigh bone and two teeth were found. The piece of skull is so small that when it was examined in 1895 by a group of the world's most famous anthropologists at Leyden, they could not determine to what animal it belonged. One group said it belonged to a man, another group attributed it to an ape, and a third group to a missing link! Dr. Rudolf Virchow, perhaps the greatest anatomist of recent times, after a careful examination, declared it to be the skull of a large gibbon. This first link in the hypothetical chain is certainly "missing"!

Pithecanthropus Erectus

2. Heidelberg man. The Heidelberg *man?* No! The Heidelberg *jaw!* Nothing is known of him except a jaw-bone with teeth well preserved. Not a fragment of the skull or any other part of the skeleton has been found. Furthermore, Prof. Birkner, of Munich, exhibits a modern Eskimo skull, the jaw of which presents the same features. (See *God or Gorilla,* McCann, p. 62.) The second link in this imaginary chain is also "missing"!

Heidelberg Man

3. Neanderthal man. The piece of skull known as the Neanderthal skull was discovered in a cave in Germany in 1856. With this skull cap were found human arm and leg bones, human pelvic bone and pieces of human ribs. Prof. Virchow said, after thoroughly studying these remains, that they were pathologically much altered: that there were traces of rickets and gout, that the Neanderthal man could not possibly have belonged to a primitive savage race. (*The Evolution and Progress of Mankind,* by Klaatch and Heilborn, p. 19).

Neanderthal Man

Huxley said: "In no sense can the Neanderthal bones be regarded as the remains of a human being intermediate between man and the apes."

The third link in our theoretical chain is also "missing"!

4. Piltdown man, otherwise known as *Eoanthropus Dawsoni* (i.e., the dawn-man discovered by Dawson). This "missing link," or ape-man, has been reconstructed by Dr. Smith Woodward from several small pieces of skull and half a lower jawbone found in a gravel pit in Sussex. The pieces were found at different times about the year 1912. The portions of skull present the characteristics of a human skull. The piece of jaw-bone is probably that of an ape. Prof. Hrdlicka, in the Smithsonian Report for 1913, said:—

Piltdown Man

> The most important development in the study of the Piltdown remains is the recent well-documented objection by Prof. Gerrit S. Miller, of the United States National Museum, to the classing together of the lower jaw and the canine with the cranium. According to Miller, who had ample anthropoid, as well as human material for comparison, the jaw and tooth belong to a fossil chimpanzee (Quoted by McCann in *God or Gorilla,* p. 8).

The Piltdown fragments were exhaustively considered by British scientists upon the first report of their discovery to the Geological Society of London, December, 1912. Sir Ray Lankester maintained that the jaw and the skull never belonged to the same creature. Prof. David Waterston, of the University of London, said that the mandible (*i.e.,* lower jaw) was obviously that of a chimpanzee, while the fragments of the skull were human in all their characters.

So the fourth link is also "missing"!

One other "reconstructed" ape-man is deserving of notice. The *Illustrated London News* of June 24, 1912, contained a picture of Mr. and Mrs. Hisperopithecus, reconstructed by Prof. Eliot Smith from a single tooth found in Nebraska by Prof. H. F. Osborn. Both these scientists regarded this tooth as sufficient evidence of yet another missing link to add to the four we have considered above Five years later the cables announced that the tooth had been positively identified as belonging to an extinct wild pig! Since then, Hisperopithecus and his wife have both been "missing"!

Is it any wonder that Prof. F. W. Jones, of the University of London has declared concerning the "missing links":

Imaginary Reconstructions

I find no occupation less worthy of the science of anthropology than the not unfashionable business of modelling, painting or drawing these nightmare pictures of imagination, and lending them in process an utterly false value of apparent reality.

Thus we see that Palaeontology has discovered large numbers of fossil apes and large numbers of fossil men. Why has it failed to find a single specimen of an ape-man? There is only one possible explanation. The ape-man never existed.

This is the reason why Sir J. W. Dawson stated:

I know nothing of the origin of man, except what I am told in the Scriptures—that God created him. I do not know anything more than that, and I do not know of anyone who does.

We have now reviewed all the main lines of evidence upon which the theory of evolution is built. We appeal to the reason and common sense of the reader to decide whether evolution is a proved fact or a specious theory.

One fact is perfectly clear and deserving of special emphasis. It is that a number of the most distinguished scientists frankly declare that no evidence of evolution has been discovered. How, then, is it possible for professors and lecturers to declare that no eminent scientist opposes evolution? What is the explanation of this strange situation? It is really quite simple. When a scientist declares himself against evolution, then the evolutionists take the offender's name off the list they label "eminent"! It is the same process by which the Modernists conclude that no eminent scholar believes in the full inspiration and accuracy of the Scriptures. If a great scholar declares his faith in the Bible as the Word of God they no longer classify him as "eminent"!

If the theory of evolution had been confined to the realm of Biology, if it had been recognized as merely a theory, and if the arguments for and against it had been fairly presented, it would long ago have passed into oblivion. But an unproved hypothesis in Biology has been carried over as a proved and accepted fact into the spheres of Psychology, Philosophy and Theology. Evolution has become the corner-stone of destructive Biblical criticism and the foundation upon which the whole Modernist position is built. Professor F. L. Patton, of Princeton, has well said: "In the crisis of today we are witnessing the greatest war of intellect that has ever been waged since the birthday of the Nazarene."

Evolution vs. The Bible

It is important to emphasize the fact that the theory of evolution has become the chief weapon of attack upon the Bible—"The Word of God which liveth and abideth for ever." The tragedy and pathos of the present situation does not lie so much in the teaching of evolution within our secular educational system. It is found in the much more appalling fact that the Theological Colleges of Protestant Christendom have capitulated to the enemy. This anti-Christian philosophy is being taught in the great majority of these institutions, and most of the theological professors who do not actively propagate it are doing little or nothing to train the future preachers to meet this enemy of the truth.

Hence, many ministers and foreign missionaries are going out without a saving message. The social gospel, the gospel of humanity, or the gospel of evolution is widely substituted for the Gospel of the grace of God.

Evolution Leads to Apostasy

The awful, though generally unrecognized spiritual disaster which has resulted is swiftly preparing for the final apostasy of Christendom, so clearly prophesied by our Lord and His inspired apostles. Modern destructive criticism, built upon the evolutionary theory, denies the infallibility of the Word of God. But the very denial proves the inspiration of the Scriptures. How did the apostles know nearly nineteen hundred years ago that false teachers would arise, "even denying the Lord that bought them," *i.e.*, denying the Deity and Atonement of the Lord Jesus Christ? (See 2 Pet. 2: 1). How did they know that on the basis of the Doctrine of Continuity (which lies at the root of the theory of evolution) these false teachers would scoff at the great truth of the Lord's Second Coming? (See 2 Pet. 3: 3, 4.) These and many other such prophecies which we see being literally fulfilled in the Theological Colleges and the theological literature of the present day prove the divine inspiration of the very Scriptures these men reject and deny.

The impregnable rock of Holy Scripture

The true Christian builds upon the Word of God. He can say with the Psalmist, "Thy Word is true from the beginning," *i.e.*, trom the first word (Ps. 119: 160). "For ever, O Lord, Thy Word is settled in Heaven" (Ps. 119: 89).

We know with certainty that the onward march of true science will continue to reveal more glorious evidences that the Scriptures are the fully inspired and wholly trustworthy revelation of God to man.

The Bible Invulnerable

The reason why so many Christians are being robbed of their faith today is that they are ignorant of the Scriptures. The enemies of the truth have persuaded them to throw away "the shield of faith," and discard "the sword of the Spirit which is the Word of God." And hence they fall an easy prey to the great adversary when he appears as "an angel of light," propagating his doctrines through those who appear as "ministers of righteousness" (2 Cor. 11: 14, 15). They "turn away their ears from the truth" and are "turned unto fables" (2 Tim. 4: 4).

We do not attempt to defend the Word of God. All we need to do is to take our stand upon it, and it will defend us from every assault of the enemy.

Principal Samuel Chadwick has reminded us that in the present conflict everything is at stake when he says:—

> If the cunningly devised philosophies of Modernism are right, I have been of all fools the most deluded; but I know whom I have believed, and I know that I know.

The Personal Appeal

On every hand men are departing from the faith, exchanging the eternal truth of God for the passing philosophies of men. The Lord is saying to His own, "Will ye also go away?" May we be enabled by Divine grace to respond, "Lord, to whom shall we go? Thou hast the words of eternal life."

FREEMASONRY

By W. Hoste, B.A.

To the ordinary observer, Freemasonry is connected with secret signs, gaudy insignia, and mysterious functions, not leading apparently anywhere in particular; but is in fact a sort of Higher Class Friendly Society; rather old-fashioned perhaps, but possibly useful, and certainly perfectly harmless, from the religious point of view, acknowledging, as it does, God as "The Great Architect of the Universe," and displaying an open Bible among its symbols. The fact that it includes Church dignitaries and Nonconformist divines, etc., in its ranks, still further veils its true character.

Initiation

No doubt some real Christians have allowed themselves to be ensnared, but their initiation should have opened their eyes. How can it be of the mind of Him who says, "Swear not at all," to take solemn oaths not to divulge a secret, still unknown, and to call down on one's person blood-curdling curses* in case of failure to keep the oaths? The ritual is really Hindu, with Bible names substituted.

A Religion

However, that such a venerable cult, to which so many "wise, mighty and noble are called," should be in deadly conflict with true Christianity, or even a rival of any religion, seems in this country a proposition too difficult even to contemplate. But any who know how in France *la francmaconnerie* is synonymous with active opposition to any form of dogmatic Christianity, will not share this difficulty, unless indeed latitudes alter cases.

---

*As the degrees advance, the penalties increase. For the first degree, your tongue is torn from its roots; for the second, your heart; for the third, your bowels, and then burnt, etc., etc., and you pray that it may be so.

In the British Empire its religious character is generally recognized as so neutral, that it starts with a great advantage, for, whereas a man cannot be a Roman Catholic and Protestant, churchman and dissenter, Baptist and Quaker, at the same time, any one may be a Freemason and remain a "faithful" member of his own church; for is it not an ethical system, rather than a religion? Listen to one of its authoritative exponents—Dr. Fort Newton, late Unitarian Minister of the London City Temple: "Masonry is not a religion, *but it is Religion* (my italics), a worship in which all good men may unite"†—the "good men" being Unitarians, Hindus, Jews, nominal Christians, Moslems, Theosophists, etc. For a Christian, then, to be a Freemason is "to be unequally yoked together with unbelievers," a thing expressly forbidden.‡ Again, "We only pursue the Universal Religion," or as another writes, "All Masons therefore whether Christian, Jew or Mahommedan . . . although we take different routes . . . we mean to travel to the same place." Alas, how many, like Bunyan's boatman, are looking to the Heavenly City, and rowing the other way! "I am the Way," saith the Lord, "no man cometh unto the Father but by Me" (John 14: 6).

Relationship to Christianity

Freemasonry utterly repudiates the exclusive claims of Christianity. "It is well," writes W. L. Wilmshurst, "for a man to be born in a church, but *terrible for him to die in one*" (my italics). Paul, on the contrary, wrote to Timothy: "Continue thou in the things that thou hast learned and hast been assured of . . . and that from a child thou hast known the Holy Scriptures which are able to make thee wise unto salvation through faith which is in Christ Jesus" (2 Tim. 3: 14, 15). Contrast this with further words of the same author: "The work of the Church ends, where the knowledge of God begins"! Another, a professed Christian minister, writes: "All candidates, Christian or otherwise, come to us in a state of darkness." Nay, rather, they

†*"The Builders,"* as quoted in *The Menace of Freemasonry.*

‡*The Spirit of Freemasonry* (Hutchinson), acknowledged by Masons to be authoritative.

come *to "a state of darkness,"* for Christ is the light of the world, and He is nowhere to be found in this system.

Social Advantages

In the article on "Freemasonry" in the *Encyclopaedia Britannica*—a dry-as-dust enumeration of the foundation of lodges, a saying "nothing with a deal of skill"—one sentence stands out: "For many years the craft has been conducted without respect to class, color, caste or creed." To the uninitiated this sounds well. The philanthrophy of the Society then overflows to the wide world without distinction. Nothing is further from the truth. You must enter it to benefit by its advantages, and you pay dearly. But that commercial and social advantages do accrue to members is a fact held out as a lure to possible candidates. In many houses of business in London, it is "considered advantageous for business purposes to insist on the higher employees being Masons."

Anti-Scriptural

"Masonry" professes to be the essence of all creeds. She certainly jealously guards the essential features of all human creeds, *viz.*, the denial of the need of atonement by the blood of Christ, and the claim to salvation by self-effort. Man is his own Saviour, and no one else is. How different is the testimony of the Bible! No salvation by works! No salvation in any other but Christ! (Eph. 2: 9; Acts 4: 12). In fact, though the Bible rests among her symbols, Freemasonry contradicts it to her votaries. It is true that a special Bible is presented to candidates at their initiation, but what is on its first page? "The Masons' Charge—testifying to what the Craft really stands for: *Masonry encourages each man to be steadfast in the faith his heart loves best*" (my italics); thus in one sentence setting aside the necessity of conversion, the evangelization of the world and the uniqueness of Christ and His work. Is it not true that any Mason who pretends that Masonry can be harmonized with Christianity is violating the constitution he has sworn to accept?

Freemasonry, viewed doctrinally, is Theosophy. But, someone may interject, Does it not speak of God, Christ, the Bible, etc.? Yes, like Theosophy, it is heavily camouflaged with scriptural expressions, but used in an unscriptural sense.

Without doubt in general its vocables are the same, but the god of Masonry at any rate is altogether other than the God of the Bible. He is a composite deity—Jehovah, Baal and On, or Osiris, rolled into one, under the initials J. B. O.* Novitiates are kept in ignorance of this; they hear the descriptive title, "the Divine Architect," and imagine that it is the God of the Bible who is meant. Whereas, if Freemasonry be true, the very idol that Jezebel set up in defiance of Jehovah, and On—one of those gods of Egypt, against which Jehovah "executed judgment"—share the Godhead with Him. Was it for nothing He gave the commandment, "Thou shalt have none other gods beside Me" (Exod. 20: 3); and said, "My glory will I not give to another, neither My praise to graven images" (Isa. 42: 8)? "Christ," too is on the lips of the Mason, but only in a list of heathen and mythical heroes—Buddha, Vishnu, Baldur, Osiris, Adonis, etc.; all on the same plane, and "but different labels of the same idea." A niche has always been offered to Christ in "the world's *pantheon*," but He claims the Throne: "Other foundation can no man lay than that is laid which is Jesus Christ;" "There is none other name under heaven given among men, whereby we must be saved." Christ "in all things must have the pre-eminence" (1 Cor. 3: 11; Acts 4: 12; Col. 1: 18).

The Bible, according to the Masonic theory, is only one chapter of a great volume, comprising the Vedas, Koran, etc., all equally God's Word.

Probably much that is going on today in the Indian and other Mission fields among professed Christian teachers who are pressing for an amalgamation of Christianity with all that is best in Hinduism, etc., may be influenced by the fact that these men, though probably not all Masons by initiation, have drunk deeply into the spirit of the Craft, and are carrying out its exact program of combining "the best elements in all religions" to form the Universal Religion. That this will prove to be the religion of the Antichrist that is to come, I have little doubt. But the Truth of God will prevail.

---

*"Lest we should offend," we will not go further and divulge the great secret of Masonry—the divine name, which no Mason may pronounce by himself, but which is sufficiently widely known outside the Craft.

HUMANISM

By Arthur H. Carter

"God that made the world and all things therein, seeing that He is Lord of heaven and earth, dwelleth not in temples made with hands; neither is worshipped with men's hands as though He needed anything, seeing He giveth to all life and breath, and all things, and hath made of one blood all nations of men for to dwell on all the face of the earth, and hath determined the times before appointed, and the bounds of their habitation: that they should seek the Lord, if haply they might feel after Him and find Him, though He be not far from everyone of us; for in Him we live, and move, and have our being, as certain also of your own poets have said, for we are also His offspring" (Acts 17: 24-28. See context).

"Because that when they knew God, they glorified Him not as God, neither were thankful, but became vain in their imaginations, and their foolish heart was darkened. Professing themselves to be wise, they became fools" (Rom. 1: 21, 22).

Genesis

As with heathenism so with Humanism. Sir Monier Wiliams points out in his great work on the religions of the East, that while flashes of light penetrate here and there, darkness prevails with all its superstitions and delusive suggestions. Out of the darkness of Romish Scholasticism, following hard upon the decline and fall of the Roman Empire—a darkness that through Divine permission well-nigh obliterated the true light that has ever shone through the intermediary of the Church of our Lord and Saviour Jesus Christ—there arose an intellectual struggle for freedom that eventually assumed the title of Humanism. A yearning after culture and freedom of thought and "the cultivation of the polite branches of knowledge" . . . developed "a system of thinking in which man, his interests and development are made central and dominant. Its tendency is to exalt the cultural and practical rather than the scientific and speculative, and to encourage a spirit of revolt against existing opinions" (*New Standard Dictionary*).

Its Pioneers

Francesco Petrarch (1304—1374), an Italian scholar and lyric poet, contemporary of Dante, initiated the Humanistic Movement, and was followed by Cardinal Bessarion (1395—1472), Bishop of Nicaea and Patriarch of Constantinople; Reuchlin (1455—1522), German Hebraist; and Erasmus (1466—1536), the celebrated Dutch theologian who studied in Paris, Oxford, and Turin, the friend of Colet and More, whose labors on behalf of the foundations of certain colleges and educational institutions in England are valued to this day. Erasmus in his struggles after intellectual liberty was said to have "laid the egg which Luther hatched."

The Greek and Latin classics lay as the foundation upon which the intellectualism of Humanism was erected, but failing to recognize as its true base Divine Revelation as set forth in the Scriptures of truth, it only led its followers into the maze of uncertainty, and provided no satisfaction for the hunger of the soul.

John Milton, the blind poet, while in association with Humanistic influences, rose above the mere intellectualism of his day through a profound sense and knowledge of the fact of Divine Revelation which nought could extinguish. Humanism broke away from what was (and still is) known as "traditional theology," and hankered after the seductive teachings of Greek and Roman philosophers.

D'Aubigné ("History of Protestantism," Book I, Chaps. 7, 8) gives the following succinct account of the Movement. "There was at that period (14th and 15th centuries) a great burst of light, and Rome was doomed to suffer by it. This passion for antiquity which took possession of the Humanists shook in the most elevated minds their attachment to the church, for 'no man can serve two masters.' At the same time the studies to which they devoted themselves, placed at the disposition of these learned men a method entirely new and unknown to the schoolmen of examining and judging the teaching of the church. Finding in the Bible much more than in the works of theologians, the beauties that charmed them in the classic authors, the Humanists were fully inclined to place the Bible above the doctors. They reformed the taste, and this prepared the way for the Reformation of the faith. . . . Still this great light which the study of antiquity threw out in the 15th century was calculated only to destroy; it could not build up. Neither Homer nor Virgil could save the church. The revival of learning, sciences and arts was not the principle of the Reformation. . . . The study of ancient literature produced very different effects in Germany from those which followed it in Italy and in France: it was there combined with faith. The Germans immediately looked for the advantage that might accrue to religion from these new literary pursuits. What had produced in Italian minds little more than a minute and barren refinement of the understanding, pervaded the whole being of the Germans, warmed their hearts, and prepared them for a brighter light. The first restorers of learning in Italy and in France were remarkable for their levity, and frequently also for their immorality. . . . Thus a new world, sprung out of antiquity, had arisen in the midst of the world of the Middle Ages. The two parties could not avoid coming to blows; a struggle was at hand. . . . In order that the truth might prove triumphant, it was necessary first that the weapons by which she was to conquer should be brought forth from the arsenals where they had lain buried for ages. These weapons were the Holy Scriptures of the Old and New Testaments. It was necessary to revive in Christendom the love and the study of the sacred Greek and Hebrew learning. The man whom the providence of God selected for the task was named John Reuchlin. . . . Luther, acknowledging all that Reuchlin had done, wrote to him shortly after his victory over the Dominicans: 'The Lord has been at work in you, that the light of Holy Scripture might begin to shine in that Germany where for so many years, alas, it was not only stifled, but entirely extinct'."

While the title "Humanism" is known of but little today, the elements of this skeptical movement are found both latent and patent in prevailing Modernism. In the United States of America, that home of strange cults, Humanism has recently been coming more prominently to the fore, and several works have appeared on the subject; but, as aptly

Humanism Today

summed up by an American critic, "Humanism is apostate Unitarianism"!

As one follows the rise of Deism, Rationalism, Higher Criticism, New Theology and Modernism, "we find the same unsatisfactory" and unsatisfying element predominating. The history of Old and New Testament Criticism reveals the fact that intellectualism apart from the recognition and experience of Divine Revelation, leads into the direst regions of skepticism and darkness of soul. The records of the mistaken "researchings" of Bolingbroke, Hume, Jean Astruc, Spinoza, Eichhorn, De Wette, Kuenen, Ewald, Bishop Colenso, Wellhausen, Drs. Cheyne, Driver and a host of others, give startling evidence of the havoc wrought to faith in the experience of those who philosophize on rationalistic lines, and refuse to bow before the supreme authority of the Scriptures of Truth, so aptly described in the Thirty-nine Articles of the Church of England as "God's Word Written."

Humanism—Deism—Modernism

Out of the Humanism of the Middle Ages eventually developed the Deism of the eighteenth century which has found its unholy fruitage in the daring Modernistic apostasy of our own times. As it ever has been, so it is today—the one great essential, the only possible solution of the problems of mind and heart and life, is to be found in that lowly attitude of mind operated upon by the Holy Spirit whereby, conscious of our sinful state by nature, mentally warped and blinded by inherent and intellectual sin, we confess ourselves undone in the presence of the glorious fact of the finished work of our Lord Jesus Christ on the substitutionary sacrificial cross of Calvary—yea, that He not only died according to the Scriptures, but was buried, and was raised again for our justification.

How sadly applicable to the intellectual darkness of Humanism is the inspired statement of the Apostle! "But if our Gospel be hid, it is hid to them that are lost: in whom the god of this world hath blinded the minds of them which believe not, lest the light of the glorious Gospel of Christ, who is the image of God, should shine unto them. For we preach not ourselves, but Christ Jesus the Lord; and ourselves your servants for Jesus' sake. For God who commanded the light to shine out of darkness, hath shined in our hearts, to give the light of the knowledge of the glory of God in the face of Jesus Christ" (2 Cor. 4: 3-6).

We augment Mr. Carter's most interesting article with an abridged extract from *The Presbyterian* of October 10, 1929:

Dr. Potter's Humanist Church

Considerable newspaper publicity has been given to the fact that on September 29, Dr. Charles Francis Potter, of New York City, formerly a minister of the Universalist Church, launched an organization to promote what is called a new religion, which he terms Humanism. It is hardly accurate to speak of Humanism as new, as it has had its representatives for generations, but certainly the movement has a vogue today that it has never previously enjoyed, and there are not lacking signs, as we pointed out last week, that it is to become the chief modern rival of Christianity. Neither is it accurate to speak of Dr. Potter's church as the only one in which the creed of Humanism is preached. As a matter of fact, in all essentials it is being preached today in many pulpits, even in those classed as evangelical. Certainly Christianity is through and through supernaturalistic, so that no naturalistic scheme of thought and life has any honest right to call itself Christian. Nothing is more certain than that Christianity de-supernaturalized is Christianity extinct; hence, if Dr. Potter is right in holding that "the so-called supernatural is only the not yet understood natural," it is high time that Christianity be relegated to the museum of dead religions. As a matter of fact, however, Dr. Potter with naturalistic thinkers in general, deals with only part of reality, and that a relatively insignificant part. They ignore the Lord God Almighty whom the heaven of heavens cannot contain, to whom the earth is less than the small dust in the balance.

Dr. Potter's Humanism

Then follows a summary of "points of difference" between Christianity and Humanism. We give the latter as a fairly true working creed in Dr. Potter's own words:

The chief end of man is to improve himself, both as an individual and as a race.

Man is inherently good and of infinite possibilities.

Man should not submit to injustice or sufferings without protest, and should endeavor to remove its causes.

There are truths in all religions and outside of religions.

The world and man evolved.

Those ideas are unimportant in religion.
Improvement comes from within. No man or God can "save" another man.
Suffering is the natural result of breaking the laws of right living.
Doing right brings its own satisfaction.

The Editor of *The Presbyterian* continues:—

While there are indications that Humanism may play a relatively large place in the thinking of the immediate future, we may be sure that such measure of triumph as it may enjoy will be short-lived. A theory of life that ignores or denies life's most significant realities cannot, in the nature of the case, have more than a short-lived triumph. Genuine Christianity can no more perish out of the earth than the sense of sin can disappear from the heart of sinful humanity, than the knowledge of God can fade from the minds of dependent creatures, than God Himself can cease to exist. The Christ of the New Testament is not only a fact of the past, He is a fact of the present, and though hand join to hand, His plans and purposes will not fail of realization.

THE KENOSIS THEORY

By A. McD. Redwood

To call the Kenosis theory a doctrine is to misuse terms. At most it cannot be called anything more than a hypothesis or theory, and that of a very flimsy kind. It is very largely a product of the "Higher Criticism."

For convenience we shall divide our subject into two sections—(1) The Examination of the Theory, (2) the Refutation of the Theory.

Whilst of course it is impossible to be too critical of any of the "learned" theories of the neo-critics, we cannot in a short article touch on more than a few of the main points. Readers are strongly advised to study one or more of the many excellent treatises written by able scholars in refutation, if they are at all troubled with the difficulties of the question.*

Examination of Theory

We proceed to consider briefly; (*a*) Definition, (*b*) Arguments, (*c*) Consequences.

Definition

(*a*) The Kenosis Theory relates to the admittedly difficult and abstruse question of the *extent* to which Christ did divest Himself of His Divine attributes in taking upon Himself the limitations involved in His becoming Man. In the words of the late Professor James Orr, D.D. (who is of course opposed to the theory, though he accurately indicates its teaching), it asserts:—

> That Jesus, in His Incarnation, emptied Himself of His divine attributes to such an extent that He shared the same infirmities and limitations of knowledge with the ordinary man. He shared alike their ignorance and their mistakes, and He was no better off than the Rabbins of His day in His knowledge of "the Law and the Prophets."
>
> In fact, some theologians would go so far as to say that "Christ did absolutely abandon relation of equality with God and His functions in the universe."

---

*Two of these are: *Our Lord and His Bible,* by Preb. H. E. Fox, M.A. (*vide* ch. 6 specially): *Sidelights on Christian Doctrine,* by Prof. James Orr, D.D.

(*b*) The Higher Critics base their hypothesis more or less upon inferences drawn from two classes of Scripture passages. The one class is composed of those very rare references to Christ's "limitations" as represented by Mark 13: 32 (others are Matt. 24: 36; Luke 2: 52, etc.). The other class of passages may be typically illustrated by such references as Matt. 12: 39, 40; Luke 16: 22, where, so the Critics state, Christ makes use of (what they are pleased to call) "popular tales" to illustrate His discourses—using them, be it very carefully noted, as if they were really historical facts!

Argument

Both sets of passages, it will be noted, make reference to Christ's knowledge, or His omniscience—which is definitely *inferred* as limited in extent. Very much is made of His statement in Mark 13: 32; whilst the other class of passages are brought in to support the otherwise slender reference. The Critics assume (without any real valid proof) the unreality, or—shall we say?—the non-historicity, of the story of Jonah, and similar passages and, therefore, Christ's use of, or reference to, such passages is made to reflect upon His knowledge of their real character. He simply shares in the mistakes and limitations of the men of His day! If He were omniscient how could He refer to "Abraham's bosom" and a "hell of conscious torment" as He did? Either He did not know, or willingly allowed these fallacies to pass unchallenged, in fact, built upon them! So that either His knowledge or His morality is involved!

Still further proof of Christ's limitations is found by the Critics in that famous passage, Phil. 2: 3-10, whereon the expression, "made Himself of no reputation" (or more correctly, as in the R. V., "emptied Himself") is founded, and from which the title Kenosis is derived (*ekenosen,* from *kenoo,* "I empty"). This expression is pushed to its utmost limits, to such an extent as to deprive Him of most, if not all, the distinctive characteristics of Deity.

It is not too much to say of most present-day Modernists what a scholarly reviewer says of a recent Modernist book: "Excision of everything in the New Testament which stands in the way of the minimizing of Jesus is the path by which the author proceeds to his conclusions."

Consequences

(*c*) These are at once apparent to any who will take time to think. In the first place, it puts our Lord on no higher a plane as regards His teaching than finite men—than the Rabbins of His day, for instance. His pronouncements, therefore, on the Old Testament cannot be trusted. In fact, the Kenosis hypothesis becomes not only a disparagement of Christ (which of course is its worst feature), but a setting aside of the integrity and authority of both the Old and New Testaments.

If we look at its history we shall find that it arose mainly in a desire to remove the strongest support of the Old Testament—our Lord's own use and vindication of it. Whatever other arguments could be brought forward to discount the Scriptures, they lost much of their force as long as Christ's use of the Holy Writings could be claimed as an authoritative imprimatur to their genuineness. The Critics themselves acknowledged this. The only thing to do, therefore, was to rob Christ of any force that might attach to His sayings. This could only be done by bringing in the Kenosis hypothesis, at first veiledly and then more emphatically. In a stroke it removed the intrinsic value of His references to the Scriptures—they and HE fell together inevitably.

Where this Theory finally lands us may not have been fully appreciated in the beginning, but Prebendary Fox puts the matter very tersely when he says, "He who cannot follow Christ at least in His treatment of the Old Testament will soon find (as some are already doing) that there are other parts also of the Master's teaching where they leave His company. And then—?" The promises He made to those who looked up to Him as Master-Teacher are, to say the least, not based on very sure foundations. "Can the lost be certain that He came to seek and save them? Can the weary and heavy laden be assured that He will give them rest?... For this alleged ignorance or nescience on the part of Jesus Christ affects no light or casual matter; it touches the most vital part of His teaching." In fact, one hesitates to consider the abyss of skepticism into which the logical termination of this hypothesis would eventually lead us, and into which, alas, many have landed.

There are at least two main grounds for rejecting this teaching, though there are a number of subsidiary ones, all of which have a cumulative effect.

Refutation

(*a*) The first reason for rejecting it is that the Critics draw altogether unwarrantable conclusions from the slender Scripture references they quote.

There is no question, of course, that Christ did submit to "such limitations as a true manhood imposed upon Him." It could not be otherwise. Apart from sin His Manhood is not some alien or strange freak, but "*solidaire* with ours" (as Moule puts it). Even so, His humanity never for a moment stands apart from His Divine nature. "The Manhood was, and is, never independently personal." This supreme truth has to be kept constantly in mind in dealing with this subject. We may quote Moule again in his statement that, "the Manhood of Christ is to be studied, not in the abstract, but in its actual, absolute, necessary harmony with His deity, under His divine Personality." His limitations, we may say, therefore, were *conditioned* by His Manhood, but uniquely and severely *circumscribed* by His Divine-Human Consciousness.

In considering, then, such references as Mark 13: 32; Luke 2: 52; Acts 1: 7, etc., we are compelled to guard against erroneous inferences. Granted that the Son did submit to certain limitations, granted that He does distinguish between His own knowledge and that of His Father regarding future events (note that He does not thus refer to *past* events), we have no warrant for inferring that Christ was in error on things that He did speak of and teach. This point Professor James Orr very clearly brings out in the following quotations from his book already named:—

Erroneous Inferences

He (Jesus) was conscious of what He knew, and of what it was not given Him to know. Within His knowledge He spoke; on what lay beyond He was silent. In what He did say His utterances were authoritative. A first mistake in this theory, therefore, is the confusing of *nescience* with *error*. If there was limitation of knowledge, it is assumed that there must be necessity of error. But this in no way follows in regard to the mind of the Divine Son. That mind was unlike every other mind...in being in absolute, constant touch with the Source of all truth. . . . Further, it is never to be forgotten that, while the Son submits to the conditions of humanity, it is still the *Son of God* who so submits, and behind all human conditionings are still present the undiminished resources of the Godhead.

In similar strain we find Dr. Handley Moule commenting upon the passages referred to:—

(Mark 13:32) . . . no doubt limits His knowledge on that one point. But the very phrase, from His lips, looks like an implicit claim to knowledge otherwise complete. And the doctrine of the Eternal Sonship, in the Gospels, makes it surely inconceivable that even that limitation of conscious knowledge should be imposed on the Son because of limitation of capacity. It was for unknown purposes of dispensation; and it was the one thing of the kind.

The Christian who deals eclectically with any positive statement of His, about fact as well as about principle, is on very dangerous ground indeed.

As regards Luke 2:52, the "increase in wisdom" no more implies stages of defective wisdom than the "increase in favor with God" implies stages of defective favor. What is implied is developed application to developed subject-matter. (*Cf.* by all means *Liddon, Bampton Lectures.* Lect. 8).*

Much could be said regarding the other texts, but it must suffice for us to emphasize *the impossibility of building so weighty a superstructure on so slender a basis.*

The very few texts that point to a certain necessary limitation on the part of the God-man cannot be separated, on any pretext, from the totality of Scripture testimony. And, as we shall see below, that testimony is unequivocal in upholding the truth that Professor Orr states so appositely—that, *"Behind all human conditionings are still present the undiminished resources of the Godhead."*

(*b*) The second reason for rejecting the hypothesis, is that our Lord's own claims are altogether opposed to it. Here

Christ's Claims

of course we touch a large subject, which strictly speaking calls for the examination of the whole of the Gospels. But the following typical passages may be taken as indicating the unequivocal bearing of all the rest—John 6:63; 8:28,

**Outline of Christian Doctrine*, p. 63.

29, 38, 40, 42, 51, 58; 12: 48-50; 14: 24; 15: 3; Luke 24: 27, 44-46.

If the neo-critics are correct in their hypothesis, then the only alternative is that our Lord made statements which are not merely exaggerated, but deliberately and flagrantly untrue. It is quite obvious that His statements concerning Himself, and theirs concerning Him, are incompatible. And if His are proved to be wrong, it seems strange that it has been left to men of the nineteenth century to find it out! We have to make choice between Him and them.

Modern methods of seeking to overcome this difficulty are inclined to be taken up with discrediting the authenticity of such passages as the above. The following sentence, as an instance, is taken from the Modernist book referred to in the beginning: "It is apparent that this writer (referring to the author of the Fourth Gospel), in his views of the Old Testament, has but little in common with Matthew and Luke and nothing at all in common with Jesus." The argument may be set out dialectically as follows:—

Critic: The Old Testament is all wrong.

Reply: But Christ set His imprimatur on it, how then can it be wrong?

Critic: Yes, but Christ was limited in His knowledge, *He* was wrong.

Reply: How can He be wrong when He claimed both equality with God and that His teaching was of God ("As My Father hath taught Me, I speak these things")?

Critic: The writer of such passages cannot be relied upon—"he had nothing in common at all with Jesus."

And so it goes on—the "scissors method," as one reviewer calls it! By such methods it would be easy to get rid of sun, moon and stars—in theory! The mariner could get rid of many a rock, many a sandbank—on paper!

We are content to take our stand by the side of John and Paul and Luke and countless other saints down the ages who believed Jesus to be what He was, God of very God, Man of very man, and accepted His teaching as Divine and infallible.

MODERNISM

By Wm. C. Irvine

Modern Modernism takes its direct descent from Higher Criticism. It builds its castles on the shifting sands of the so-called "assured results" of "critical Scholarship." But the true origin of this deadly heresy can be traced to a garden—which garden all Modernists do their best to legendarize—therein the first tragedy of Modernism took place.

Its Origin

"As for Modernism," said the Warden of a Madras College, "people make a mistake when they think it is a new fad or that it is of a mushroom growth. Modernism, as a certain mode of thinking, is as old as Mother Eve." How very true, for Satan was the first of the cult and on his first introduction to—or rather intrusion on—the human race, his first words were: "Yea, hath God said, Ye shall not eat of every tree of the garden?"

Herein lies the very essence of Modernism:—

"Yea"—a diplomatic affirmative.

"Hath God said"—an artfully expressed doubt immediately negativing the affirmation, presented in the form of a question.

"Ye shall not eat of EVERY tree of the garden?"—a falsification of God's utterance: "Thou shalt not eat of It."

Are any of the germs of Modernism missing?

Its modern revival can be traced through Spinoza, a Dutchman, who lived towards the end of the 17th century and wrote a book to prove that Ezra was the author of the Pentateuch: through Jean Astruc, who lived in the middle of the 18th century: Eichhorn, who took up his theories, and De Wette the German, soon followed by Julius Wellhausen, of whom it is asserted that, when he was told that British higher critics still believed in the Old Testament Scriptures as inspired, he said: "I knew the Old Testament was a fraud; but I never dreamed of making God a party to the fraud as these Scotch fellows do."

The most characteristic marks of Modernism can be clearly traced in some heresy, in well-nigh every century.

Characteristic Marks

A reader of *The Southern Methodist* tabulated some of the chief features of the Gnostic Heresy of the first century, of the Marcionites of the second century, of the Neo-Platonic Heresy and the Manichean Heresies of the third, and the Pelagian Heresy of the fourth century. It is almost a monotonous repetition! If we give one, we practically give all. Here is his outline describing the Gnostic Heresy of the first century:

"Claimed to have a deeper and truer view of Christianity.
"Rejected the inerrancy of the Holy Scriptures.
"Belief in one's self is belief in God.
"Christ delivers men by His coming and not by an atonement.
"Rejected the virgin birth of Jesus.
"Ridiculed orthodoxy.
"Salvation by illumination."

Anyone writing a thousand years hence might fairly summarize the teachings of Modernism as found above.

Dr. Ernest Gordon in *The Leaven of the Sadducees* (p. 221) says:

> Strauss gathered up in masterly fashion the whole literature of free thought which preceded his day. It would be a fruitful undertaking to examine whether there is a single objection, argument, sneer, wound in Christ's body, to be found in American theological literature which cannot be traced back to the *Leben Jesu* or to Strauss' minor writings.

In a footnote he says: "'These sections (of the *Leben Jesu*),' says Schwetzer (Ques. 84), 'marked out the ground which is now occupied by modern critical study.'"

In the face of the above, well may the reader marvel at the repeated claims of the Modernists to new light, etc., which so constantly is found in their writings.

Before entering further into our subject it might be well

to give a few utterances of Conservative scholars concerning Modernism. That practically all scholarship, as many Modernists have claimed, is on their side, is simply untrue. We can find space for but a few.

Conservative Scholars and Modernism

A. H. Finn, whose monumental work, *The Unity of the Pentateuch,* is still unanswered, says:

> In a very careful study of the criticism of the Pentateuch, I have found reason to object to strained interpretations, circular arguments, beggings of the question, unsubstantiated assertions, and other questionable methods; and similar blemishes are not absent from the criticism of the New Testament.*

Robert Dick Wilson, Ph.D., D.D., whose erudite knowledge of classical and biblical languages was unequalled by any living scholar, said:

> I've seen the day, when I've just trembled at undertaking a new investigation, but I've gotten over that. I have come now to the conviction that *no man knows enough to assail the truthfulness of the Old Testament.* Whenever there is sufficient documentary evidence to make an investigation, the statements of the Bible, in the original texts, have stood the test.†

Sir Wm. Ramsay, whose research work is so well known, said:

> The Modernist theologian knows all that I do not know. He has no hesitation; he fixes the limits of the possible and knows exactly what is impossible....He knows all things, and he is content and happy in his utter ignorance...He believes in the so-called laws of nature, and thinks that he knows... The Modernist is no more than a survival from the remote past.‡

Sir Wm. Ramsay was a one-time higher critic, but through his own discoveries in the realms of archæological research he became a firm believer in the inspiration and inerrancy of Holy Writ.

**Liberal Theology (so called)* by A. H. Finn, p. 15.
†*Is the Higher Criticism Scholarly?* by R. D. Wilson, p. 10.
‡*Modernism versus the Bible,* by A. J. Pollock, p. 31.

The same writer quotes the following by *Professor Sayce* in his great work *Monument Facts and Higher Critical Fancies* (pp. 17, 18):

> In dealing with the history of the past we are confronted with two utterly opposed methods, one objective, the other subjective, one resting on a basis of veritable facts, the other on the unsupported and unsupportable assumptions of the modern scholar. The one is the method of archæology, the other of the so-called "higher criticism." Between the two the scientifically trained mind can have no hesitation in choosing.

This is rather bitter medicine for those who are constantly making the assumption that their "assured results" are the findings of modern science.

Sir Robert Anderson, K.C.B., LL.D., in the sixth edition of *The Bible and Modern Criticism*, writes:—

> The Higher Criticism at once degraded into what it is today—a skeptical crusade against the Bible, tending to lower it to the level of a purely human book (p. 43).

J. Gresham Machen, D.D., in *What is Faith?* says:—

> The retrograde, anti-intellectual (*sic*) movement called Modernism, a movement which really degrades the intellect by excluding it from the sphere of religion, will be overcome, and thinking will again come to its rights (p. 18).

James M. Gray, D.D., in *Modernism*, states that:—

> Modernism is a revolt against the God of Christianity.
> Modernism is a revolt against the Bible of Christianity.
> It is a revolt against the Christ of Christianity.

H. W. White, D.D., Editor, The China Fundamentalist:

> Some day we may recognize that Modernism is Bolshevism, and descends to the lowest methods of fighting the Gospel (*C. F.*, July-September, 1929).

We conclude with a severe but unquestionably true censure of Modernism, by *Dr. T. T. Shields* of Toronto, who has long and faithfully contended for the Faith:

> Modernism, when it is finished, is *sheer lawlessness;* it rejects all authority except the authority that resides in the

individual himself. *Modernism is of the "Old Man," and the Old Man, even though he wear the Gown and Hood of a Professor of Philosophy, is always an Anarchist,* he "is not subject to the law of God, neither indeed can be." Modernism is a *naturalistic religion.* It grows out of the pride of the human mind that magnifies men and minimizes God; it holds that authority in religion is in *man's own consciousness,* rather than objectively in the Book as the revelation of God Himself.

What defence and answer do Modernist leaders make to all these and other charges? Practically none.

Podsnappery*

In *Our Mutual Friend,* Dickens, in his inimitable style, portrays the character of a fairly large section of society, whose importance in this little world of ours, if taken at their own value, is indisputable. He commences by saying: "Mr. Podsnap was well to do, and stood very high in Mr. Podsnap's opinion."

A few lines on we read:—

> Thus happily acquainted with his own merit and importance, Mr. Podsnap settled that whatever he put behind him he put out of existence. There was a dignified conclusiveness—not to add a grand convenience—in this way of getting rid of disagreeables which had done much towards establishing Mr. Podsnap in his lofty place in Mr. Podsnap's satisfaction. "I don't want to know about it; I don't choose to discuss it; I don't admit it!" Mr. Podsnap had even acquired a peculiar flourish of his right arm in often clearing the world of its most difficult problems, by sweeping them behind him, "and consequently sheer away," with those words and a flushed face. For they affronted him.

There is a Podsnappery Society among certain scholars today, as certainly as there was amongst the élite in the time of Dickens. I was reminded of this Society as I read an article from the pen of Dr. Hugh W. White, of China, in the *Bible League Quarterly, April-June,* 1930. A short extract will suffice to illustrate the point:—

> We commend the straightforward methods of Dr. Hay Watson Smith, and as for the writer in the *Review* "which is quite inconsequential so far as my point is concerned," while

*From the *Bible League Quarterly,* July, 1930, by the editor, *Heresies Exposed.*

he aims to keep an even keel, he repeatedly speaks of the anti-Bible men with the highest respect, but when he comes to genuine scholars, James Robertson, James Orr, Robert Dick Wilson, C. Boutflower, men with arguments for the authenticity and accuracy of the Bible which are absolutely unanswerable, he simply does not attempt the impossible. Instead of facing their arguments, he condescendingly waves them aside as well-meaning but impotent traditionalists.

Now that is just what the higher critics of yesterday and the Modernists of today are continually doing—for their own "great convenience" they just wave aside the arguments and facts they cannot meet, and ignore the works of conservative scholars, such as H. C. G. Moule, H. E. Fox, James Orr, R. D. Wilson, A. H. Finn, J. Tuckwell, W. B. Dawson, J. Gresham Machen, A. Rendle Short, and a host of others—it is a good way of getting "rid of disagreeables"!

Can you not almost hear one of them saying: "Why, sir, I have the 'assured results' of the critics, and don't you know 'all scholars believe or agree' with us? No"—and with a wave of the hand—"I have no time for these traditionalists; 'I don't want to know about it; I don't choose to discuss it; I don't admit it' "—and the matter is "put out of existence."

By such Podsnappery-logic plus the flourish of the right arm, the arguments of conservative scholars, the researches of conservative scientists and the finds of conservative "and other" archæologists are "swept sheer away."

Can it be shown from the actual words of Modernists that the testimony of many recognized leaders in evangelical circles is warranted? In the sixth edition of *Heresies Exposed* the Editor of *The Witness*, Mr. Hy. Pickering, has a collection of a goodly number of such utterances. We can but quote a few of them:—

Modernists' Attack on the Bible

Dr. Lyman Abbott: "An infallible book is an impossible conception, and today no one really believes our Bible is such a book."

Professor Shailer Matthews: "As for higher criticism, we not only use it in the study of the Bible, but we believe any person who does not use it is not studying the Bible wisely or efficiently (So say Russellites, Mormons, Christian

Scientists and others, of their books.—*Ed.*). Most skepticism in college students is due to the extreme teachings of the inspiration of the Bible."

Dr. Fosdick: "From naive acceptance of the Bible as of equal credibility in all its parts because mechanically inerrant (which no one teaches.—*Ed.*), I passed years ago to the shocking conviction that such traditional Bibliolatry is false in fact and perilous in result." He speaks of the Trinity as an "arithmetical absurdity" (*The Modern Use of the Bible*, pp. 273, 188).

The Editor of the *Christian Century,* January 3, 1924: "The Bible of Fundamentalism is one Bible; the Bible of Modernism is another."

Dean Inge at the 12th Conference of Modernist Churchmen, Oxford: "They had discarded two infallibilities — the infallible Church and the infallible Book."

Bishop Barnes: "The Old Testament is Jewish literature. In it are to be found folklore, defective history, half-savage morality, obsolete forms of worship based on primitive and errononeous ideals of the nature of God, and crude Science."

Professor Geo. Jackson, alluding to the Mosaic authorship of the Pentateuch, said: "It was a gigantic and wholly impossible concession."

Professor Peake: "It is no longer possible to insist on the literal accuracy of the Gospel narratives." Also: "Much in Genesis 1-11 is of mythical origin."

Dr. Glover: "The New Testament writers wrote as well as they knew how."

Canon Streeter: "The Christian is aware that the infallibility of the historical records of the life of Christ is questioned by the majority of competent scholars."

Space forbids more, save an example of what is being openly stated in our day. The following is from the *Evangelical Christian* of April, 1930:—

> I doubt if there is any other book which ranges from such sublime heights to such degrading depths as the Bible. The Bible was not written by God. If God wrote the Bible He would have done a better job of it. If written now, it could not be sent through the U. S. mails. It contains a wide range of materials not suited for children.

All scholars agree that the trinitarian references in the Bible are pious forgeries. The question of the divinity of Jesus is not worth a hill of beans. We must scrap the Bible before we can attain church unity. It has no part in the 20th century civilization.

Sad to say, the ravings of this poor skeptic were from the platform of a convention whereat 5,000 delegates attended from various Protestant churches in the State of Ohio, U.S.A. The Editor of the *Evangelical Christian* comments: "How such a man could be invited to speak on a supposedly Christian platform at a convention of supposedly Christian ministers and laymen, passes our comprehension. That his words should have been received without a storm of protest and repudiation, is a sad commentary on the state to which the Christian Church, in large measure, has sunk."

Thus the Modernists leaders scoff at the Scriptures being infallible: claim that apart from *their* works it cannot be efficiently studied: discard much of the Old Testament as being defective, obsolete, erroneous and crude: assert that the Gospels are inaccurate and the writers uninspired: that much of the Bible is mere folklore, of half-savage morality, containing pious forgeries, and should be *scrapped!*

How is it that many true Christians with all this in view and much more, are constantly charging Fundamentalists with using extreme language about Modernists, yet never open their mouths to rebuke the Modernists, for *their* extreme language about *the Word of the Living God,* and their attack upon almost every vital doctrine therein?

"For fourteen hundred years," says Dr. Jefferson, "the sun was misinterpreted. It made no difference to the sun. Ptolemy had a wrong conception, but the sun kept right on shining. He flooded every day with light, and went out into the fields every summer and aided the farmers in bringing in their crops." The meaning of this parable is obvious!

We must examine some of the methods used by the leaders of this school.

Its Methods We quote from *"Modernism versus the Bible."* p. 10:

Canon Cheyne is the name of a well-known English Higher Critic, who followed in the steps of Wellhausen, and even surpassed him in his wild guesses. Bishop Welldon writes of him: "At the hands of such a critic as the late Dr. Cheyne it (higher criticism) aspires to fix dates not only of particular books, but even of particular chapters and even verses in the same book. Dr. Cheyne's method of treating the Psalter and the Prophetical books falls *little short of insanity!*"

In *"Is Higher Criticism Scholarly?"* (p. 52), Dr. R. D. Wilson says:

Critics who are attempting to prove the late date of a certain document are wont to cite the words in that document which occur nowhere else, except possibly in another work claimed as being late, and in the Hebrew of the Talmud. Such evidence is worthy of being collected in order to show the peculiarities of an author, but it does not necessarily have anything to do with proving the date. For there are three thousand words in the Old Testament that occur five times only or under, and fifteen hundred that occur but once. Besides, such words occurring elsewhere in the Talmud are found in every book of the Old Testament and in almost every chapter. If such words were proof of the lateness of a document, all documents would be late; a conclusion so absurd as to be held by nobody.

From *Liberal Theology* (*so called*), by A. H. Finn, we quote the following from p. 17:—

Another tendency is to lay down as inevitable axioms what are really highly debatable propositions; such as "Perfect humanity is Deity under human conditions;" "There is no distinction between natural and supernatural;" and "The Church fears new truth rather than loves it."* This last I venture to characterize as mere libel. The Church fears no *truth,* whether known of old or newly discovered, though it may hesitate to accept unquestioningly what are asserted to be *truths,* but may after all prove to be human speculation or theory.

Dr. H. C. Morton, the Editor of *The Fundamentalist,* has well christened higher criticism—"Guess Criticism." Perhaps one of the best examples of this is Wellhausen's "imaginary discovery" of twenty-two authors for the Books of Moses!

A. J. Pollock writes:

We may well ask, was there any occasion in all the literature of the world, when an editor produced a volume made up

*From *Modern Churchmen.*

of the writings of twenty-two different authors, more or less, and succeeded in foisting them upon a whole nation as the writings of one of their greatest men, and received as such without question for many centuries? And yet, this is what we are asked to believe in the case of Moses and the Jewish nation.

Not to be outdone, C. H. Cornell of Konisberg claims the authors to be twenty-six!

But the "Polychrome" Bible (or, many-colored) reveals the length to which the critics were prepared to go. Professor J. L. Campbell, D.D., in his book *The Bible Under Fire,* tells us that the critics had never produced a more scholarly body of men than those who produced this "Rainbow" Bible, which has since "been ridiculed out of court." On page 15 of his book, Dr. J. L. Campbell gives a long list of their names, saying: "They are mentioned here to show that their friends cannot evade the responsibility of this undertaking." He then says:

> Now as a sample of the length to which they went let us turn to the Polychrome edition of the book of Judges by Dr. Moore of Andover (Mass.). He actually professes to have so analyzed this book that he is able to show that the 24 verses included between chapters 2: 6 and 3: 6 are made up of 23 different fragments all spliced together. Extracts vary much in length, but in 13 cases he claims to show that three words are from one author, while the context is from another. In ten cases he claims that two words are from one author and the context from another, and in eight cases he would have us believe that one single word is from one author and the context from another, one of these words being the personal pronoun "I" (Judges 6: 16).

Other equally puerile examples are given. Is it to be wondered at that Bishop Welldon should state that their work falls *"little short of insanity"*?

Its Morality

We open this unhappy section of our article with a quotation from Mr. E. C. Cratill in *The Morning Star,* who clearly expresses a charge made very frequently against the higher critic:—

> If he did in the commercial world what he does in the religious world he would be dismissed summarily. If he be-

trayed his trust in the army or navy he would be shot at sunrise. The Modernizer in the pulpit has not been honest enough to put on his true colors and boldly declare himself an unbeliever in the Scriptures, an ally of Unitarianism and Universalism.

Some may say that is pure assumption, mere assertions however emphatic prove nothing. Well, let the *Modernist* decide the point. Rollin Lynde Hartt, a layman, says:—

Rash measures would have been ruinous. Accordingly the Modernists clothed their unorthodox ideas in orthodox verbage, or trusted to letting the time-honored creeds die from neglect.

Albrech Ritschl, the German theologian, credited as the Father of Modernism, defended the principle that *it is right and proper*, in order to lay the fears of conservatives, to express new theological opinions in the old familiar words. And ever since Ritschl's day, theological counterfeiting or two-facedness has been in fashion amongst his followers.—*Modernism*, p. 8. By J. M. Gray, D.D.

Dr. Dinsdale T. Young, at the annual meetings of the Wesley Bible Union in 1925, said of more advanced men:—

These men had got not only a New Theology but a new Morality. Living on the pay given them to preach one set of doctrines, they were deliberately advocating the very opposite.

Dr. Ernest Gordon in *The Leaven of the Pharisees*, writes:—

Dr. Fosdick's colleague at Union, Prof. Fagnani, writing *In Praise of Heresy*, says of heretics: "One who really cares for the church instead of resigning and withdrawing is conscientiously bound to remain in and bring as many of his brethren as possible around to his way of thinking," the church meanwhile paying his bills while he wrecks it. Dr. Rainsford urges young men to enter the Episcopal ministry, "to stay in it, and fight within to liberalize it." So David Hume was wont to urge men of free-thinking tendencies to take orders.

Surely nothing further need be said on this count.

So much has been written about these disappointments,

and so often have the critics been smitten by their own boomerangs, that a couple of short extracts from an able article by W. Hoste, B.A., in the *Bible League Quarterly*, July-September, 1930, must suffice:—

Assured Results

We hear much of "the *assured* results of modern criticism," but "ephemeral" would seem a better description. The conjectures of Astruc gave place to the Document Theory of Eichorn, and that to the "supplement theories" of Tuch, Stähelin and De Wette. These again were superseded by the theories of Ewald and Hupfield; and they in their turn by those of Graf, Kuenen and Wellhausen. For long the last named has been the teacher to which the British School of Criticism has bowed; but his theory in its turn has been attacked by the French critic, Maurice Vernes, and so the "assured results" seem to be an ever-varying quantity. . . .

Before he died, Dean Wace left on record an important statement to the effect that "the results of criticism, that are said to be 'assured,' are not the results of unanimous criticism, but are opposed by other men, who are themselves critics of high standing." In other words, the critics are agreed in opposing the Scriptures, as usually understood, but they cannot agree as to how best to do it. It is the old story over again, "But neither so did their witness agree together" (Mark 14: 59).

1. The critics were all agreed (till 1887) that Israel was illiterate and hence Moses could not have written the Pentateuch, and that writing was not known in his day. Sir. R. Anderson says: "The attack on the Pentateuch was based on the assumption that the Mosaic Era was a barbarous age." Professor Sayce calls this "a baseless assumption due to the ignorance of the critics." In 1887 the Tel-el-Amarna tablets proved that the critics had blundered again. But they merely shifted their ground of attack and assured the public that Moses could never have written such a code of law as is in Exodus 20. That, on account of its advanced morality, etc., this chapter must be dated much later. This, too, was unfortunate as the "Code of Khamurabi" was discovered in 1891. Writing was proved to have existed a thousand years before *Abraham*, and the critics were silenced! Not a bit of

Ascertained Blunders

it, they suavely told us that Moses obtained his code from Khamurabi.*

2. "Of 'the assured results of modern criticism' none is more assured than that 'the Mosaic books' are literary forgeries, the work of the Jerusalem priests of the exilic era. But whatever else may be said of that hypothesis, it is exploded by the fact that the Pentateuch is the Bible of the Samaritans" (Note to the Seventh Edition of *The Bible and Modern Criticism,* by Sir R. Anderson, K.C.B.).

This is a polished shaft which pierces the heart of criticism.

3. Astruc's surmise that the book of Genesis was written by two writers, on account of the use of the names Jehovah and Elohim, became the basic principle on which higher critics built their theories regarding the many sources from which the early books were compiled—*e.g.,* some of the supposed writers are known by the following symbols: J1, J2, J3, E1, E2, E3, P1, P2, P3, D1, D2, D3, R1, R2, R3—incidentally proving (!) the lateness of the passage thus labelled.

From time to time critics have been challenged to determine composite writings, and whenever they have accepted, have dismally failed. "Coleridge," we are told, "was probably the last scholar to do this with Shakespeare, and Macaulay pronounces his effort 'pure nonsense'." But perhaps Professor C. M. Mead's argument with regard to "Dictation, Style and Doctrinal Content" that Romans was written by four different authors who used the names "God," "Lord," "Jesus" and "Christ" respectively, is as clever a piece of work (covering 87 pages) as could well be mentioned.

"It was written," Professor J. L. Campbell, D.D., tells us in *The Bible Under Fire,* p. 28, "wholly to expose the absurdity of the critical method. But the amusing part of it all was that the Germans took him seriously and reviewed his work with warm commendation, as a new, valuable contribution to the study of Romans. Imagine their chagrin when Dr. Mead had to disabuse them of their false impression and

---

*See *The Bible and Modern Science,* p. 43, and *Bible League Quarterly,* July-September, 1930.

tell them that it was intended simply as an exposé. He signed himself 'E. D. McRealsham'."

Space forbids us to give more than one other extract, also from Dr. Campbell's book, pp. 36, 37:—

"Sinai could not be prior to Judges," said the critics. During the period of the Judges the Israelites were too low down morally to have before that time the high spiritual standards of Sinai. Therefore the law must have come after Judges. This is evolution again applied to the Bible. By parallel reasoning we could show that Christianity was so corrupt during the Dark Ages, say from the tenth to the fifteenth century, that the New Testament with its high spiritual and moral ideal could not have existed prior to this time. The people were not yet far enough advanced. The New Testament must have come into existence later, say at the time of the Reformation.

Its Fruitage

Our Lord has said: "Beware of false prophets which come in sheep's clothing, but inwardly they are ravenous wolves. Ye shall know them by their fruits. Do men gather grapes of thorns, or figs of thistles? Even so every good tree bringeth forth good fruit; but a corrupt tree bringeth forth evil fruit. . . . Wherefore by their fruits ye shall know them" (Matt. 7: 15-20).

Let us see what fruit Modernism produces.

"Already there are complaints," says Professor John Horsch in *The Failure of Modernism,* p. 41, "from circles in which Modernist views have been adopted, that there is a noticeable lagging of the mission interest. The following is a case to the point. Recently Bishop Joseph F. Berry, of the Methodist Episcopal Church (North), complained of the marked trend toward Modernism in the denominations which he represents. And now comes the significant news that the Methodist Board of Foreign Missions has been compelled to cut its mission appropriations for fields outside the United States by thirty-three and one-third per cent. The reduction ranges from twenty-two per cent for Africa to forty-six per cent for Europe and North Africa."*

*That was a few years ago. Since then the M. E. Mission in India, and other missions, have made further cuts in both men and money.

A. H. Carter, the Editor of the *Bible Witness*, in pp. 7, 9 of *Modernism: The Ruthless Destroyer of Child Faith*, says:

> The burden of the effect and result of the teaching of Modernism upon the intelligence and faith of our young people has pressed heavily. Since those far-off days havoc has been wrought universally to an appalling extent until at the present time one becomes inundated with deplorable facts of this wholesale method of destruction to faith of our boys and girls.

He goes on from a letter quoted: "Truly the outlook," says the writer, "is bad enough, and black enough, regarding the schools of our country (Britain) and the pervading and leavening influences of Modernism by means of them" (p. 14). He gives touching incidents, one of a five-year old child who, after returning from school, said: "Mummy, I won't trouble to say prayers tonight, there is no God, so it is not worth while!" And another whose girl friend said: "Do you mean to say your mother is silly enough to believe that stuff (the Bible)? I thought she was too clever for that"—the speaker was about 11 years old!

Is it surprising that in an article appearing in the *N.C.C. Review,* February, 1928, a writer from the homelands should say: "In many countries which have in the past been the mainstay of the Christian missionary enterprise, we are faced today with a serious decline of missionary influence, especially among the younger generation."

Its fruitage on the Mission Field is simply disastrous. The late J. Wilkie, D.D., at a Missionary Union in India gave a lecture on Modernism and its effect in India. Pointing out how it was side-tracking missionaries from gospel effort to social and economic developments, and how it "encouraged the magnifying of everything connected with Hinduism, as if by praising and flattering them we were going to win them," he said: "But to me one of the most serious effects is that which Modernism is having upon Indian workers themselves." Then after saying that all knew how among Indian workers were many men of independent thought, and earnest Christian mind, whose influence had told for the gospel, he shows how the Indian "naturally follows one that he calls his Guru or teacher, and that most of them are comparatively poorly educated and so unqualified for entering the lists with the Higher Critics."

We must close this section of our article by citing the effects this baneful teaching has on some of its propagators. Huxley said: "If Satan had wished to devise the best means of discrediting '*Revelation*' he could not have done better" (*Life*, vol. 2, p. 118), and as A. J. Pollock says, Huxley "was not biassed in favor of the Bible."

The same writer tells us that Dr. Marcus Dods, a thoroughgoing higher critic, confessed plainly at the end of his life: "I am a backslider," and "I take no interest in prayer." He confessed that "he had not prayed for years," and he died under a spiritual cloud. His compeer Dr. A. B. Bruce, "the greatest pioneer of our time in theological thought," died "without a single Christian conviction;" and Dr. Cheyne died "a Bahaist, that is, a sort of Mohammedan."

As an example of its deadening effect take Kanamori's experience whilst a Professor in the Doshisha College, Japan. We are thankful to record that though he "lost everything," he has regained it through simple faith in God's Word. Here is his experience in his own words as given by W. Bell Dawson:

> I was brought up in puritanic strictness of doctrine and practice, so when I read those easy-going Modernist books I felt as though I was coming out of a frozen zone into the warmth of the tropics. I enjoyed the reading of those Modernist books so very much that I was completely carried away by their clever arguments. . . . When I embraced this Modernism and Higher Criticism I lost my Christian message entirely, and I became a messageless man. . . . When I lost faith in the absolute divine authority of the Bible, and faith in the deity of Jesus Christ, I lost everything. I could still preach the moral precepts of the Bible, and thought that perhaps I could apply them to some of the social questions of the day. But I could not preach the central fundamental doctrine of Christianity, salvation by the blood of Jesus shed upon the cross (*The Scriptures and the Mistakes of the Critics*, p. 24).

If it is true that "by their fruits ye shall know them," what must our verdict be of this first and last day heresy, which is destroying the faith of young children in God's Word and Person: undermining the faith of converts on the

Mission Field: greatly reducing gifts for spreading the gospel and robbing its propagators of hope for the future?

The assured fruits of Modernism are seen:

In the BUD it *empties* the Scriptures of their authority.
In the BLOSSOM it *empties* the individual of *spiritual power.*
In the FRUIT it *empties* the churches of *worshippers.*
This we submit is the true KENOSIS of MODERNISM.

Lecturing in the year 1930 on Modernism the Principal of an Anglo-Chinese School in Malaya after stating that Modernism is "willing to investigate," "Modernism . . . makes experiments," "Modernism is searching for new values," Modernism is testing the "old ideas of the Bible," opened his heart and "lifted the lid" by saying: *"At times we are completely dazed to know what to believe and what to practise or how to do things."*

Not only are they "dazed" but so are those who follow these blind guides. The Archbishop of York recently stated of the young people of today: "Their predominant characteristic, so far as the seriously-minded are concerned, was bewilderment."

A state of "BEWILDERMENT," of being "COMPLETELY DAZED," is the assured result of their shrouding the WORD OF GOD with the grave-clothes of unbelief—the WORD which should be "a lamp" unto our feet, and "a light" unto our path (Ps. 119: 105). Whoso followeth them shall walk in darkness.

MORMONISM

By A. McD. Redwood

It will be best in studying this sinister subject—which is strictly more than a heresy, but rather a "black-hand cult," using the language of Holy Scripture to hide its true character—to consider a little of its origin and the character of its founders.

Two names are recognized as the chief of the "prophets" of Mormonism—Joseph Smith and Brigham Young. We concentrate chiefly on the former, as he was really the main factor in the founding of Mormonism.

Joseph Smith

Joseph Smith was born of rather notorious parents, in Sharon, Windsor Co., Vermont, U.S.A., on December 3rd, 1805. We are told that his "father sold blessings, and his mother was a fortune-teller" — though this does not tell the real tale of their evil character. Concerning their fourth child, Joseph Smith, Jr., we quote the following by Dr. Edmund B. Fairfield, late President of Michigan College*:

It was in August, 1850, that I found myself spending a week in the immediate vicinity of Palmyra and Manchester (U. S. A.). Three men were mentioned to me who had been intimately acquainted with Joseph Smith from the age of ten years to twenty-five and upwards. The testimony of these men was given under no stress of any kind. It was clear, decided, unequivocal testimony, in which they all agreed. "Joseph Smith is simply a notorious liar." "We never knew another person so utterly destitute of conscience as he was." "The thing for which Joseph was most notorious was his vulgar speech and his life of unspeakable lewdness."

---

*The quotation is taken from a recent booklet, *The Mormons or Latter-Day Saints,* by Rev. D. H. C. Bartlett, M.A., published by Chas. J. Thynne & Jarvis, Ltd., London, to which authority we are indebted for much of the historical information. We commend it to any who wish to know more.

Smith was extremely superstitious, became known for his strange dreams which he spoke of freely, developed a mania as a "money digger," and professed to be able to locate buried treasure. He attracted the attention of one Sidney Rigdon, a disappointed Baptist minister, who himself had degenerated into being a charlatan to gain money. Between them, chiefly under Rigdon's influence, they hatched up a story in which Smith declared he had seen a vision of an angel in his room at midnight, "who took him to a hill four miles from Palmyra, where they unearthed a stone box which contained a number of *gold plates* covered with writings, and fastened together with gold rings. Together with the gold plates, he says, he found a sort of wonderful pair of spectacles —two crystals set in a silver bow—which he called Urim and Thummim. When the illiterate Smith put on these supernatural spectacles he found he could not only read but could translate the mystic writing! Concealed then behind a curtain, he dictated, in the first place to Martin Harris—and when he was tired of acting as amanuensis, to Oliver Cowdery —the contents of this golden book! The result, Smith tells us, was the *Book of Mormon*—that is the sacred book of the Mormons."

The Gold Plates

In order to complete the fraud, Smith declared that the "golden plates" were carried off, together with the spectacles, etc., by the angel as soon as he had dictated their contents!

Concerning this so-called "Bible," it has been believed by some that it originated in a historical novel written by one Solomon Spaulding, a Presbyterian preacher, who died of consumption at Conneaut, Ohio, in 1816, before it could be published. This MS. was said to be found by Sidney Rigdon in the printing office of Patterson and Lamdin of Pittsburgh, who resolved to turn it to his own financial benefit. He presumably originated the idea of getting this book published in the manner described, and in Smith he found a ready tool, adding to it passages of Scripture, and possibly many of the "almost forgotten tales of the monk Cyril and the Abbot Joachim," who thrived as founders of a new "schism" in the thirteenth cen-

Book of Mormon

tury, and from whom the title "The Everlasting Gospel" (applied to the Mormon "revelation") may have been derived.*

Such an origin does not speak well for its so-called "divine character"! Joseph Smith had the colossal effrontery to palm off this fraud upon a credulous public as the very "oracle of God," and Brigham Young, who succeeded him, declared of the book:

"Every Spirit that confesseth that Joseph is a prophet, and that the Book of Mormon is true, is of God, and every Spirit that does not is of Antichrist!"

Polygamy

After this event Smith proceeded to found the Mormon Church with himself as "seer, translator, prophet, apostle of Jesus Christ, and elder of the Church." He followed a checkered career, once having to flee precipitately with his accomplice Rigdon to escape from the law because of their flotation of a bogus bank concern. Eventually he settled in a sparsely populated part of Illinois, where he was out of immediate reach of the law. Here he took to open polygamy and led his followers to do the same. He justified his conduct by a convenient "revelation" which was incorporated in a book, *Doctrines and Covenants*, held in almost equal repute with the *Book of Mormon.* Here is an extract from one of the Sections:

37. Abraham received concubines, and they bear (bare) him children, and it was accounted unto him for righteousness, because they were given unto him, and he abode in My law. . . .

---

*Since printing the eighth edition of *Heresies Exposed* we have received a communication challenging the correctness of the statement that the Book of Mormon originated in a historical novel by one Solomon Spaulding. This paragraph has appeared in each edition since 1917, was written in all good faith, and was unchallenged for twenty years. Further enquiries have been set on foot, but no conclusive evidence has been received either to corroborate or refute this theory. [August 1960]

52. And let Mine handmaid, Emma Smith, receive all those that have been given unto My servant Joseph, and who are virtuous and pure before Me (Section 132).

There is much more, but we forbear nauseating the reader.

Brigham Young

Things went from bad to worse, until the chief of his own followers rose in revolt, determined to expose him. A free fight led to Smith and his brother being imprisoned, but before the law could deal with them as they should have been dealt with, an armed mob rushed the prison and both Smith and his brother were killed. This had the opposite effect to what a proper trial and lawful punisment would have had, and Smith's followers used the occasion successfully to weave around his name a halo of martyrdom, Rigdon was now excommunicated by his rival Brigham Young, the senior of the "twelve apostles." The latter became the leader of Mormonism, and in order to escape the laws of the United States he took himself and all his followers to the State of Utah, which then belonged to Mexico, where they founded the now famous headquarters, Salt Lake City. This was in 1847. In 1877 Brigham Young died in Salt Lake City, leaving a fortune of £400,000, seventeen wives, and fifty-six children!

During his time and after, a fierce struggle arose between the United States Government and this immoral cult over the question of polygamy, which threatened the very stability of moral law. In the end, in order to save their very existence as a "lawful community," they submitted to the Government, recognized the law, and openly abandoned polygamy. But all students of the system are agreed, upon unimpeachable evidence, that whatever may be the outward conduct as before the law, Mormons *still* teach and practise polygamy—and not merely as a kind of "privilege" but as a *"rule of faith."*

We quote the following by the Rev. D. H. C. Bartlett (Rector of Nailsea, England), whose book we have already mentioned:—

Polygamy Propagated

In a few weeks, in 1907, Mormon "Elders" taught four pure English youths living in my parish, a number of texts from the Bible to use in defence of polygamy, and which they had been made to believe upheld polygamy. At the same time the same "Elders" placed in the hands of two girls, communicants of my Church, aged 21 and 18, respectively, their *Ready References*, a work which was at that time on sale at their Liverpool depot. It contains eleven pages devoted to the teaching of polygamy in the plainest language. The article on the subject is headed *"Patriarchal Marriage,"* and begins thus:—

"Traditions and prejudices of centuries, the man-made creeds of the day, and the laws of all nations professing a belief in Christ, unitedly inculcate the idea that it is sinful for a man under any circumstances to have more than one living and undivorced wife at the same time. A careful perusal of the Scriptures will, however, reveal the facts that the practice which is now considered so heinous is in accordance with the divine law given to the ancient Israelites and that never has received the divine condemnation."

This article closes with various quotations, among which we read:—

"The prohibition of polygamy is not only a prohibition of what nature permits in the fullest manner, but of what she requires for the reparation of States exhausted by wars, etc. It (polygamy) was practised. . . without doubt by some of His (Christ's) own disciples."

And this is the teaching which visiting Mormon "Elders" are putting into the hands of young English girls; and in order to get an unsuspected entrance for these vile productions into pure English homes, they actually bind up these *Ready References* at the end of an Oxford copy of the New Testament!—and in such manner that no ordinary person would suspect the presence of the poison.

We add a further reliable testimony, somewhat abridged, from *The Christian* (London), dated February 10th, 1921 (our italics):—

Oaths and Secrecy

A writer in the *Watchman-Examiner*, Rev. W. E. La Rue, explains Mormonism and shows it to be a terrible menace to America's welfare. "The system has been *at variance with the moral sentiments of every community* in which it sought to live. It was only after it had been forcibly expelled from the bounds of civil society, and had settled down in the wilderness of Utah, unrestrained by the moral sentiments of any, *that it was able to live out its religion. . . .* Its whole history has been darkened by many incidents that arouse suspicion. *Mormons have openly and confessedly lied to shield the existence of polygamy;* they have openly broken their promises to the Government to abandon it in faith and practice. . . . There are two elements in Mormon religion which serve as powerful factors in binding its adherents to the system. The first is that of mysticism. Its most outstanding manifestation consists in the fact that every Mormon wears on his body an *endowment garment,* containing figures and symbols of things very vital to him. These garments are bestowed upon the Mormon convert after due discipline in the secret temple ceremonies of the Mormon Church. There are secrets regarding this which Mormons dare not divulge. Another element of mysticism is the practice of *baptism for the dead.* Under the view that no person can be saved without baptism, this doctrine has been devised in behalf of those who have died without it. When it has been revealed to some leading Mormon that some remote relative in the spirit-world desires liberation, the process is that some living Mormon is baptized by immersion in his behalf, and thus he is liberated. So they believe! These doctrines, and many others, *are not offered as subjects of instruction to those who first come in contact with Mormonism.* Many of the preachments of the elders seem innocent and harmless, and if questions are asked regarding things more mysterious, citation is made to the words of Jesus: "I have many things to say unto you, but ye cannot bear them now." Thus the convert is led on *until he is tied to the system* by oath and obligations very difficult to break. In this organization we have an illustration of religious autocracy scarcely duplicated in the history of mankind. It is the reorganization on the part of the people of the right on the part of priesthood to command them in matters secular as well as spiritual, that has made the Mormon Church as far as organization is concerned, a spectacle of wonderment before the world.

Its Doctrine

Such is the cult, and such its antecedents that go under the name "Mormonism." Not only by its moral code does it stand condemned at the Bar of Truth, but by its altogether revolting teaching concerning the Deity—although strictly it is not surprising, for a fountain of slime cannot pour forth a lifegiving stream! We give here an extended quotation from a well-known writer* and student of contemporary thought, whose testimony is beyond question:—

---

*D. M. Panton, B.A.

It teaches that God is on exalted man, once a man on earth as we are now, ever changing and advancing, but never absolutely perfect. Joseph Smith, second only to Brigham Young among their "prophets," says: "God himself was once as we are now, and is an exalted man, and sits enthroned in yonder heavens: it is the first principle of the Gospel to know that he was once a man like us; yea, that God the Father of us all dwelt on an earth, the same as Jesus Christ himself did."

Their *Doctrines and Covenants* (Sec. 130: 22) declares:

"The Father has a body of flesh and bones as tangible as any man's;" "and this being," says Joseph Smith, "cannot occupy two distinct places at once." But who is this huge man in the heavens? The answer is almost past belief; but it comes from no less than their supreme prophet, Brigham Young: "Adam is God, the Supreme God, the Creator of this world, our God, and the only God with whom we have to do. He is our Father and our God. Who is the Father? The first of the human Family."

"Adam," says the *Pearl of Great Price* (p. 60), "is the Father of All, the Prince of All, and the Ancient of Days."

All Christian Churches are therefore anathema; Mormonism is the sole Church of the living God, to which all nations are required to submit. "All the Churches," says Mr. Orson Pratt, "preach false doctrine *and are under the curse of God.*" How solemn all this is when we remember that Mormonism has a vast world-wide propaganda; that in 1912 it had more *than a thousand missionaries in England, distributing annually five million tracts and between one and two hundred thousand volumes; that its agents have again and again been expelled from Germany as a menace to morality, and that its organization is unsurpassed, cemented by secret and terrible oaths.*

Let all beware of this Satanic delusion!

The following is a verbatim quotation from p. 50 of Brigham Young's Journal of Discourses, Vol. I:—

Now hear it, O inhabitants of the earth, Jew and Gentile, Saint and sinner. When our father Adam came into the garden of Eden, he came into it with a "celestial body," and brought Eve, "one of his wives," with him. He helped to make and organize this world. He is MICHAEL, "the Archangel," the ANCIENT OF DAYS! about whom holy men have written and spoken—He "is our" FATHER "and our" GOD, "and the only God with whom WE have to do." Every man upon the earth, professing Christians or non-professing, must hear it, and "will know it sooner or later."

When the Virgin Mary conceived the child Jesus, the Father had begotten him in his own likeness. He was "not" begotten by the Holy Ghost. And who is the Father? He is the first of the human family, and when he took a tabernacle, it was begotten by *his* Father in heaven after the same manner as the tabernacles of Cain, Abel, and the rest of the *sons and daughters of Adam and Eve.*

PSEUDO-CHRISTIANITY or MODERN RELIGIOUS EDUCATION

By A. L. Wiley, Ph.D.

Undoubtedly, Modernism's most effective ally is the system of Religious Education taught in the Educational Institutions and in the different denominational Sunday Schools in Europe and America, and also on the Foreign Mission fields. A study of any of the modern systems of Religious Education will reveal clearly that it is predominantly Unitarian. The history of Educational institutions in America during the last half-century shows that a general movement has been in operation to transfer what were formerly Evangelical institutions into schools to propagate Unitarianism and thus convert Evangelical Christianity into Unitarianism. A study of most American educational institutions will show that the conversion of the institutions has met with great success. During this same period Unitarianism, as a denomination, has been at a standstill. Instead of seeking additions to Unitarianism, the Unitarian leaders are seeking to transform the Evangelical Christian Church into a Unitarian body. Unitarians under cover of other denominational names are found working industriously in nearly all schools to transform them into Unitarian schools. Professor Troeltsch said, "We cannot use force on the Evangelical Church, but we have another weapon in order to overpower it. That is to appoint the greatest possible number of radical and liberal professors, and then it will of itself and from within go to pieces." To hasten this transforming process, Unitarian leaders have succeeded in appointing "University Pastors" in many institutions, and in some cases where there have been no Unitarian students. But in order to succeed in a complete transformation of these schools into Unitarian schools and the Evangelical Christian Church into a Unitarian body, the appointment of professors and "University pastors" had to be followed by the adoption in all institutions of courses of Religious Education which should be distinctly Unitarian. To make such courses absolutely effective they had to begin in the primary department of the Sunday School and continue until the students should pass out of the university full-fledged Unitarians.

In order that there should be uniformity of the Unitarian kind in all Religious Education, the Religious Education Association of America was set up. This Association was founded by Professor Harper of Chicago University, and in its earlier stages was largely controlled by the Theological School of his University. Its members include Jews, Rationalists, Freethinkers, Unitarians and some so-called Evangelicals.

The Sunday School Council of the Evangelical denominations was organized in 1910, and began to issue the International Graded Lessons. This organization was formed because the radicals were unable to get a foothold in the International Sunday School Association. The new organization was composed of official representatives of the various denominational agencies for Sunday School promotion, and of course was radical in opinion.

After much opposition this new organization succeeded in merging with the old Association under the title of the International Sunday School Council of Religious Education. Though the convention which merged the two Associations voted that the name should be "The International Sunday School Council of Christian Education," the word "Religious" was substituted for "Christian." A little later the leaders changed the name to "The International Council of Religious Education." This Council states that the Religious Education Association has decided to maintain *advisory relations only* with the Committee of the Council in view of the fact it (the Religious Education Association) comprehends within its scope religions other than the Christian religion. In spite of this statement it is evident that the Council is controlled by the Association and predominantly Unitarian.

The present-day Religious Education, sponsored by nearly all the denominations, for Sunday Schools and other schools, emanates from the Religious Education Association, which is parent and guide to all the rest.

The aim of all modern Religious Education is to change "the goal of Christian effort, from that of Individualistic salvation to the Socialization of Man." The Bible account of the creation is a myth and the Evolutionary hypothesis is proposed as the route along which social progress is achieved. Miracles are tabooed and regeneration is ruled out. "The facts of conversion are manifestations of natural processes." The efficacy of the blood of Christ and the vicarious atonement are laughed out of court. "Jesus' death was the sane demonstration that the one unfailing way in which sinners may be saved, is the way of love and complete self-sacrifice." The death of Jesus Christ has no other meaning according to modern education than this. Miracles cannot occur and our Lord never arose. "Acceptance at their face value of the biased and naive chronicles of the Jewish and Christian writers is one of the baneful aspects of 'Evangelical' Bible teaching." So-called miracles are easily explained away. "The fish from whose mouth the coin was taken by Jesus, was really sold, and the proceeds paid the tax for Peter and his Lord."

The "new Religious Education accepts the psychology of religion which begins with nature worship—and works up to the worship of humanity." In such worship there is no place for prayer. Prayer becomes an unprofitable and often harmful exercise. The methods used in this new Religious Education are said to be the methods of Jesus, of Moses, of Paul, of Mahommed, and "are to be studied with open minds." "All those using the Bible as the text, either as literature or for purposes of dogmatic doctrinal teaching, miss entirely the scientific method." "The only foundation for a course of Religious Education is life itself." "It would seem wise to utilize all the great Bibles, all literatures, all histories, the arts and sciences, because science has certainly given us great help in living."

This is what is being taught to the children of our schools and universities, all over the world. This form of Religious Education is spreading rapidly throughout India, sponsored often by Evangelical Missions and churches. In many schools nature worship is supplanting the worship of God and un-Christian poems are replacing the Psalms and other portions of the Bible, in the Sunday Schools.

How long will Missions and Churches in India and elsewhere tolerate this insidious and thoroughly organized attack on evangelical Christianity and on our Lord Himself, to transform the Church into a Unitarian body and to reduce our Lord to a mere man?

"Hereby know ye the Spirit of God: every spirit that confesseth that Jesus Christ is come in the flesh is of God: and every spirit that confesseth not Jesus, is not of God: and this is the spirit of the antichrist, whereof ye have heard that it cometh; and now it is in the world."

(*With acknowledgments to Dr. Ernest Gordon*).

ROMAN CATHOLICISM

By Wm. C. Irvine

We are desirous in this article of proving from Rome's *own statements* that her system of teaching is both unscriptural and false. Let her own mouth condemn her, "For by thy words thou shalt be justified, and by thy words thou shalt be condemned" (Matt. 12: 37).

Our first charge is that she is an Idolatrous Church.

But it may be asked, Does Rome really teach the worship of idols? Archdeacon Sinclair, writing on *Image Worship*, said:—

Idolatry

The twenty-fifth session of the *Council of Trent* decrees that the images of Christ and the Virgin Mary, and of the other saints, are especially to be had and retained in the churches, and that honor and veneration are to be paid to them.

From the *Protestant Alliance Magazine*, July, 1922, we cull the following:—

The Creed of *Pope Pius IV* teaches thus:—

"I most firmly assert that the image of the Christ, of the Mother of God, ever Virgin, and also of the other saints ought to be had and retained, and that due honor and veneration are to be given them."

The Catechism of the *Council of Trent* says:—

"It is lawful to have images in the church, and to give honor and worship unto them,"

"Images of the saints are put in churches as well, that they may be worshipped."

Rome and the Bible

Our next charge is that Rome is hostile to the Bible, and both prohibits, and when unable to do that, discourages the reading of the Scriptures among her adherents.

Pope Pius VII, in 1816, denounced Bible Societies as "a crafty device by which the very foundations of religion are undermined, a pestilence which must be remedied and abolished." The authorized

Catholic Dictionary records, with apparent satisfaction, that Leo XII, Pius VIII, and Pius IX have likewise, in their turn, warned Catholics against the Protestant Bible Societies. Leo XIII, in 1897, prohibited "all versions in any vernacular language made by non-Catholics, and specially those published by the Bible Societies." In the same document, he altogether prohibited "vernacular versions even by Catholics, unless approved by the Holy See or published under the vigilant care of the bishops, with annotations." Rome knows that an open Bible, without Notes, spells her ruin. For no Scripture teaches anything about Purgatory, the worship of Mary or the saints, or upholds the Confessional, the Mass and the priesthood. (Quoted in *The Indian Christian,* November, 1922).

(Rev.) Dr. Cahill declared that "he would rather the Catholic should read the worst books of immorality than the Protestant Bible—that forgery of God's Word, that slander of Christ."—(Roman Catholic *Tablet,* December 17, 1853, p. 804).

"Do you allow your flock to read the Bible at all?" said a writer in the *Contemporary Review* to a friend of his, a parish priest. "No, sir, I do not; you forget that I am a physician, not a poisoner of souls."—April, 1894, p. 576.

Rome's greatest enemy is God's Word. Rome's hostility to the free circuiation of the Bible is a matter of history. Even to this day in Roman Catholic countries, the Bible is almost unknown, and the public burning of Bibles (sent out by the Bible Societies) in South America is an object lesson how she still seeks to hinder the circulation of God's own Book whenever she has the power. Bibles were burnt in Rome as recently as 1923, in the public street.

Further, the Church of Rome makes BLASPHEMOUS CLAIMS for her priests and particularly for the Popes of Rome. Pope Pius X uttered the following words:—

Rome's Blasphemous Claims

The Pope is not only the representative of Jesus Christ, but He is Jesus Christ Himself, hidden under the veil of the flesh. Does the Pope speak? It is Jesus Christ that speaks. Does the Pope accord a favor or pronounce an anathema? It is Jesus Christ who pronounces the anathema or accords the favor. (*Protestant Alliance Magazine,* March, 1922).

Further, from the same Magazine of February, 1922, we read:—

OUR LORD GOD THE POPE.—These words appeared in the Roman Canon Law: "To believe that our Lord God the Pope has not the power to decree as he is decreed, is to be deemed heretical.—*In the Gloss "Extravagantes" of Pope John XXII Cum inter, Tit. XIV, Cap. IV. Ad Callem Sexti Decretalium, Paris,* 1685.

LORD GOD THE POPE.—Father A. Pereira says: "It is quite certain that Popes have never approved or rejected this title 'Lord God the Pope,' for the passage in the gloss referred to appears in the edition of the Canon Law published in Rome in 1580 by Gregory XIII."

THE POPE AND GOD THE SAME.—Writers on the Canon Law say, "The Pope and God are the same, so he has all power in heaven and earth."—*Barclay Cap. XXVII,* p. 218. *Cities Petrus Bertrandus, Pius V.—Cardinal Cusa supports his statement.*

THE POPE, BEING GOD, CANNOT BE JUDGED.—Pope Nicholas I declared that "the appellation of God had been confirmed by Constantine on the Pope, who, being God, cannot be judged by man."—*Labb IX Dist.*: 96 *Can.* 7, *Satis evidentur, Decret Gratian Primer Para.*

The horrrible blasphemy of all this may well shock the reader. Much more evidence of the kind is easily produced to show that Popes, priests and people of this apostate church actually dare to claim these preposterous pretensions.

Not only, as seen above, does this apostate church claim for a mere man an equality with God, but, despite the clear word of Scripture: "THERE IS ONE GOD, and ONE MEDIATOR between God and men, the Man Christ Jesus" (1 Tim. 2: 5), she CLAIMS for a MERE WOMAN this POSITION which belongs to Christ alone.

Her Intermediaries

In "Glories of Mary" by Liguori, whose writings at the time of his canonization were declared to be absolutely free from error, he teaches that Mary is not only to be appealed to as Advocate and Mediator, but actually teaches that she is more merciful than our blessed Lord Himself. He writes:—

He who is under the protection of Mary will be saved; he who is not will be lost . . . O immaculate Virgin, we are under thy protection, and therefore we have recourse, *to thee alone,* and we beseech thee to prevent thy beloved Son, who is irritated by our sins, from abandoning us to the power of the devil. . . . Thou (Mary) art my only hope. . . . Lady in heaven, we have but one advocate, and that is thyself, and thou alone art truly loving and solicitous for our salvation . . . My Queen and my Advocate with thy Son, whom I dare not approach (From *Judge Fairly,* p. 5).

With equal truth may it be also affirmed that, by the will of God, Mary is the intermediary through whom is distributed unto us this immense treasure of mercies gathered by God, for mercy and truth were created by Jesus Christ. Thus as no man goeth to the Father but by the Son, so no man goeth to Christ but by His Mother. Pope's Encyclical dated 1891, as published in the *Tablet,* October 10, 1891. (Quoted in *The Claims of Rome,* p. 61).

We cull the following from an excellent article in the *Evangelical Quarterly,* by Dr. W. Graham Scroggie, which is very much to the point:—

There is no truth more dear to Protestants than that of *the direct access of the soul to God.* Yet such a privilege Romanism both forbids and denies. Rome does not forbid access to God, but denies that it can be *direct,* and so introduces a host of intermediaries, chief among whom are the *Virgin Mary,* the *departed Saints, the Officials of the Roman Church*: Pope, Cardinals, Bishops, and Priests; not to speak of the Mass, Images, and Pictures.

Such teaching and practice are a plain denial of the revealed will of God for men; but it is much worse, for *no one can invoke the Virgin or the Saints without investing them with Divine attributes and putting them in the place of God Himself and His Son Jesus Christ.*

That Romanists do this *they* do not deny . . .

Never for a moment must we allow either the *Blessed Virgin,* or *Departed Saints,* or *Popes,* or *Cardinals,* or *Bishops,* or *Priests,* or *Masses,* or *Images,* or *Pictures,* or *Cardinals,* or *Traditions,* or *Indulgences,* or *Sacraments,* or *Confessionals,* or *Monasteries,* or *Nunneries,* or *Pilgrimages,* or *Purgatory* to stand between our souls and God. The prodigal can come straight to the Father, and the sinner to the Saviour. It is because we *believe* this, *experience* this, and *preach* this, that we are Protestants.

We will now glance briefly at three of Rome's most characteristic teachings, all of which are in direct conflict with the revealed will of God in the Scriptures. No wonder Rome burns Bibles!

The Mass

In the most uncompromising language the Roman Catholic Church deliberately teaches, despite the statement of Scripture to the contrary, that in the sacrifice of the MASS the priest makes a PROPITIATORY SACRIFICE FOR THE SINS OF THE PEOPLE. The Scripture says:—

> "So Christ was *once* offered to bear the sins of many" (Heb. 9: 28); "But this Man after He had offered *one* sacrifice for sins *for ever*, sat down on the right hand of God" (Heb. 10: 12); "For by *one* offering He hath perfected for ever those that are sanctified" (v. 14)—see also Hebrews 7: 26, 27.

The tremendous significance of these passages is, if possible, strengthened when we remember that the Epistle to the Hebrews is the one and only book in Scripture that unfolds the glorious work of Christ, as our Great High Priest, in the heavenlies.

Now let us see what Rome teaches:—

> The Council of Trent at its twenty-second session in A. D. 1562 had the Mass for its subject of consideration, and passed a decree containing nine explanatory chapters, and nine canons.
>
> Pope Pius IV confirmed the decree of the Council of Trent at the conclusion of their sessions, and in these words he summed up the doctrine of the Mass:—
>
> "I profess that in the Mass there is offered to God a true, proper and propitiatory sacrifice for the sins of the living and the dead"!
>
> This same Pope was the author of The Tridentine Canons, which contain the following:
>
> "If any man shall say that in the Mass there is not offered to God a true and proper sacrifice, let him be accursed." (From *The Advent Witness*).

Surely such language brings its own curse on the head of him who dares to utter it. For Paul the Apostle, who was made a minister "to fulfil the Word of God" (Col. 1: 25), wrote to the Galatians: "As we said before, so say I now again, If any man preach any other gospel unto you than that ye have received, *let him be accursed*" (Gal. 1: 9).

The Confessional

"It is a significant fact that the confessional in the present form was not instituted and forced upon the people until after the vow of perpetual celibacy was forced upon the clergy. It was in A.D. 1215, during the darkest ages of the Church, at the 4th Council of Lateran that Pope Innocent III made auricular confession an article of faith in the Church of Rome. This fact is conclusive proof not only of the worthlessness of the institution, but of its evils and dangers."*

And yet the result of not using the confessional is taught to be eternal punishment!

In *Catholic Dogma,* by Father Müller, C.S.S.R., the following catechism is found on p. 67:—

Q. Are Protestants willing to confess their sins to a Catholic bishop or priest, who alone has power from Christ to forgive sins?
A. No, for they generally have an aversion to confession, and therefore their sins will not be forgiven them throughout all eternity.
Q. What follows from this?
A. That they die in their sins and are damned.

The dangers of the Confessional to the priest are widely acknowledged by Catholic dignitaries themselves. Liguori says:—

Oh, how many confessors have lost their own souls and those of their penitents on account of some negligence in hearing confession of women! . . . Oh, how many priests who before were innocent of similar transactions which began in the spirit (what spirit?—*Ed.*) have lost God and their own souls."†

Who is to blame? Why, obviously the system that compels celebate priests to hear confessions from women, young and old. Give ear to what an ex-priest has to say of how a priest is prepared for the confessional:—

The most shameless libertines could not read without blushing the filth which is contained in the books of moral

***Truths you should know,* Jovinian, p. 41.

† Tom. ix p. 145 n. 93, Cap. x and p. 104, Mechlin Edition. 1845.

theology; and it is upon these books that the education of the young clergy in the seminaries is founded . . . after four years devoted to the study of all possible and imaginary indecencies, what will be their conduct, when, in the flower of youth, they find themselves all alone with a beautiful girl, with a young bride who lays open her heart, and entrusts such youths with all her weaknesses? Unhappy victims of the Confessional! It is for you to answer.†

And what shall be said for their methods, learned from their textbooks? Here is a sample:—

The prudent Confessor will endeavor, as much as possible, to induce his (the penitent's) confidence by kind words, and then proceed from general to particular questions—from less shameful to more shameful things: not beginning from external acts, but from thoughts, such as, Has not the penitent been troubled, inadvertently as it were, with improper cogitations? Of what kind was the thought indulged? Did he experience any unlawful sensations?‡ And so on . . .

Good Confessors, says Liguori, begin to investigate the cause and seriousness of the disease by interrogating concerning the habit of sinning—the occasion—the time—the place—the persons with whom—the combination of circumstances (Prax. Conf. 6).

Is it surprising that confessional boxes have been called "spider parlors full of senseless flies," "priestly spider dens," "sinks of iniquity"?

We again make use of Dr. Scroggie's article:—

Purgatory

The Doctrine of Purgatory, for which there is in Scripture not the slightest warrant, is one of the most abhorrent doctrines of the Roman Church.

The priest, summoned to the bed of a dying man, administers to him *extreme unction,* and solemnly pronounces *full and final absolution;* and yet, after the man is dead, *money is cruelly extracted* from his mourning relatives and friends to *pay for masses* to be said in order to *shorten the period of his torment in purgatory.*

Anything more utterly absurd and wicked could not be imagined. How different is the Protestant teaching, that at death the spirit of the believer, relying entirely on the merits of Christ, goes immediately into the Divine Presence, and is for ever with the Lord.

---

†*Confession: a Doctrinal and Historical Essay,* pp. 111,112.

‡Bailly in *The Confessional Exposed,* by G. E. A. Watling.

Paul declares that to depart is to be with Christ, which is far better: A Voice from Heaven says, "Blessed are the dead which die in the Lord;" and the Master Himself says to the faithful servant, "Well done, enter thou into the joy of thy Lord."

We will now give the oath which all converts to the Roman Catholic Church have to take:—

I (name), having before my eyes the Holy Gospels, which I touch with my hand, and knowing that no one can be saved without that faith which the Holy, Catholic, Apostolic, Roman Church holds, believes and teaches: against which I grieve that I have greatly erred, inasmuch as I have held and believed doctrines opposed to her teaching;

I now, by the help of God's grace, profess that I believe the Holy, Catholic, Apostolic, Roman Church, to be the only true Church established on earth by Jesus Christ, to which I submit myself with my whole heart. I firmly believe all the articles which she proposes to my belief, and I reject and condemn all that she rejects and condemns, and I am ready to observe all that she commands me.

What slave-mentality!

Cardinal Wiseman writes thus of converts to Protestantism:—

Perversion to Rome

The history of every case is simply this: that the individual by some chance or other, probably through the influence of some pious person, became possessed of the Word of God, the Bible; that he perused this Book; that he could not find in it Transubstantiation, or Auricular Confession; that he could not discover in it one word on Purgatory or on worshipping images. He perhaps goes to the priest, and tells him that he cannot find these doctrines in the Bible. His priest argues with him, and endeavors to convince him that he should shut up the Book that is leading him astray. . . . But he perseveres; he abandons the communion of the Church of Rome—that is, as it is commonly expressed, the errors of the Church—and becomes Protestant. (See Isaacson's "*Road from Rome,*" page 248).

Space forbids us to say anything of the debasing and immoral practices of Praying for the Dead, of Rome's cruel treatment of "Heretics," of her belief that unbaptized infants go straight to Hell, of the immoral and blasphemous sale of

Indulgences, etc., etc., all of which form part of her propaganda, and are utterly contrary to the express teaching of Holy Writ.

Yet there are some "Protestants" who are seeking union with Rome!!

Dr. Scroggie has well said: "Rome, too, wants a re-united Christendom, but only by the capitulation of all the Churches to herself. The fox has no objection to the geese, provided they are all *inside* her. But a re-united Christendom on these terms would be the greatest blunder and crime in the history of religion."

RUSSELLISM, or, JEHOVAH'S WITNESSES

BY WM. C. IRVINE

THE self-styled "Pastor" Russell is dead, but the heresies he spent his life in spreading are very much alive; and India has become one of the dumping-grounds for his literature.

Dr. Dixon, late of Spurgeon's Tabernacle, says of Russellism: *"Its plan of Salvation is a plan of Damnation."* Concerning its testimony with regard to Jesus Christ, Dr. J. M. Gray of the Moody Bible Institute, Chicago, says, *"It contradicts almost every fundamental revelation."* And Dr. I. M. Haldeman, of New York, sums up Millennial Dawnism* as *"the wicked and blasphemous system* which teaches the annihilation of our Lord Jesus Christ." Such a threefold testimony is not easily discounted.

"To the Law and to the Testimony: if they speak not according to this word, it is because they have no light in them." Let us compare some of Russell's teachings with that of the inspired Word of God.

Its Christology

In Vol. 1, *Divine Plan of the Ages,* p. 179, Russell writes:—

> When Jesus was in the flesh, he was a perfect human being: previous to that time he was a perfect spiritual being. Since his resurrection he is a perfect spiritual being of the highest or Divine Order. . . . It was not until the time of his consecration, even unto death, as typified in baptism at thirty years of age, that he received the earnest of his inheritance of the divine nature.

Compare what the Scripture says of Christ in Isa. 11:5; Micah 5: 2; Matt. 1: 23; John 1: 1-3; Col. 1: 13-18; Rom. 9: 5; 1 Tim. 3: 16; Heb. 1: 7-10.

---

* This was the name by which the cult was originally known.

Again, note his teaching concerning Christ as Man, Vol. II, *The Time is At Hand*, p. 107. We read:—

> We must bear in mind, also, that our Lord is no longer a human being. . . . Since he is no longer in any sense or degree a human being, we must not expect him to come again as a human being.

What saith the Scripture: Luke 24: 39; 1 Tim. 2: 5 and Acts 1: 11? "This *same* Jesus . . . shall *so* come in *like manner* as ye have seen Him go into heaven."

Further, with reference to the resurrection of our Lord, concerning which the Apostle Paul says, "If Christ is not risen your faith is vain" (1 Cor. 15: 17), Russell would have us believe that:—

> Our Lord's human body, however, was supernaturally removed from the tomb. . . . We know nothing about what became of it except that it did not decay or corrupt (Acts 2: 27, 31). Whether it was dissolved into gases, or whether it is still preserved somewhere as the grand memorial of God's love, of Christ's obedience, and our redemption, no one knows (Vol. II, p. 129).

But we do know, and that on the authority of Christ Himself; read John 2: 19-22; Luke 24: 39.

Dr. James M. Gray writes:

Its Theory of Future Life

> As explanatory of this, Millennial Dawnism is wrong, to begin with, in its definition of Life, holding it to be simply a principle common to all beings whether God, man, animals or plants. All existence results from the impartation of this principle into organism, the nature of the existence resulting from the nature of the organism. Man results spontaneously from the impartation of this principle into a human organism, and by similar reasoning the extinction of his being follows the separation of the two.
>
> It is this that gives color to its teaching about the sleep of the soul, and that when a man dies he passes out of existence until the resurrection. The answer to this is cumulative.
>
> In the first place, the New Testament teaches that death does not mean extinction of being. Christ said: "Let the dead bury their dead" (Luke 9: 60), when He was referring to the living. Paul said, "You hath He quickened who were dead

in trespasses and sin" (Eph. 2:1). John said: "We know that we have passed from death unto life because we love the brethren" (1 John 3:14).

In the second place, the New Testament teaches that the penalty for sin is more than extinction of being. The rich man "lifted up his eyes in hell being in torments" (Luke 16:23). Christ said it had been good for Judas if he had not been born (Matt. 26:24), which is inconsistent with the theory that he has ceased to exist.

In the third place, if everlasting punishment means only extinction of being, then everlasting life must mean only continuation of being which is the boon even of Satan himself, who is to live for ever (Rev. 20:10).

In the fourth place, if death means extinction of being, how can there be a resurrection, for this implies the coming back to life of the same person who passed out of it, otherwise a resurrection would be a new creation.

In the fifth place, the Scripture especially says that the soul continues to exist, for Christ warns us in Matt. 10:28, not to fear them "that kill the body, but have not power to kill the soul." And even this says nothing about the spirit. Man has a spirit as well as a soul, and it is by his spirit he becomes the offspring of God, and his spirit never dies.

In the sixth place, the Bible shows us men living after death, Abraham for example, Moses, Samuel. . . . In the sixth chapter of Revelation John has a vision of those to be beheaded in the great tribulation and shows them anticipatively, as souls existing after such beheading (*Haldeman*).

Finally, if death means extinction of being, then Jesus Christ became extinct at Calvary—annihilated, as Dr. Haldeman expresses it. And no wonder, as he says, that to break the horror of such a thought, Millennial Dawnism should teach that after such extinction He was created over again not as a man indeed, but somewhat after His former estate as an invisible spirit. But if Jesus Christ was annihilated then the gulf between Deity and humanity remains unbridged, redemption is a failure and salvation beyond the hope of fallen men.*

Russell's books being full of "damnable heresies" concerning the Person of Christ, any believer who has been induced to buy his literature ought to burn it, whatever it may have cost him; nor should we receive his followers in our houses (2 John 7), lest we become partakers of their evil deeds.

Many of Russell's publications have been issued under the name of the *International Bible Students' Association* and

**Errors of Millennial Dawnism,* James M. Gray, D.D.

that of the *Watch Tower Bible and Tract Society.* His agents have been known to say that they are selling books for the "Bible Society," and many have been induced to buy them thinking they must be sound if issued by the "Bible Society," *i.e.*, the British or other Bible Societies. The Movement is or has been known as *Millennial Dawnism, International Bible Students' Association* and later as *Jehovah's Witnesses.* There is a reason for this chameleon-like characteristic. "There are certain men crept in unawares, who were before ordained to this condemnation, ungodly men, turning the grace of our God into lasciviousness, and denying the only Lord God, and our Lord Jesus Christ" (Jude 4).

In Many Names

"Death of the Founder of 'Millennial Dawn.' Usually a man's faith shines brightest as he nears the confines of Eternity. The test of all tests is then applied. The self-styled 'PASTOR' RUSSELL, founder of the Movement, seems to have miserably failed at the supreme moment. He died in the Sante Fé train on its way to Kansas City on Oct. 31, 1916, his traveling companion, Mr. Menta Sturgeon, alone being with him. The published details of his last days indicate how the gloom of night settled on the prophet of Millennial Dawn. Here are extracts (*italics ours*).

The Last Days of its Founder

Oct. 16.—The public meeting at Lansing was well attended: but for some reason the interest waned and *many left*: so much so that Brother Russell spoke of it afterwards and *seemed puzzled.*

Oct. 24.—He went to dinner with us, talking pleasantly to every one, and was *as humorous as usual;* but he ate nothing, although the dinner was excellent.

On *Oct.* 30, evidently realizing that death was approaching, Mr. Sturgeon says: "We inquired respecting the Seventh Volume (*of Scripture Studies*) and received his answer, *'Some one else can write that.'* We are satisfied. He had spoken concerning the *smiting of the Jordan,* the *payment of the penny,** and the writings of the Seventh Volume; and this was enough."

---

*We had not before read of the introduction of this Romish custom into Russellism.

On *Oct.* 31 the conductor and the porter of the train were called in by Mr. Sturgeon, who said: "We want you to see how a great man of God can die." Alas, alas, he who had so well "staged" his system and "boomed" himself, failed in the drama of the last moment, and so passed into Eternity silent and sombre. No "dawn" on his horizon, no farewell note of victory, no reconciliation to his divorced wife, no recantation of his numerous denials of the Deity of Christ, the value of His Atonement, His bodily Resurrection, the Second Coming, eternal punishment and other cardinal truths; no sorrow for the thousands whom he had turned from *light* to *darkness*, not even an admission that his prophecy that "The harvest of this age . . . ends with the overthrow of Gentile power in A. D. 1914" had passed unnoticed by God or man. Thus closed the career of one of the greatest of the "many *false prophets*" (1 John 4:1) of these last days (*The Witness*).

SEVENTH-DAY ADVENTISM

By Wm. C. Irvine and A. McD. Redwood

Seventh-Day Adventism, Christian Science, and Theosophy have one thing in common at least—they all had hysterical, neurotic women as their Founders!

Genesis

Mrs. Ellen G. White was the founder of the "ism" of this article, though she got her cue from one William Miller of Low Hampton, N. Y., U. S. A. Concerning Mrs. White, "Dr. William Russell, a chief physician in the Seventh-Day Adventist Sanatorium at Battle Creek, long a Seventh-Day Adventist, wrote in 1869 that Mrs. White's visions were the result of a diseased organization or condition of brain or nervous system." Dr. Fairfield, likewise an Adventist, and for years a physician in the same Sanatorium, wrote in 1887 that he had no doubt that her visions were "simply hysterical trances. Age itself had almost cured her."* We may well pity the poor woman in her ill-health, but we cannot be sentimental about the seriousness of her teachings, *which amount to blasphemy and are directly opposed to the Word of God.*

Mrs. White's standard work is *The Great Controversy between Christ and Satan,* which has run through several editions. This contains an authoritative account of the Seventh-Day Adventism teaching. Of this book, however, (Rev.) D. M. Canright (who was intimate with her for years) writes in his volume *Seventh-Day Adventism Renounced*: "She often copies her subject-matter without credit or sign of quotation from other authors. Indeed her last great book, *The Great Controversy,* which they laud so highly as her greatest work, is largely (mainly in its historical parts) a compilation of Andrews' *History of the Sabbath; History of the Waldenses,* by Wylie; *Life of Miller,* by White; *Thoughts on Revelation,* by Smith, and other books." "The Pastors'

---

*A. J. Pollock, *Seventh-Day Adventism.*

Union of Healdsburg, California, investigated the matter, and published many instances of her plagiarisms." In spite of such facts, however, the publisher's preface reads, "We believe she has been empowered by a Divine illumination to speak of some *past events* which have been brought to her knowledge *with greater minuteness than is set forth in any existing records,* and *to read the future with more than human foresight!*"

Such a genesis is not very reassuring. In religious matters at least, one expects to find the source for new light coming from a more lofty and spiritual plane. A stream never rises higher than its source; and if this stream of a "new faith" is no higher in source than represented, it does not augur well for subsequent developments. Alas, we do not need to go very far into the depths to find out the muddy and unwholesome character of this that is called Seventh-Day Adventism. William Miller, the progenitor, was found out to be a very false and dangerous prophet, but this much can be said of him—that he *stopped short* after repeated failures in his own line, from going into the wholesale theories and vapid imaginings advocated by the later Mrs. White, albeit these new theories *were built upon his discarded foundation!*

We indict Seventh-Day Adventism on *four main counts,* leaving out lesser (though none the less false) theories.

Attitude towards Atonement

Seventh-Day Adventism denies the Biblical Doctrine of the Atoning Sacrifice of Christ as the only means of man's salvation.

This is the first serious indictment. We shall prove it from Mrs. White's own writings, so that we may not be accused of misrepresentation or exaggeration:

> The ministration of the priests throughout the year in the first apartment of the sanctuary (which sanctuary Mrs. White places in heaven and not on earth!—*Ed.*) . . . represents the work of ministration upon which Christ entered at His ascension. . . . For eighteen centuries this work of ministration continued in the first apartment of the sanctuary. The blood of Christ, pleaded in behalf of penitent believers, secured their pardon and acceptance with the Father, yet their sins still remained upon the books of record.—*The Great Controversy.*

Can it be *unreasonable* for us to inquire, What in the name of all that's reasonable does this mean? Sins pardoned and *yet still on the books!*

(*a*) *Seventh-Day Adventism denies the finality of the work of Christ on the cross,* hence it makes Christ's last cry on the cross, "It is finished," to be a lie!

As in typical service there was a work of atonement at the close of the year, so before Christ's work for redemption of men is completed, there is a work of atonement for the removal of sin from the sanctuary. This is the service which began when the 2,300 days ended (according to Mrs. White this was in the year 1844! Evidently the nineteenth century was more wonderful than we had imagined!—*Ed.*), At that time, as foretold by Daniel the prophet, our high priest entered the most holy to perform the *last division* of his solemn work to *cleanse the sanctuary* . . . in the new covenant the sins of the repentant are by faith placed upon Christ, *and transferred, in fact, to the heavenly sanctuary* . . . so the actual cleansing of the heavenly (sanctuary) is to be accomplished by the removal, or blotting out, of the sins which are there recorded. But, *before* this can be accomplished, there must be *an examination of the books of record to determine who,* through repentance of sin and faith in Christ, are entitled to the benefits of His atonement. The cleansing of the sanctuary therefore involves a *work of investigation*—a work of judgment. Those who followed in the light of the prophetic word saw that, *instead of coming to the earth* at the termination of the 2,300 days in 1844 (as Prophet William Miller had so dogmatically and widely proclaimed.—*Ed.*), Christ then entered into the most holy place of the heavenly, to *perform the closing work of atonement* preparatory to his coming.—*Ibid.*

We have given this extended quotation on purpose to show a fair specimen of Mrs. White's writings and teachings. Here then are the facts—William Miller prophesied that Christ would come (hence the name Adventist) in 1844, but He did not! So Mrs. White steps in to save the situation. A mistake has been made—it was not to earth but to the "heavenly sanctuary" He came. Why? Her fertile imagination was equal to the question—to complete the work of atonement, and to carry on something she calls "investigative judgment," all preparatory to His coming to earth at some later date! She assumes therefore; (i) there is a sanctuary in heaven, though the Bible says nothing about it being in heaven; (ii) there is sin *in heaven,* though the Bible says nothing about it; (iii) that in some mysterious way not explainable the sanctuary has to be a kind of "mediator" and bear the sins of the believer for at least a time; (iv) this sanctuary needs cleansing nevertheless; and (v) this cleansing and investigating *began* in 1844. We find it difficult to decide whether to be shocked at its rank heresy, or to pity the one who can write such balderdash. But there is worse ahead.

Seventh-Day Adventism declares Satan to be the joint sin-bearer, and the vicarious substitute of the sinner.

Satan the Sin-bearer

It was seen also that while the sin-offering pointed to Christ as a sacrifice, and the high priest represented Christ as Mediator, *the scapegoat typified Satan,* the author of sin, *upon whom the sins of the truly penitent will finally be placed.* When the high priest by virtue of the blood of the sin-offering removed the sins from the sanctuary, he placed them upon the scapegoat. When Christ, *by virtue of His own blood, removes the sins of His people from the heavenly sanctuary at the close of His ministration, He will place them upon Satan,* who in the execution of the judgment must bear the final penalty. The scapegoat was sent into a land not inhabited, never to come again into the Congregation of Israel. So will SATAN be for ever banished from the presence of God and His people and *he will be blotted from existence in the final destruction of sin and the sinner.*—(*The Great Controversy*).

Dr. D. Anderson-Berry gives but a just estimate of this rigmarole in his book when he says:

We have the choicest doctrine of the Gospel, justification by faith, utterly contemned and set at naught. Nay, more, as if that were not enough to damn their doctrine, they dare to substitute for Christ's finished work on the cross, SATAN'S vicarious suffering in bearing away the sins of the people of God into a land of utter annihilation. It does not lessen the blasphemous grossness of the idea to say that it is wholly imaginary, the figment of the addled brain of a hysterical woman. *It merely explains it!*

If ever there was a "damnable heresy" (see 2 Peter 2: 1) surely it is here! Mrs. White professes to found all this teaching on Leviticus 23 and the book of Daniel. We confidently hand both books, yea, the whole Bible itself, to any mature, sane-thinking Christian and challenge him to find anywhere in the whole sixty-six books of the Divine Library, one jot or tittle of evidence or proof (set forth according to fundamental and eternal principles of exegesis), for such consummate trash. It seems an insult to offer such stuff for the serious consideration of a reasonable mind.

With this, compare the following few texts (selected out of a vast number) from the Word of God itself, and then ask yourself, reader, which you are prepared to believe and stake your soul's destiny upon.

"Without shedding of blood there is no remission" (Heb. 9: 22).

"The blood maketh atonement for the soul" (Lev. 17: 11).

Scriptures and Atonement

"Redeemed by the precious blood of Christ" (1 Peter 1: 19).

"Who His own self bare our sins IN HIS OWN BODY on the tree" (1 Peter 2: 24).

"Made peace through the blood of His cross" (Col. 1: 20).

"Made nigh by the blood of Christ" (Eph. 2: 13).

"He that believeth on Him is not condemned" (John 3: 18).

"There is therefore now NO CONDEMNATION to them which are in Christ Jesus" (Rom. 8: 1).

"Justified freely by His grace through the redemption that is in Christ Jesus" (Rom. 3: 24).

"The blood of Jesus Christ His (God's) Son cleanseth us from ALL SIN" (1 John 1: 7).

Seventh-Day Adventists teach that the Lord Jesus Christ inherited a sinful, fallen nature.

It may surprise and pain the reader to learn that the above statement is actual FACT. If such is a foundation-stone on which the Seventh-Day Adventist church is founded, how can it stand? Such is not the Christ we have learnt to know—not the Holy Lord of Holy Writ.

Christ's Humanity

The following extract, taken from one of their own

publications—*Bible Readings for the Home Circle,* makes this astounding statement (p. 115, 1915 edition):—

In His humanity Christ partook of our sinful, fallen nature. If not, then He was not "made like unto His brethren," was not "in all points tempted like as we are," did not overcome as we have to overcome, and is not, therefore, the complete and perfect Saviour man needs and must have to be saved.

In other words they say, If you do not accept our teach ing on the "sinful, fallen nature" of Christ, you have no Saviour! This writer continues:—

The idea that Christ was born of an immaculate or sinless mother,* inherited no tendencies to sin, and for this reason did not sin, removes Him from the realm of a fallen world, and from the very place where help is needed. On His human side, Christ inherited just what every child of Adam inherits—a sinful nature. On the divine side, from His very conception He was begotten and born of the Spirit. And all this was done to place mankind on vantage-ground, and to demonstrate that *in the same way* everyone who is "born of the Spirit" may gain like victories over sin in his own sinful flesh. Thus each one is to overcome *as Christ overcame* (Rev. 3: 21). Without this birth there can be no victory over temptation, and no salvation from sin, John 3: 3-7. (Their italics.)

Let us examine somewhat carefully the above teaching.

The Scripture tells us that we are partakers† of God's holiness (Heb. 12: 10); God and Christ are one (John 10: 30); yet above we are assured that Christ "partook of *our sinful, fallen* nature!" What a contemptuous denial of Scripture! Are we not distinctly told that He was "holy, harmless, *undefiled,* separate from sinners?" How could He be at once "*holy*" and "*undefiled*" and at the same time *partake* of our "fallen nature;" *inherit* what we as sinners inherited, and yet be "without sin" ("sin apart," R. V.; see Heb. 7: 26; 4: 15)?

---

*This, the writer perfectly well knows, is a doctrine which is held by no body of evangelical Christians—it is Roman to the core.

†"—to take, receive, *with*" (*Young*).

After publishing the above quotation with these and other comments in *The Indian Christian* for January, 1927, we received a letter from the Editor of *Oriental Watchman*, the official organ of the Seventh-Day Adventist people in India, in which he sought to explain the teaching which he says "is orthodox to the very core!" We can only give short extracts as the letter covers more than five type-written pages. He says:—

> I wish to affirm definitely just the contrary of your conclusion by saying *that if Jesus did not take our fallen nature in His own person* (his italics) by His incarnation, fallen humanity is left without a saviour. . .
>
> There was but one kind of humanity in the world that Jesus could have taken, and that is fully described in Romans, chapter three, where Paul describes it as sinful and fallen, and beyond all hope if left to itself.*
>
> He who was holy and undefiled, had sin imputed unto Him. The sinful nature which He bore was not that which came by the sins of His own doing, for it is written of Him: "*Who did not sin,* neither was guile found in His mouth" (1 Pet. 2: 22), but they were the sins of imputation—sins committed by others which were laid upon Him.

He also quotes 2 Cor. 5: 21, and draws attention to Isaiah 53.

So, then, we are to understand that Christ carried the burden of imputed sin His whole life long, not only on the

---

*He apparently does not know that: "Sin is no property of humanity at all, but the disordered state of our souls" (*Faussett*).

W. Kelly says: "Not a trace of evil was in Christ. He was man as truly as the first Adam—Son of man as Adam was not, but Son of Man which is in heaven—a Divine Person, yet none the less a Man. But for these very reasons He was capable and competent, according to the glory of His Person, to be dealt with by God for all that was unlike Him in us. Had there been the smallest taint in Him, this could not have been done. The perfect absence of evil in this one Man furnished the requisite victim; as in Himself and all His ways the divine nature found satisfaction and delight. Would He then bear all? Be willing to go down to the depth of the judgment of all men, according to God's estimate of the evil of our nature? The entire, unbroken, unmitigated judgment of God fell upon Him in order to deal with it and put it away for ever. No less, I believe, is the force of Christ's death for us."

cross, for it was at His birth He *inherited* His human nature. Again if Christ inherited a sinful, fallen nature, when did He disinherit it? Do they teach that He who is the same yesterday and today and for ever, has taken His "sinful, fallen nature" to God's right hand?

Let us now turn to orthodox teaching on this point. Dr. I. M. Haldeman of New York says of Christ:—

> He was begotten of God from the seed of the woman, by and through the Holy Ghost. That which was begotten was not a person, but a nature—a human nature. This human nature was holy, Scripture calls it "that Holy Thing." It was the holiness produced by and out of the Holy Ghost. It was the holiness produced by and out of God. It was, therefore, in its quality the holiness of God. Since its quality was the holiness of God, there was no sin in it, and no possible tendency to sin. This holy, sinless human nature was indissolubly joined to the eternal personality of the Son.

Dr. Griffith Thomas on Romans 8: 3* says: "Observe the wonderful fulfilment of this verse. Thus we have the Deity of Christ, 'His own Son,' the Incarnation 'in the likeness of sinful flesh,' that is, He was like us in all things except sin—Christ's flesh was not sinful, never the seat of sin; and His atonement 'for sin,' which means 'as an offering for sin'."

Dr. C. I. Scofield says: "Our sins were borne 'in His body,' but not in His nature."

Were the teaching of the Seventh-Day Adventist church true we would have a monstrosity—Deity inheriting a sinful nature!

If this could have been so there could have been no sinless sacrifice, no hope for sinners, no Saviour. And how could it have been written: "The prince of this world cometh, and hath NOTHING in Me" (John 14: 30). Further the Scripture says, "In Him Is No SIN" (1 John 3: 5)!

---

*Rom. 8: 3 is nicely balanced. "Sinful" necessitates "likeness." "Sinful flesh" would have meant that He Himself had needed a Saviour. "Likeness of flesh" would have meant that the Humanity of the Saviour was unreal—later the Docetic heresy (*C. F. Hogg*).

Seventh-Day Adventism believes in Soul-sleep after death and Conditional Immortality.

Soul-sleep This indictment will not take up much of our time, as we deal with both these heresies elsewhere in this booklet (see separate articles). Mrs. White says:—

Upon the fundamental error of *natural immortality* rests the doctrine of *consciousness in death,* a doctrine like eternal torment, opposed to the teaching of the Scriptures, to the dictates of reason and to our feelings of humanity.

The theory of *eternal punishment* is one of the false doctrines that constitute the wine of the abominations of Babylon. . . . They received it from Rome, as they received the false Sabbath.

Will the Seventh-Day Adventists explain then why Paul could use such language as, "Absent from the body, present *with the Lord";* and, "to be with Christ, which is FAR BETTER"? Will Mrs. White tell us what "natural immortality" means, and who is so foolish to preach it, when we see thousands dying around us every day? Will Mrs. White or any of her disciples dare to set up "the feelings of humanity" against the plain Word of the Living God—"*These* (*i.e.,* sinners) *shall go away into everlasting punishment: but the righteous into life eternal"?* (See the article on Soul-sleep).

The fourth indictment is that Seventh-Day Adventism tries to force the believer back under Law and so away from Grace, by their Sabbath teachings.

The Sabbath As the Seventh-Day Adventists materialized the sanctuary in heaven, they were forced to materialize everything. So besides an actual sanctuary in heaven, with candlesticks, curtains, table of showbread and ark, they were forced to add within the ark the two tables of stone, and call upon all to put themselves under the law. Mrs. White at first refused to believe that the Fourth Commandment was more binding than any other. Elder Bates urged its great importance until Mrs. White had a convenient vision, in which she asserted she was taken to heaven, and shown the sanctuary and its appointments! A description of her vision is given: "Jesus raised the cover of the ark, and she beheld the tables of stone on which the ten commandments were written. She was amazed as she saw the Fourth Commandment in the very centre of the ten precepts, *with a soft halo of light encircling it.*"

The Adventists have found a handle for their teachings in the erroneous way Christians speak about the first day of the week (the Lord's Day) as if *it* were the *Sabbath.*

The Adventists claim that Christians being still under the Law of Moses, are bound to keep the "least of its precepts," and therefore must keep the Sabbath. They also state that Protestants acknowledge that the Roman Catholic Church, away back in the year A.D. 364, at the Council of Laodicea, changed the Sabbath or Seventh day to Sunday or the First day. Neither statements are tenable when judged in the light of Scripture and early Church history.

1. The Sabbath was given as a "sign" and "perpetual covenant" between Jehovah and Israel, as is most clearly stated in Exod. 31: 12-18. The ten commandments, of which the law of the Sabbath is the fourth, were written with the finger of God on tables of stone. These commandments are called "the ministration of death" and "the ministration of condemnation," "written and engraven in stone" (2 Cor. 3: 7, 9), which ministration, the Holy Spirit tells us, is "done away" and "abolished" (vers. 11, 13), and in its place we have "the ministration of the Spirit" and "the ministration of righteousness" (vers. 8, 9). Hence in Colossians 2: 16 we read, "Let no man therefore judge you . . . of a sabbath day" (R. V.), see also Rom. 14: 5, 6. Again we read in Colossians 2: 14 that the "handwriitng of ordinances" was "blotted out" and "nailed" to Christ's cross (as of old, bills were nailed to the doorpost when paid), for Christ has fulfilled the law on our behalf, met its every claim.

Further, Scripture emphatically teaches our position of *freedom from the law, e.g., "Ye are not under the law but under grace"* (Rom. 6: 14; see also Rom. 7: 4, 6; Gal. 5: 18); indeed the Epistle to the Galatians was written to establish this very thing. The rebuke given to those who sought to bring the Gentile converts under the yoke of the law as given in Acts 15, still holds good for legalizers, such as the Seventh-Day Adventists: "Now therefore why tempt ye God, to put a yoke upon the neck of the disciples, which neither our fathers nor we were able to bear?" (v. 10).

The Adventists say:—

> Christ further declares that whosoever breaks even so much as one of the least of the precepts of the law . . . shall be called the least . . . in the kingdom of heaven." See *Signs of the Times* (Extra No. 15, p. 50).

If this still holds good, why do Adventists ignore circumcision? Again, if Christians are bound to observe "the least of the precepts of the law," why did the great Council of Jerusalem (Acts 15), when writing to the Gentile converts, declare their freedom from the law, and write of those who had sought to make them keep the law, as those who "troubled you with words subverting your souls" (v. 24)? If the keeping of the Sabbath was to be observed, why was it not enjoined here? Why was it never enjoined to believers in a single passage of the New Testament?

Before going further it might be well to note *how* the Sabbath was to be observed. Someone has put it thus:—

> It was to be kept from sunset to sunset (Lev. 23: 32). If within twenty-four hours any burden was carried (Jer. 17: 21), any fire kindled (Exod. 35: 3), any cooking done (Exod. 16: 23), the Sabbath would be broken; the penalty for which was death (Num. 15). Were this law observed by Adventists they would all quickly be exterminated, as the above rules they consistently break. How very inconsistent he is who preaches to others to keep the Sabbath when he does not keep it himself. Surely this man's religion is vain.

D. M. Panton has well said:—

Moral and Ceremonial Law

> An honest, if uninstructed, error is very prevalent among the Churches of Christ, and affords the Seventh-Day Adventist the fulcrum for his lever. It is said that the ceremonial law, and the civil law of Israel, have been abolished but not the moral law, and that the Sabbath as occurring in the Decalogue, is part of the unrevoked moral law of God. But (1) most remarkably no inspired writer ever makes any such distinction between "moral" and "ceremonial" law; the ceremonial law (*e.g.*, Lev. 19) contains laws as purely moral as any in the Decalogue, and had we been delivered

from the ceremonial, while remaining under the moral, Paul would most surely have said so—an utterance he never makes. (2) The Sabbath, in its nature, is itself a ceremonial law: the moral law is all law which appeals to the conscience, and needs no written revelation; but as to which day to observe, or whether to observe any day at all, conscience is silent. If we are to distinguish between the moral and the ceremonial law, on the ground that one is passed, and the other still in force, then—as the Sabbath is purely ceremonial law—*it is passed.* But the most important point still remains. (3) I, as a Christian, obey all law that is moral in the Decalogue, not because it is in the Law, *but because it is in the Gospel.* Worship of God only is enjoined fifty times in the New Testament; idolatry is forbidden twelve times; profanity four times; honor of father and mother is commanded six times; adultery is forbidden twelve; theft six; false witness four; and covetousness, nine times. "The Ten Commandments," as Luther says, "do not apply to us Gentiles and Christians, but only to the Jews." So therefore, Paul, in all his fourteen epistles, never once names the Sabbath—except in a single passage where, classing it with the entire law, he declares it has been totally abolished. So the early Church held.

Now as to the second claim, viz., that at the Council of Laodicea the Roman Catholic Church changed the Sabbath from the Seventh to the First day. Whatever may have happened at that Council, we submit that the Sabbath was not changed. For no decree of man could or can change God's covenant. What did take place, so far as we can learn, was "to in a manner quite abolish" the observation of the Sabbath for Christians. That is, that they made it illegal *for Christians* acknowledging the sway of Rome, to observe the Sabbath as their day of worship. But let it be well noted, large numbers of Christians were at that time, and long before, observing the first day of the week as their day of worship. The assertion of the Seventh-Day Adventists is entirely misleading as is proved from the following extracts:—

Seventh and First Days

(i) THE EPISTLE OF BARNABAS about A.D. 100.

"Wherefore, also *we keep the eighth day with joyfulness,* the day also on which Jesus rose again from the dead."

(ii) THE EPISTLE OF IGNATIUS: A.D. 107.

"Be not deceived with strange doctrines, nor with old fables, which are unprofitable. For if we still live *according*

to the Jewish Law, we acknowledge that we have *not received grace*. . . . If, therefore, those who were brought up in the ancient order of things have come to the possession of a new hope, *no longer observing the Sabbath*, but living in the observance of the Lord's Day, on which also our life has sprung up again by Him and by His death."

(iii) THE WRITINGS OF JUSTIN MARTYR: A.D. 145-150.

"And *on the day called Sunday* all who live in cities or in the country gather together in one place, and the memoirs of the apostles or the writings of the prophets are read. . . . *But Sunday is the day* on which we all hold a common assembly, because it is the *First day of the Week* on which God . . . made the world; and *Jesus Christ our Saviour on the same day rose from the dead*."

(iv) APOSTOLIC CONSTITUTIONS: Church life in the 2nd Century.

"*On the day of the resurrection of the Lord*—that is, the Lord's Day—assemble yourself together without fail, giving thanks to God and praising Him for those mercies God has bestowed upon you through Christ."

(v) IRENAEUS: A.D. 155-202.

"The Mystery of the Lord's Resurrection may not be celebrated on any other day *than the Lord's Day*, and on this alone should we observe the breaking off of the Paschal Feast."* (Our italics all through).

As a matter of fact, the first day of the week—the Lord's Day—was selected *not in place of the Sabbath*, but as a day in which to celebrate our Lord's death and resurrection. As a writer has well said: "It is a day of thanksgiving and liberty to the Christians, and a day which they delight in regarding as unto the Lord (Rom. 16: 6). It is the Lord's Day, as John called it in Rev. 1: 10. On that day Jesus rose the Head of a new creation. On the Lord's Day He appeared to His disciples. On the Lord's Day the Holy Ghost was given. On the Lord's Day the door of the kingdom was unlocked and 3,000 souls entered in. On the Lord's Day

---

*These quotations are taken from Dr. D. Anderson-Berry's book *Seventh-Day Adventism*—he was a scholar of no mean repute. He states that these are "*extracts all made by myself*, so that ignorance of the context might not mislead me; the portions omitted I have omitted since they do not affect the sense, and merely cumber the pages."

the disciples came together to break bread in remembrance of Him (Acts 20: 7)."

In answer to the following question, *The Witness* (Scotland) gives the accompanying lucid reply from the able pen of the late David Baron, one of the most eminent and learned of Jewish believers:—

Jewish Believers

How can a Hebrew Christian be shown that he must not keep the Seventh-day Sabbath seeing it is written: "The children of Israel shall keep the Sabbath, to observe the Sabbath throughout their generations for a perpetual covenant" (Exod. 31: 16)?

There is no necessity to "show" or teach the Jewish believers that they "must" not "keep the Sabbath" as if the Gospel made the non-observance of the Seventh-day rest compulsory or a condition of true discipleship. . . . When more fully instructed, and as he grows in grace and in the knowledge of Christ, he will be brought to see for himself that the Jewish Sabbath has no significance in this dispensation and in relation to those whose calling is a heavenly one, and whose destinies are bound up not with time but with eternity. . . .

The Sabbath is thus essentially connected with the old marred creation, with the imperfect Mosaic dispensation, and with the typical redemption from Egypt. But Christians are children of the new creation, and are in the dispensation not of the Law but of the Spirit. "With Christ's resurrection," says an old writer, "the Seventh-day Sabbath expired, transmitting its sanctity and its privileges to the *new* Sabbath—the first day of a new week, which became our day of rest (and of worship) in the power of a new creation."

The Editor of *The Witness* well says: "Sticklers for keeping the exact 'Seventh Day,' or Sunday, or 'Lord's Day,' have a difficulty in the way days have been calculated and thrown about. In 1582 Gregory XIII found a miscalculation and decreed to drop October 5-14 and to drop 3 leap years in every century. In England 11 days (September 3-13) were dropped in 1752, in addition to other changes."

"SOUL-SLEEP"

By Wm. Hoste, B.A.

This materialistic notion, itself hardly worthy to be dignified as a "heresy," is the handmaid of various heresies, *e.g.*, Christadelphianism, Conditional Immortality and other systems, which deny to man conscious existence between death and resurrection.

Phrase Unscriptural

The "sleep of the soul" is a phrase as foreign to the Scriptures as is the doctrine attached to it. Believers, and believers only, are said to "fall asleep" when they die, and the sleeping is always connected with the body, but the persons who have slept are viewed as "with Christ," *e.g.*, "Them also that sleep in Jesus will God bring with Him" (1 Thess. 4: 14); that is, the departed saints (not their bodies in the cemeteries) till then in spirit with their Lord, will be brought with Him when He comes and will be re-united to their bodies in resurrection.

False Premises

Others, like the late Dr. Bullinger,* go further than "soul-sleep;" they hold that the soul is merely a combination of body and spirit, and that when these are parted at death, nothing survives to sleep. This is the Christadelphian conception, which Dr. B. supports with a wealth of illustration: "A rifle is made up of 'stock and barrel' (Dr. B.'s rifles apparently have no "locks"!); a watch of 'works and case'; separate these, where are the rifle and the watch?" One would have thought existing still, in their separate parts! Certainly one has seen the works of a watch going on a jeweller's bench without the case!

**e.g., his booklet, The Rich Man and Lazarus;* answered by the present writer in his *The Intermediate State.*

So Scripture teaches that the spiritual part of man still functions, though parted from the body. Man is not a combination of body and spirit merely, but is tripartite, as 1 Thess. 5: 23 teaches: "Your whole spirit and soul, and body be preserved blameless (or entire) unto the coming of our Lord Jesus Christ." The spirit is the seat of the understanding (1 Cor. 2: 11); the soul of the affections (1 Sam. 18: 1). They are distinct, but never divided. The soul unites the spirit, the higher nature of man (originally created as the link with God), and the body.

Re-creation not Resurrection

If this soul-extinction theory were true, what these men call resurrection would be the re-creation of an extinct personality, a thing unknown in Scripture, and where would be the link of responsibility between the old and the new? It is precisely on the survival of the personality of the defunct that the Lord bases His argument for resurrection: "I am the God of Abraham, the God of Isaac, and the God of Jacob. God is not the God of the dead, but of the living" (Matt. 22: 32). Note it does not say, as these teachers would have us believe, "of those who *will live* again," but "of the *living*." In Luke 20: 38 five more words are added which affirm the same truth with added emphasis, "for all live unto Him." This is clearly not a mere assertion that "all will be raised," for the Sadducees were too clever to be silenced by a mere assertion of the point at issue.

Existence and Life

These teachers persistently confuse "life" and "existence" and yet Dr. Bullinger in his *magnum opus*, *The Critical Lexicon*, under the word "live" (*zao*) gives as the meaning "to live," and not "to exist," for "a thing can exist without living." Therefore, "ceasing to live" is not the equivalent of "ceasing to exist." A man may die as far as this world is concerned, "his thoughts (or purposes) in that very hour perish" (Ps. 146: 4); "no longer does he know anything," that is, he is completely out of touch with the world —but it is not therefore true that he is out of touch with spiritual realities, or that he forgets the past. Death is not a cessation of existence, but a separation of existence.

All this is brought out in the story of the rich man and Lazarus in Luke 16. There we see two men in the intermediate state, the one in Hades, tormented, the other in Paradise, comforted. The rich man recognizes Lazarus under his new conditions, and Abraham, whom of course he had never seen; he remembers his five brethren still on the earth, and though he knows nothing of them actually, he realizes from what he once knew of them, that they sadly need warning "lest they also come into this place of torment."

The Lord knew the impression His words must convey, and could speech be more explicit? Nevertheless we are asked to believe that He was only adopting a tradition of the Pharisees which, however, He knew to be untrue, to crush them in argument—a maneuver no decent man of the world would adopt. We utterly refuse to give the slightest value to such reasonings, which are not only dishonoring to Christ, but an insult to our intelligence. Even Mr. Rotherham, for years Editor of an "Annihilationist" journal, while discussing our Lord's words to the dying robber, does admit as an argument in favor of the meaning usually assigned to them, that, "no ingenuity of exposition can silence the testimony of Luke 16: 23-25, to conscious comfort of separate souls in Abraham's bosom." Our Lord never failed to witness against the traditions of the Pharisees (though even Pharisees may hold some truth); but where is a hint that He is adopting anything from them or did not believe what He said was true? The very suggestion is sheer blasphemy.

Sheol and Hades

All through the Bible special words, "*sheol*" and "*hades*," are used for the place of departed spirits, as distinguished from the tomb where the body lies. The Revisers in their preface state, "The Hebrew '*sheol*' signifies the abode of departed spirits, and corresponds to the Greek '*hades*' or the underworld . . . it does not signify 'the place of burial.'" But why such a place if there are no departed spirits to inhabit it? Other words are used for a burying-place, such as "*shah-gath*," constantly translated "pit," e.g., Job 32: 18, 24; or "grave," Job 32: 22; or "corruption," *e.g.*, Ps. 16: 10; 49: 9; Jonah 2: 6. Psalm 16 is specially important: "Thou wilt not leave My soul in hell (*sheol*), neither wilt Thou suffer Thine Holy One to see corruption." Between death and resurrection our Lord, far from becoming an extinct personality, as the "soul-sleepers" profanely teach, went to Paradise the very day He died, where the repentant robber found Him soon after according to His promise and, as it is expressed in Ephesians 4: 9, "He descended into the lower part of the earth."

When Jacob, however, speaks of rejoining his son Joseph, whom he supposed had been devoured by some wild beast and therefore not buried at all, he used the word "sheol"—the unseen world. Then there is another word, *"kehver,"* which also means a literal grave (*e.g.*, Is. 53: 9), "He made His grave with the wicked," and in Gen. 50: 5 this is the word Jacob uses when referring to his literal grave in Canaan. David, too, spoke of going to his dead child who was not yet in his grave, which shows that he did not confuse, as these teachers do, the sepulchre with the spirit-world. The same is true of *"hades"* (derived from "not" and "to see") which never means a tomb—*"mnema"* and *"mnemeion"* are employed for that—but the "unseen world." Nor do these represent a place of silence, as is asserted by the soul-sleepers, as Isa. 14: 9; Ezek. 32: 21; and Jonah 2: 2 show, and as we have clearly seen in Luke 16.

Any attempt at communication with the departed is forbidden in the Scriptures, and spiritists are in flagrant disobedience to God's Word, and the dupes of demons; but that in no way affects the fact that the spirits of the departed are in a state of consciousness; indeed, goes to prove it.

All depends of course on the resurrection of Christ, whether for the present enjoyment of the redeemed with Him, or for future completed blessing, when "the dead shall be raised incorruptible." These teachers insist on connecting all blessing with the resurrection of the believer, but 1 Cor. 15: 17 is clear: *"If Christ be not raised,* your faith is vain; ye are yet in your sins" (so much for the living). "Then they also which are fallen asleep in Christ are perished." Naturally, if Christ were not raised and ascended, no believer could be with Him now or ever. This is borne out by the apostle's own testimony in Phil. 1: 23: "For I am in a strait betwixt two, having a desire to depart and to be with Christ, which is far better." There are two alternatives in this passage and only two, dying or living, or in other words, "departing to be with Christ," or "abiding in the flesh." Had he consulted his own wishes, he would have chosen to depart, but for their sakes he was willing to "abide in the flesh."

Philippians 1:24

A far-fetched attempt has been made by Dr. Bullinger, in order to suit the exigencies of the "soul-sleep" theory, to make a third thing out of the "departing"* as though it meant "the coming of the Lord;" but this cannot be admitted, for then the alternative of ver. 24 would be ruled out, as the Philippians would be gone too. Though this "departing to be with Christ" would not involve the full blessing of resurrection glory, it would be "far better" than the deepest joys of communion the apostle had ever experienced. If we compare the teaching of 2 Cor. 5, we shall find this confirmed. The apostle knows he and all believers have awaiting them in heaven "a house not made with hands" to replace the present tabernacle of the body in which now he and they were groaning. This permanent spiritual body would be revealed at the coming of the Lord, and those thus clothed upon would never pass through the "unclothed" state and be "found naked." This is the condition of the man in the "intermediate state," and could never be normal, for man was created to inhabit a body. But so ardent was the desire of the apostle to be with Christ, that he was willing rather to face the abnormal unclothed state, that is, to be *"absent from the body"* in order to be "present with the Lord." It is clear that this cannot refer to resurrection, as then believers will be ***present with the body,*** as well as with the Lord.

---

*Dr. Jackson, O.M., Regius Professor of Greek at Cambridge, and Dr. Edwin A. Abbott, a world-wide authority on N. T. Greek, to whom I submitted a few years ago Dr. Bullinger's suggestion as to Phil. 1: 23, both ruled it out as inadmissible.

The assertion that, even if the soul survives, it is unconscious, because bereft of those bodily organs, brain, etc., on which man is dependent for perception or sensation of any kind, is further negatived by the teaching of 2 Cor. 12: 1-4. The apostle here narrates an experience he had had fourteen years before. He remembered vividly being caught up to the third heaven, and also it would seem on a separate occasion into Paradise, when he heard unspeakable words, "which it is not lawful for a man to utter." "Then," says the soul-sleepist, "he must have been in the body, otherwise he would neither have known or heard anything." Twice, however, the apostle assures us he did not know whether he was "in the body or out of the body," God only knew. Paul was clearly not a "soul-sleepist."

Consciousness Continues

To sum up, the intermediate state, far from being one of unconsciousness is one (1) of conscious existence (Luke 16: 26); (2) of immediate experience (Luke 23: 43); (3) of vivid experiences (Phil. 1: 23; Luke 16: 24); (4) of recognition and remembrance (Luke 16: 25); (5) of irrevocable destiny (Luke 16: 26).

SPIRITISM

Sometimes Misnamed Spiritualism

By Wm. C. Irvine

Warnings

The Scriptures fail not to warn those living in the last days that many shall abandon the faith, "giving heed to *seducing spirits and doctrines of demons* through the *hypocrisy of men* that speak lies" (1 Tim. 5: 1, 2, R.V.). These spirits are well described as "seducing spirits," for they first seek to gain the victim's confidence and then to undermine his or her faith in the Word of God. When tempting Christ, Satan quoted (rather, misquoted) Scripture, and so do modern mediums; but like Satan in the garden of Eden, they soon seek to cast doubt on the Word of God and to belittle its authority.

Could anything be clearer than the following Scriptures:—

> "And the soul that turneth after such as have familiar spirits, and after wizards, to go a-whoring after them, I will even set My face against that soul, and will cut him off from among his people. . . . A man also or woman that hath a familiar spirit, or that is a wizard, shall surely be put to death: they shall stone them with stones: their blood shall be upon them" (Lev. 20: 6, 27).

Growth of Spiritism

It was stated that in 1894 in North America alone Spiritism claimed 16,000,000 adherents, and that in the whole world there were 200 journals entirely devoted to its cause. Since the War, numbers caught in this awful delusion must have greatly increased. How far this cult has made inroads on Christian circles in the East we do not know; but we are saddened to see that a paper voicing Indian Christian interests, recently gave a somewhat favorable review of a book purporting to be a record of succession of private séances between a well-known scientist and his dead son.

Not all Trickery

Although much that passes for spirit manifestation is pure trickery, doubtless real communications are at times received from the spirit-world. Were it not so, Spiritism would have collapsed long ere this, but as Tennyson has said, "A lie which is half a truth is a harder matter to fight than a lie outright." Many grief-stricken souls in their agony have sought for comfort in the hope that Spiritism holds out to them, of getting access to their beloved dead through a medium; little realizing the dread danger they run through tampering with forbidden things. With a host of enlightened Christians we believe that what messages are received from the spirit-world are *not received from the souls of those who have passed through the veil, but from demons who impersonate them.*

The seeking after familiar spirits and the desire to get in touch with the dead is strongly and clearly forbidden by God in His Word:

Forbidden

"And when they shall say unto you, Seek unto them that have familiar spirits and unto wizards that peep and that mutter; should not a people seek unto their God? for the living to the dead? To the law and to the testimony: if they speak not according to this word, it is because there is no light in them" (Isa. 8:19, 20).

"*There shall not be found among you . . . a charmer, or a consulter with familiar spirits, or a wizard or a necromancer. For all that do these things are an abomination unto Jehovah.* . . . For these nations, which thou shalt possess, *hearkened* unto observers of times, and unto diviners; but as for thee, the Lord thy God hath not suffered thee so to do" (Deut. 18:10, 12, 14).

Do the leaders of Spiritism speak according to the Word?

In a standard work entitled *Spirit Teaching*, by an Oxford M.A., the personality of the Lord Jesus is denied (p. 250), the Bible account of the Fall of Man is a "legend and misleading" (p. 158), "future bliss" is not by faith in "notions of atonement and vicarious sacrifice" (p. 91), but by "merit that man lays up for himself by slow and laborious process" (p. 159). It denies resurrection, judgment to come and man's eternal destiny!

Dr. Wisse, a noted Spiritist, said:—

Anti-Christian

All testimony received from advanced spirits only shows that Christ was a *medium* or reformer in Judea; that He is now an advanced spirit in the sixth sphere; but that *He* never claimed to be God and does not at present! (See article *Unitarianism*, p. 193).

At a Spirit Conference held at Providence, Rhode Island, U. S. A., at which eighteen States were represented, the following pernicious resolutions were passed:—

1. To abandon all Christian ordinances and worship.
2. To discontinue all Sunday Schools.
3. To denounce sexual tyranny.
4. To affirm that animal food should not be used.

Let 1 Timothy 4: 1-3 be compared with the above last two clauses!

This anti-Christian character of Spiritism is witnessed to by other authenticated testimonies as well.

"Spiritualism," says (Rev.) Thomas Waugh, "is a deadly foe to Christianity, *and I have never known a Christian embrace it without becoming a backslider!* What Paul calls a 'communion of demons,' acquired at a table of demons, invariably drives from the communion of the Table of the Lord (1 Cor. 10: 21). Here is a remarkable testimony from a clerical advocate of Spiritualism as foremost as any. Recently in *Light* the Rev. Fielding-Ould, a London clergyman who has spoken on the platform of the National Spiritualist Alliance, and whose writings are recommended by Sir Conan Doyle, wrote thus:

No one has a right to call himself a Christian unless he believes in the Divinity of Jesus Christ. He may be a person of estimable character and greatly developed spiritually, but he is not a Christian. Take away the truth of our Lord's Divinity, on which the Church is erected, and the whole elaborate structure falls into ruins. *It is upon that rock the great vessel of modern Spiritualism is in imminent danger of being wrecked.* In the Spiritualist hymn-book the name of Jesus is deleted, *e.g.*, "Angels of Jesus" reads "angels of wisdom." *At their services His name is carefully omitted in the prayers,* and the motto of every man is, "Every man, his own priest and his own saviour." Christian spiritualists (!) who rejoice in many of the revelations of the séance, are alarmed. They are quite prepared to allow every man to make his own decision, but that the movement as a whole should be identified with Theism and that they themselves should be considered as having renounced their faith and hope in Jesus Christ, is intolerable. *Spiritism is utterly discredited and condemned if it can be shown that the communicating spirits are the authors responsible for the anti-Christian tendency.*

D. M. Panton, B.A., commenting upon the above, well says: "Mr. Fielding-Ould's language is that of a man who suddenly finds himself on the crater's edge of a live volcano." He then proceeds:*

Still more decisive is the testimony of an Oxford physician, Dr. C. Williams. He says:

I am writing this not from choice and with a feeling of pleasure, but quite against my natural inclination, and with a feeling which is most painful. For the subject of spiritualism is as distasteful to me, and fraught with such unpleasant and painful memories, that were it not for a stern sense of duty, I should never be essaying the task. What, then, is my reason for attempting it? My reason I may say at once, is this: *Spiritualism is, to my certain knowledge, such a deadly foe to the Christian religion* that unless it is promptly and effectually dealt with and its true nature shown—and this must necessarily be done by those who know it, intimately and from personal experience, by those who know all about it and not merely "something" of it—I feel sure that before long our erstwhile Christian England will see its churches and places of worship practically emptied and the halls of the deadly enemy of the Christian Faith crowded to the doors with those who not long ago were Christians. And I make this statement deliberately and advisedly, *for almost without exception everyone who becomes a spiritualist, sooner or later loses faith in the Christian Religion, nearly always gives it up altogether, and ultimately ends by becoming the bitter foe of that Faith which he formerly loved and esteemed.*

---

*In the *Bible League Quarterly*, Jan.-March, 1921. (The italics are ours except in the first sentence quoted.—*Ed.*)

A word of warning must now be sounded to those who are in danger of being captivated by this wile of the Devil.

Disastrous Results

We give three instances showing how Spiritism has affected its victims:—

1. The most remarkable case of mediumship I have met with was that of a young lady, who commenced with a little seemingly innocent table-turning at a children's party, and finished up by death in a mad-house. (*Reader Harris, K. C.*).

2. Writing of a lady of his acquaintance Mr. F. Swanson says:—

Up to the time that her husband came into contact with Spiritism, he was all that could be desired. When he took to Spiritism he came in touch with a certain Spiritist woman, who claimed affinity. The result was this, that the man cruelly deserted his wife, and left her to die, as she is dying today, of a broken heart. That man today is passing as a leading official of a Spiritist circle in England.

3. As a young man Mr. Reader Harris, K.C., went with his father to the house of Dr. Gully, a leading Spiritist in Malvern, where Mr. Home, the great Spiritist writer and lecturer, lay dying. He tells how they went to make Mr. Home's will:—

But found it impossible to proceed, because of the rapping of spirits and general turmoil among the furniture of the room. Demons were already there in all their power to claim their victim, who had long yielded to them!

Dr. Beattie Crozier, the eminent physician, says:—

Three of my friends, men of eminence who really believe in Spiritualism, have told me they have forbidden the very name of it in their homes, as if it were a thing accursed; because, by the "black magic" which is always a part of it, it so often leads to insanity and death. "But for the fearful, and unbelieving, and abominable, and murderers, and fornicators, and SORCERERS, and all liars, *their part shall be in the lake of fire and brimstone, which is the second death*" (Rev. 21:8).

In the Editorial of *The Christian* (London), March 1st, 1917, on *The Snare of Spiritualism* the writer well says:—

Triviality is the very hall-mark of spirit communications, and its most damning refutation. . . . That Spiritualism is beset with the gravest dangers, often resulting in moral degradation, madness and even death, its advocates admit.

We append two striking extracts, the first from an article by D. M. Panton culled from *Living Waters,* and the other from *The Life of Faith* by Dr. A. T. Schofield, the famous Harley Street Physician:—

Spiritism and the Blood

Spiritualism is a planned and determined overthrow of the Christian faith. Dr. A. C. Dixon says: "Do you believe in the atoning work of the Lord Jesus Christ for salvation? Do you believe that the atoning blood removes the guilt of sin from the sin-stained soul? *Ask the medium that.* I have been asking that question all over the world for forty years: if there is any Spiritualist under the stars who believes that the blood of Jesus Christ cleanses from all sin, and if I can find one who does, I am willing to apologize for all that I have said. *I have never met one yet."* And here is the answer of Sir A. Conan Doyle: "The whole doctrine of original sin, the Fall, the vicarious Atonement, the placation of the Almighty by blood—all this is abhorrent to me. *The spirit-guides do not insist upon these aspects of religion."* For the horror of what may happen now is but a faint shadow of that which is to come.

A. T. Schofield's Condemnation

By the lips of Sir A. C. Doyle it denies the foundations of the Christian faith. It also makes a gross parody of heaven, denies *in toto* the resurrection, either of Christ or man, and the judgment to come.

Its dangers are terrible, and are incurred by all who dabble with the cult. Professional mediums suffer terribly in body, mind and morals, and the vast majority are victims to vice or drink. All spiritist leaders have given warning of these dangers, but Mr. A. F. Sennet's disclosures are the most awful, and those he dare not print, certainly more so. Indeed, these and the worst horrors of Bolshevism are so akin that one cannot doubt their common origin from the pit. To say that such obscene and bestial devils, as possess their victims as truly today as by the Sea of Galilee, are in any sense human, is an intolerable libel on humanity. Indeed their existence proves the falseness of spiritism and the fact of evil spirits in the other world.

With regard to attempts at necromancy, there is as vet no scientific proof of any communications with the dead, in spite of the most determined efforts. Before Mr. F. W. H. Myers, the distinguished author of "St. Paul," died, he resolved to make necromancy an undoubted fact, and before he passed away wrote a long communication in a sealed envelope, and gave it to Sir Oliver Lodge, saying that after his death he would reveal the contents of the envelope, which could then be opened. Mrs. Verrall, the medium, after his death, received this communication as she thought from Mr. Myers, and it was sent to Sir Oliver Lodge, who then on December 13, 1904, sent a circular letter to the Council of the Society of Psychical Research, and in their presence and in their rooms the communication was read. Then the letter was opened, and its contents were found to be absolutely different, and the experiment proved a total failure. Not only so, but in 1910 the President of the S. P. R. declared that no message from Mr. Myers had as yet been proved authentic. Moreover, Myers himself had forgotten he ever was a member of the S. P. R.

In the same way these supposed deceased spirits will give long messages for the "departed spirits" of men who are yet alive, from the imaginary brother and sister of only sons, and indeed from any suggested myth. The whole atmosphere is steeped in fraud. The *modus operandi* of the major part of the spiritual phenomena is very imperfectly understood. A small minority are due to the incursion of spirits (non-human) from another world, but the majority are the result of collective hypnotism or telepathy and the marvels of unconscious mind.

The trance is simply a condition of auto-hypnosis by which the medium is enabled to read and reproduce the unconscious minds and memories of the medium. It is thus that most messages supposed to come from the next world really come from this. But enough has been said to show the character of the cult, and when we consider the utterances of its latest apostle, Sir A. C. Doyle, who declares that our blessed Lord was a superior sort of medium, and he only regrets that He often lost his tongue, our minds recoil from the blasphemy, and I think every Christian should make the firmest stand against any traffic with spiritism in the present day. The supposed messages from the dead are delusions and the whole is steeped in injustice and fraud.

When the true spiritual life is more deeply cultivated and better known, Christians will be better able to detect the false spirits of this dangerous modern cult.

SWEDENBORGIANISM

By Wm. Hoste, B.A.

Emanuel Swedenborg was the son of a Swedish Lutheran bishop and was born at Stockholm in 1688. He was early interested in religious questions, and was remarkable in many ways for his mechanical skill and knowledge of science, as then taught.

Swedenborg

His mind was of the poetical and speculative order, and it was in the midst of speculations on the human soul, with which he seems to have overtaxed his brain, that he was stricken down at the close of 1744 with fever and delirium; an illness which, it is charitable to suppose, affected his mind for the rest of his life. In the spring of 1745 came his life crisis. He had over-eaten himself one day, he tells us, when all around him things grew misty and the walls seemed covered with loathsome crawling creatures; next a man appeared to him, who afterwards declared himself to be "God, the Lord, the Creator and Redeemer of the world," or in other terms, the Lord Jesus Christ, and commissioned him to hold converse with the unseen world and record his experiences. The connection, on the face of it, seems strange—a surfeit of over-eating, a hallucination of disgusting reptiles, and then a revelation of the Lord Jesus Christ.

What simplifies our examination of Swedenborgianism is its claim to be, not a mere new sect or offshoot of Christianity, *but a new dispensation,* as distinct from Church Christianity as that was from Judaism. The old Church is affirmed to have come to its end in 1757 when, as some will be surprised to learn, the last judgment took place. Swedenborg says he was present; though why he was not judged himself does not appear clear. However, all this is opposed to Scripture and facts. The Lord promised that "the gates of hell

A New Dispensation

should not prevail" against His Church, and we know we have "received a kingdom that cannot be moved," and a succeeding dispensation of Christianity to the Church dispensation is a pure invention without foundation. Is it not too much to ask us to believe that there has been no true Church testimony on the earth since 1757, except that of a little handful of self-commended Swedenborgians?

If, however, a new dispensation did begin in 1757, might we not expect it to be marked by an increase of spirituality, holiness of conduct, submission to God's Word and separation from the world? None of these marks is apparent. Swedenborg's heaven reminds one of the heaven of the Spiritists—a replica of earth with spiritual cigars, whiskey, armchairs, debating societies, lending libraries and —the antipodes of the heaven of the Apocalypse, neither holy nor happy, but "earthy, sensual, devilish," for even the devils and the lost make raids into it. Swedenborg once saw "an execrable rabble in heaven."*

"Heavenly Love!"

But is the system marked by special holiness? The predominant subject in the teacher's mind was "conjugal love," which was indeed in his view "heavenly love in its highest form," and is according to him a great subject of interest and conversation among the angels.† In spite of our Lord's denial, they *do* "marry and are given in marriage" in heaven! There are passages in Swedenborg's writings so grossly indelicate, Dr. Pond assures us, that they ought never to have been translated. Swedenborg gives 55 cases in which a married man may judge himself free to be unfaithful to his marriage vows; and in certain cases he permits and even recommends flagrant immorality.‡

**Swedenborgianism Examined*, p. 91, to which I refer my readers for further information, and to which I acknowledge my indebtedness in preparing this article.

†*Arcana Celestia*, pp. 2735, 5053, and *Conjugal Love*, pp. 54, 64-65, 229, 367, 457 as quoted by Dr. Pond, p. 150.

‡*Swedenborgianism Examined*, pp. 163-167.

A Fanciful System

Is, then, Swedenborgianism subject to the Word of God? By his fanciful system of "correspondences" — which Swedenborgian writers* themselves being witness, no one can rightly interpret the Scriptures can be made to mean anything or nothing. One instance must suffice. The story of the 42 children destroyed by bears in 2 Kings 2: 24 is thus interpreted: "Elisha represented the Lord as the Word. Baldness signifies the Word, devoid of literal sense, thus not anything. Forty-two signifies blasphemy. And bears signify the literal sense of the word, real indeed but not understood."† I hope my readers are edified. To some such interpretations must appear as the ravings of a disordered mind. And why all this talk about the literal word, when Swedenborg rejected Ruth, Job, Chronicles, Nehemiah, Ezra, Esther, Proverbs, in the Old Testament, and all but the four Gospels and the Apocalypse in the New, only because these books could not be made to work out on the "correspondence" system. But, alas, a disordered heart beats behind a disordered mind! Swedenborg's antipathy to the doctrines of grace amounted almost to a monomania. He *never* ceased to travesty and vilify the doctrine of the Trinity, accusing his opponents of being tritheists: he replaced it by a Unitarianism which made the Lord Jesus Christ, the one God, substituting for the glorious Three in One, Father, Son and Spirit, a nominal Trinity, "essential divinity, divine humanity (*sic*), and a divine preceding" (see notes on pp. 160, 161). The Lord Jesus is not honored by such daring perversions of the truth, but profoundly dishonored. In fact what remains when the divinity of the Godhead has been destroyed?—not Jesus, the Son of God, but "another Jesus." In reality His Person is denied (1) in His essential Deity, for He could have no existence as the Eternal Son without the Father:‡ (2) in His true humanity, for the divinity took the place of the human spirit: and (3) in His intrinsic

---

**e.g.*, Mr. Tulk, see Swedenborgianism Examined, p. 65, footnote.

†*Apocalypse Revealed*, p. 573.

‡I am well aware Swedenborg strenuously denied the eternal Sonship of Christ.

holiness and sinlessness, by the blasphemous attribution to Him of "great moral impurities and imperfections." "We are therefore called upon to work in ourselves, in *our* human nature, the same kind of work which He wrought in His."*

Atonement not Vicarious

He was equally opposed to the atonement in any vicarious sense. To him it was *"a subjugation of the powers of evil,"* or, as one of his followers puts it, "the reconciliation of the human nature to the divine;" but Christ *bearing our sins and judgment,* shedding His blood to make atonement to God on account of sin, all this was anathema to Swedenborg, and is to his followers today. This antipathy to spiritual doctrine meant in his case a corresponding dislike to the most precious saints of all time who have been used of God to establish these truths, and whose memory is fragrant in the Church. He professed to see David and Paul, for instance, in the unseen world, *associated with the worst of devils;* from Luther and Calvin and other well-known servants of God he affirmed to have heard the most abject confession of hypocrisies and heresies; in the case of his own contemporaries, the Moravian brethren, devoted missionaries for the most part, many of whom had laid down their lives for Christ's gospel, and of whom the world was not worthy, he did not scruple to affirm that he saw them choosing hell, so great had been their hypocrisies. How far could Swedenborg adopt the language of the apostle: "We know that we have passed from death unto life, because we love the brethren?"

Separation Unnecessary

But, perhaps, the system has a high standard of devotion and separation from the world. Nothing could be further from the truth. It deprecates all such extremes. "They who renounce the world and live in the Spirit procure to themselves a sorrowful life, which is not receptible of heavenly joy."† Men must "live in the world" and enjoy "the concupiscences of the body and the flesh" (*sic*). Besides this,

---

*See *Swedenborgianism Examined,* p. 83.

†*Heaven and Hell,* p. 528.

Swedenborg recommends the following "diversions of charity," "the delights and pleasures of the bodily senses . . . convivialities, feasts, entertainments, and all kinds of merry-makings, games which are played at home with dice, billiards and cards."* Such morality might suit well some Mr. Facing-both-ways of Vanity Fair; one fails to recognize it as Christian ethics. Certainly if this be heavenly-mindedness, few need fail to attain the standard.

To accept this evil system, we are asked completely to revise our doctrinal and ethical standards, and to do so on the sole ground of Swedenborg's visions, backed up by no miracles or signs, and by no testimony but his own. They do not bear a moment's investigation from the astronomical or scientific standpoint, being full of absurd blunders and mis-statements of the science of the day. He did leave two tests, which he urged his adepts to follow up. He asserted that "the most ancient Word" written by Noah would be found among the inhabitants of Great Tartary, and that there exists in Central Africa an important branch of the New Church.† But neither the one nor the other has ever been proved to have any real existence. We may be sure that the master's visions of the heavens and the hells, and the accounts of his visits to the heavenly orbs have no higher claim to our consideration.

Unworthy of Credence

The question may be asked how such an unchristian system can ever have gained adherence or have persisted to the present day. I think the answer is plain. The system responds in a very marked way to three dominant factors in the natural heart of man: his love of the marvellous, his dislike for the doctrines of grace, and his craving for pleasure; especially when these are found combined in a religion of high pretensions under the imposing title of "The New Jerusalem descending out of Heaven from God."

[We received a letter from an official of The Swedenborg Society of India in which he says: "The delay is mainly due, however, to there being hardly a single statement in

---

**Charity*, p. 117.

†*Swedenborgianism Examined,* p. 199.

the article that can be allowed to pass unchallenged; indeed there are instances of single words (in quotations) even being refutable, as, for example, where 'proceeding' has been substituted for 'preceding' and 'conjugal' for 'conjugial' (the latter word having no reference to the carnal side of marriage, which, *like Mr. Hoste,* (his italics) the Sadducees of Christ's time had in mind; *conjugial* love is *spiritual,* and comes from a marriage of *minds*)."

Beyond general charges, these are the only definite "mistakes" pointed out. We sent the letter to Mr. Hoste, amongst other things he says: "As for his quibbles about misrepresentations and garbled quotations, *unless he lies,* he cannot bring any forward. Probably one or two misprints may have crept in, but what I am supposed to gain by substituting 'preceding' for 'proceeding' I do not quite see. There is no such word as 'conjugial' in Webster or, I believe, in the English language. Swedenborg's mind was full of the 'conjugal' question. He can't invent words and ask his critics to differentiate."—*Ed.*]

THEOSOPHY

By A. McD. Redwood

Theosophy is not a religion, but a revival of "Ancient Wisdom" which "lies behind all religions alike." Its own definition is:—

Genesis

An all-inclusive synthesis of truths, as it deals with God, the Universe, and Man and their relations to each other.

With such a self-appointed mission, this re-born baby of Man's inflated imagination comes to us for examination. Where did it come from? Who gave it birth? Just as Seventh-Day Adventism was inspired by Mrs. White, a neurotic woman, subject to cataleptic fits; and Christian Science by Mrs. Eddy of similar temperament; so Theosophy was cast upon a world already deluded, by "Madame Helena Petrova Blavatsky, a spiritualistic medium born at Ekaterinslow, South Russia, in 1831." We are informed by the *Modern English Biography* (F. Boase), that she married twice; the first husband, an old man nearly seventy, whom she deserted three months after marriage; and the second a young lad of sixteen years who went mad the day after marriage. She led a regular bohemian life and kept a gambling hell in Tiflis in 1863. Between 1848 and 1857 she professed to visit Tibet and there learnt the secret of the Mahatmas. In 1871 Madame Blavatsky set up a spiritualistic society in Cairo. There she got into trouble for tricking the public and fleecing them of their money by deception. She founded the Theosophical Society in 1875 and died in England in 1891. She wrote the book *Isis Unveiled,* and experts have declared that it is filled with plagiarisms and trickery. She had a violent temper, and was anything but attractive in appearance.* Such was the founder of Theo-

*A. J. Pollock in *Scripture Truth.*

sophy. Strange vessel indeed out of which we are invited to drink the clear waters of truth! "We cannot dissociate a system from its Founder"—not even Theosophy. Now contrast this with the Divine record of the Founder of Christianity--"Who did no sin, neither was guile found in His mouth" (1 Pet. 2: 22). "God anointed Jesus of Nazareth with the Holy Ghost and with power: who went about doing good, and healing all that were oppressed by the devil; for God was with Him" (Acts 10: 38). "Never man spake like this Man" (John 7: 46). And He could challenge the crowd—"Which of you convicteth Me of sin?" (John 8: 46). He could also declare with sublimity—"I am the Way, the Truth, and the Life." "In Him was Life, and the Life was the Light of men."

We next ask, What does this "All-inclusive Synthesis" teach us? Does it help us in our fight against sin? Does it give us hope for the future? Does it tell us of a Personal Saviour? Let us first put down some statements made by the leaders of this cult:—

Theosophy's Denials

1. The next matter impressed on the student is the denial of a personal God, and hence, as Madame Blavatsky has pointed out, Agnostics and Atheists more easily assimiliate Theosophic teachings than do believers in orthodox creeds (Mrs. Besant, in *Why I became a Theosophist*, pp. 26, 27).

2. We believe neither in vicarious atonement, nor in the possibility of the remission of the smallest sin by any god, not even by a personal Absolute or Infinite, if such a thing could have existence (*Key of Theosophy*, p. 135).

3. The Historic Christ, then, is a glorious Being belonging to the great spiritual hierarchy that guides the spiritual evolution of humanity, who used for some three years the human body of the disciple Jesus* (*Esoteric Christianity*, p. 140).

Now what does all this amount to?

1. Theosophy — this Expositor — this comprehensive Illuminator of Ineffable Truth, denies the existence of the very Fountain-head of all Truth!

Here is a piece of the "Ancient Wisdom"! Personally we prefer the unsophisticated doctrines of the Old Book,

*A Gnostic heresy—*Editor.*

which declare—"He that cometh to God must believe that HE IS." "I AM JEHOVAH and there is none else." "This is the TRUE GOD and Eternal Life."

2. Theosophy denies even the *possibility of forgiveness of sin.* Hence it is in direct conflict with the Word of the Living God "who cannot lie." And *that* first puts all men into one category—"All have sinned and come short of the glory of God," and then offers salvation to all—"If thou shalt confess with thy mouth Jesus as Lord, and shalt believe in thy heart that God raised Him from the dead, thou shalt be saved" (Rom. 10: 8-10, R. V.). We prefer to believe God, and let Theosophy be the liar!

3. Theosophy teaches us that Christ was not any higher than an angel, that He is engaged in "evolving" humanity (whatever that may mean to the All-Wise), and that He was impersonated by a human disciple named Jesus! Leaving that nonsense and turning to the Sacred Word, we read the sublime and dignified words of John 1: 1-14: "In the beginning was the Word," etc.

We could go on, but sufficient has been said to indicate the utter variance between this self-styled Illuminator, and the Word of Almighty God. It has no foundation to build on. But having taken away our foundation, what has this system? Having denied the Creator Lord, and reduced His truth to the level of its own puerile speculations, what does it give us in their stead? It claims to have a "gospel for the weary world." We are informed that "Theosophy is a doctrine of common-sense." Let us examine these claims.

There are three primary "doctrines" that are put forward as their "gospel." These embody evidently all the "common-sense" the system is capable of, so we are on the tip-toe of expectancy! What are they?

Reincarnation

1. First there is the theory of *Reincarnation.* This is a "pivotal truth." It means, "We live on the earth not once, but many times." What proof is there that such is the case? Let Mrs. Besant answer:—

> The only proof of this doctrine . . . must in the nature of things, lie for us in the future, if it exists at all (*Why I became a Theosophist*).

Mrs. Besant must be very easily satisfied! Personally we want *proof*. And could proof be forthcoming, we would want to know, What good does this doctrine do us? Does it make men better? Does it relieve the world's sorrow and sin? The answer is, No. The truth is, that it is nothing but an incoherent collection of puerilities, based upon imagination, without proofs, without any material or spiritual value. As a writer has said, we prefer to believe in the Bible doctrine of Resurrection, which rests first on the historical facts, and on Divine Revelation—giving us the glorious hope of a glorious future.

2. The next thing they offer us is the dogma known as *Karma*. It is "the twin principle of Reincarnation." What does Mrs. Besant say of it?

Karma

Even among Theosophists belief in Karma is more an intellectual assent than a living fruitful conviction (*Karma*).

A recent writer has said concerning it: "It opens the door to superstition, and exalts crude fancies to the dignity of a philosophy." Here again there is neither proof nor value. Even amongst themselves it is a *theory*, without any "fruitful conviction." In these days we want to be able to say, "We know," or else it is valueless practically. The Word of God declares in opposition, *"The wages of sin is death, but the gift of God is eternal life."* Here is a divine, living, authoritative declaration—as simple for the simple as it is profound for the profound thinker.

3. The third thing is the *Mahatmas* (*lit.*, "Great Souls"). These are supposed to be exalted beings in whom are summed up the accumulated knowledge of all the past. Let us suppose for a moment that such masters do exist somewhere. What about them? Does their knowledge help us in this life? Let us see.* Koot Homi, who with Master Morya, founded the Theosophical Society, and led Mr. Sinnet into the occult mysteries, revealing to him the outline contained in his *Esoteric Buddhism*, was one of these Mahatmas. He evidently

Mahatmas

**Theosophy, its Theories v. Bible Truth*, Geo. Aldridge.

helped Mr. Sinnet also to write *The Occult World*, in which there is a letter from him. This letter (and book) was read by a Mr. Kiddle, an American Spiritualist, who found to his astonishment that it contained lengthy extracts, *without acknowledgment, from a speech which he himself delivered a year before the book was published!* Mr. Kiddle "wondered that so great a sage as Koot Homi should need to borrow anything from so humble a student of spiritual things as myself!" Here's a fly in the ointment! We say very politely: If that is a sample of your sage's knowledge, we prefer to remain very ignorant; for where "ignorance is bliss, 'tis folly to be wise."

Mrs. Besant tells us:—

> Unless it is true that the soul of man comes back life after life to earth . . . then, indeed, the Mahatma would be an impossibility. . . . Reincarnation is taken for granted in the whole of this teaching ("*The Masters*").

And so we may go on piling up theory upon theory, like building castles in the air. In spiritual matters, however, the issues are so great, so awful, we dare not take anything *for granted.* This is poor stuff to give us indeed for the wholesome truths founded on God's Everlasting Word, which the Theosophist would ask us to deny.

There is one more belief the Theosophist has come to hold within recent years, and that is the advent of a World Teacher.

For many years now the Order of the Star in the East has given more or less publicity to this new idea. We do not propose to go into the matter except to state that this supposed World Teacher is identified with a young Hindu named Krishnamurthi, who was trained at Oxford. Mrs. Besant and Mr. Leadbeater of the Theosophical Society of India have been the principal promoters of this "Krishnamurthi cult." He has been heralded as the Messiah, and active centres of propaganda have been created in Australia, Adyar (India), and other countries.*

Krishnamurthi

*Since this was written it has become evident to all, including Krishnamurthi, that he is not fitted for this role.– *Editor.*

In an article in the *Sunday School Times* (of Philadelphia) for March 13th, 1926, there appeared a brief statement by Dr. E. Stanley Jones, a widely-known Methodist Missionary in India, in which he says concerning Krishnamurthi:—

He has received divine honors in India and in the West. I had a long interview with him, found him of average intelligence, of rather lovable disposition, of mediocre spiritual intuitions, and heard him swear in good, round English! I came away feeling that if he is all we, as a race, have to look to in order to get out of the muddle we are in, then God pity us.*

Can a Christian be a Theosophist? Mrs. Besant says, YES:—

Christian Theosophists?

No man in becoming a Theosophist, need cease to be a Christian, a Buddhist, a Hindu; he will but acquire a deeper insight into his own faith.

The Bible says, No:—

What communion hath light with darkness? What concord hath Christ with Belial? Or what part hath he that believeth with an infidel? And what agreement hath the temple of God with idols? For ye are the temple of the Living God. . . . Wherefore come out from among them and be ye separate, saith Jehovah, and touch not the unclean thing (2 Cor. 6:14-18).

We append this choice clipping from the writings of Dr. W. Graham Scroggie:—

Theosophy

Christianity is the final religion. Christ Himself is God's last word. The Theosophists are looking for a greater, but we know from the New Testament that a greater need not be expected. The Christ has come. I speak quite reverently when I say that God has exhausted His vocabulary. He has spoken His last word. If there is any hope for the world, it is to be found in Christ. If it cannot be found in Christ, it cannot be found at all.

---

*This statement is taken from Dr. Stanley Jones' book, *The Christ of the Indian Road.* Krishnamurthi has since resigned the honor of aping the Messiah. We wonder what must be the feelings of those who worshipped this self-dethroned tin god.

UNITARIANISM

By Wm. C. Irvine

In the city of Poona many years ago, a friend attended services held in two places of worship, one in the morning and the other at night. In the one he was assured from the pulpit that he was living in the "Great Tribulation" and in the other that he was now in the Millennium! The latter speaker may now see his mistake, probably the former is more convinced than ever that his view is right—of course both were wrong. Today one might enter a church in the morning and hear the Deity of Christ denied or questioned, and in the evening from another pulpit be assured, from a disciple of the New Theology School that *man* is Divine!

Christ's Deity Denied

This foundation truth—the Deity of Christ—is assailed from almost every point of view. We have the *frontal* attack by those known as Unitarians: the *flank* attack by Russellites: and the still more dangerous tactics of that far-famed *sapper and miner corps—the Higher Critics.* The first deny that Christ is God: the second declare that whilst on earth our Lord was nothing more than a "perfect human being," and the last assure us that He laid aside His Godhead, and was therefore as unreliable as His fellow-Jews of the first century.

Unitarians teach to worship Christ is idolatry, and so it is *if* Christ be not God: the followers of "Pastor Russell" accept as gospel truth their "Pastor's" exposition as found in his book, *The Divine Plan of the Ages,* in which it is asserted that, "It was not until the time of His consecration, even unto death as typified in baptism at thirty years of age, that he received the earnest of his inheritance of the divine nature:" and the "Higher Critics," to evade the evidence Christ gave to the authority of the Old Testament Scriptures, conceived the blasphemous *Kenosis* theory, the deadliness of which is well illustrated in the following blunt assertion by one of their number:

> The objection is raised that Jesus and the apostles clearly considered these accounts to be fact and not poetry. Suppose they did; the men of the New Testament are not presumed to have been exceptional men in such matters, but shared the point of view of their time (Prof. Gunkel's *Legends of Genesis*, p. 3).

Nor must it be imagined that this fundamental doctrine is attacked only by those mentioned; many others might be cited.

Attitude to Deity

The Deity of Christ, if discredited, causes the collapse of Christianity, for, as someone has truly said, "Christianity is Christ"—this Satan well knows. Concerning the doctrine touching the Person of our Lord, the "beloved disciple" warns us in his second epistle, in the following solemn words: "He that abideth in the doctrine of Christ, he hath both the Father and the Son. If there come any unto you, and bring not this doctrine, receive him not into your house, neither bid him god-speed: for he that biddeth him god-speed is partaker of his evil deeds." That there would be many in the last days of the Church's history who would thus deny their Lord is clearly foretold by the Apostle Peter in his second epistle, "But there were false prophets among the people, even as there shall be false teachers among you, who privily shall bring in damnable heresies, even denying the Lord that bought them, and bring upon themselves swift destruction, and many shall follow their pernicious ways; by reason of whom the way of truth shall be evil spoken of." Hence in our day it is incumbent on every faithful servant of Christ to be alive to the danger that threatens; to warn his fellow-Christians, and to rebuke those teaching false doctrine concerning our Lord's Person. This entails bearing the cross, for nominal and half-hearted Christians, who desire to walk in the smile of the world, are never tired of calling all such "uncharitable," "narrow-minded," "heresy-hunters," etc.

Some evil doctrines are dangerous because they deceive us into imagining ourselves to be saved when we are still in our sins, *e.g.*, Baptismal Regeneration: others are dangerous because they take us off our guard and leave us exposed to the wiles of the devil, *e.g.*, Eradication: others because they bring us into a wrong relationship, *e.g.*, the Universal Brotherhood of Man: others because they lead us to question the inspiration of the Scriptures, *e.g.*, Higher Criticism: but the one we are dealing with undermines the *very foundations* of Christianity, presenting us with a shell without a kernel, a body without life, and a religion without a Saviour.

Christ's Claim

It is sometimes stated that Christ never claimed Deity for Himself. We were confronted with this astounding statement some time ago when travelling in the train. Nothing is simpler than to prove the falsity of such a question. Could anything be plainer than His words:—

"My Father worketh until now, and I work" (John 5: 17). The Jews understood by this that He made Himself equal with God, ver. 18, and Christ did not deny it. He justified it, vers. 19, 20.

"Say ye of Him whom the Father hath sanctified, and sent into the world, Thou blasphemest; because I said, I am the Son of God?" (John 10: 36).

"Before Abraham was I AM" (John 8: 58). Note the results of this assertion and the Jews' charge when before Pilate (John 19: 7).

"I and the Father are one" (John 10: 30). Again note the attitude of the Jews on hearing this.

But, as Dr. Dale has pointed out, such texts are by no means the most impressive proof we have of Christ's Deity. He compares proof-texts to salt-crystals cast up by the sea and left upon the shore. "These are not," says he, "the strongest, though they may be the most apparent proofs that the sea is salt; the salt is present in solution in *every bucket of sea-water*." So indeed it is with the doctrine of the Deity of Christ, everywhere throughout the sacred pages may it be found in solution. In both the Old and New Testaments Divine titles, perfections and attributes are ascribed to the Christ: He Himself, not only as seen above, asserts His Deity, but exercises the chief prerogative of God, in forgiving sins, accepts and approves of human worship, and asserts His omniscience, omnipresence and omnipotence.

"I am Alpha and Omega . . . saith the Lord, . . . the Almighty" (Rev. 1: 8).

But not only do Unitarians (and of course others also) go astray on the doctrine of the Deity of Christ, they are grievously in error on the fundamental doctrine of the Trinity.

Doctrine of the Trinity

The Unitarians declare that the doctrine of the Trinity proclaims three Gods, and not One. There is only one Uni-personal God, they say, and He is not Christ, nor the Holy Spirit. Hence Christ is in no sense an object of worship. They are the lineal descendants of the Arians of old, though they are also sometimes called Socinians.

In all this, of course, they stand condemned by the Scriptures, which are the sole authority and source of this doctrine. Only a few points can be stated here.

At the outset it should be clearly understood that whilst this is a *doctrine of revelation* alone, it is arrived at by *induction* from the totality of Scripture evidence, and not stated in so many words. The word "trinity" does not occur in Scripture, and yet the *doctrine* of the Trinity is clearly witnessed to. But no finite mind can ever comprehend fully the mystery of the Godhead. It is not a subject for intellectual speculation or theorizing; it is to be accepted on the evidence of the Word and acted upon. Scripture assumes by its whole language and the existence of one God, manifested in three Persons, a Trinity in Unity. How this can be is to us impossible to understand, but the fact remains: "Hear, O Israel: Jehovah our God is one Jehovah" (Deut. 6: 4; Mark 12: 29). Nothing could be plainer than that. At the same time, we see evidence for *three Persons* in the Godhead: the Father, the Son and the Holy Spirit. In the words of the late Bishop of Durham: "Each has His nature, the entire Divine nature, which is quality not quantity: Each is truly God. Each is necessarily and eternally one in Being with the Others: there are not three Gods. Each is not the Others: there are three Persons." In proof of this we get such texts as 2 Cor. 13: 14; 1 Cor. 12: 4-6; 1 Pet. 1: 2;

Rev. 1: 4, 5; and finally the "cardinal text," as Professor Orr calls it, "Baptizing them in *the name* of the Father, and of the Son, and of the Holy Ghost." Here we have *one name,* not three names.

In the Old Testament there is at least the suggestion of the Trinity in Unity: (1) in the plural noun *Elohim,* God, which is always used with a *singular* verb; (2) again in a large range of passages a Being appears whose character is at once that of Messenger and Master, Angel of Jehovah and Jehovah. See, *e.g.*, Gen. 16: 10; 22: 12; 31: 11-13; Num. 22: 32; Josh. 5: 13; 6: 2; Isa. 3: 9; Mal. 3: 1. "Such passages at least adumbrate the truth that the divine Unity is not such as to exclude inner Relation" (*Moule*).

IF:—Christ's Deity Seven Times Questioned and Seven Times Affirmed.

1. *The IF of Satan*:—"IF Thou art the Son of God command that these stones be made bread" (Matt. 4: 3).

Deity Affirmed

God's Testimony:—This *is* My beloved Son, in whom I am well pleased" (Matt. 3: 17).

2. *The IF of the Jews*:—"IF Thou be the Christ, tell us plainly" (John 10: 24).

Christ's Testimony:—"*I am* the Son of God" (John 10: 36).

3. *The IF of the passers-by*:—"IF Thou be the Son of God, come down from the cross" (Matt. 27: 40).

The Centurion's Testimony:—"Truly this *was* the Son of God" (Matt. 27: 54).

4. *The IF of the Chief Priests*:—"IF He be the King of Israel, let Him now come down from the cross and we will believe Him" (Matt. 27: 42).

Nathanael's Testimony:—"Thou *art* the Son of God; Thou *art* the King of Israel" (John 1: 16).

5. *The IF of the Rulers*:—"Let Him save Himselt IF He be the Christ, the chosen of God" (Luke 23: 35).

Peter's Testimony:—"Thou *art* the Son of the living God" (Matt. 16: 16).

6. *The IF of the soldiers*:—"IF Thou be the King of the Jews, save Thyself" (Luke 23: 37).

Pilate's Testimony:—"This *is* the King of the Jews" (Luke 23: 38).

7. *The IF of the malefactor*:—"IF Thou be the Christ save Thyself and us" (Luke 23: 39).

The other malefactor's Testimony:—"Dost not thou fear GOD, seeing thou art in the same condemnation?" (Luke 23: 40).

The Gospel IF

"IF thou shalt confess with thy mouth Jesus as LORD, and shalt believe in thy heart that God hath raised Him from the dead, thou shalt be SAVED" (Rom. 10: 9, R.V.).

"THE UNITY SCHOOL OF CHRISTIANITY"

By H. A. Ironside, Litt. D.

The test of any system is its teaching as to Christ. If wrong as to Him, we may be sure the entire body of doctrine is unscriptural. When this standard of judgment is applied to what is known as "The Unity School of Christianity," fostered originally by Mr. and Mrs. Charles Fillmore, and now advocated by many thousands of health and prosperity seekers, it proves to be as truly opposed to real Biblical Christianity as any heresy referred to in this volume. To the Unity people the true Christ of God is unknown. According to them, Jesus was a man of unusual spiritual insight and abandonment to the will of God. The Christ is the cosmic spirit of the Universe, the Deity, which abode in Him and dwells in every man, and even in every creature. The Christ is in fact the universal life. The system is thoroughly pantheistic.

They teach that the term "Unity" refers, not as naturally might be supposed, to the unity of the Godhead, but to the unity of all life with the one life, the divine. Jesus apprehended this in the fullest sense, hence He could say, "I and My Father are One." Every enlightened person can say the same. Jesus was a son of God in the same sense that all are sons of God: the divine was within Him as in all of us.

Unlike Eddyism, or so-called Christian Science, with which it practically agrees as to Christ, the Unity School admits the reality of the body and its ills, but insists that the recognition of one's own deity gives deliverance from sickness, infirmity and distress of every kind. Testimonials are adduced in abundance, of sick people who became well through constant insistence on their own deity, of those who for years struggled with poverty, who became wealthy because of their recognition of their invincibility as divinely able to do all things through the recognition of this inward being, and so to conquer opposing forces.

Unity uses Biblical terms with unbiblical meaning and hence is likely to deceive the very elect. It speaks of sin, redemption and atonement, but none of these words mean to the adherents of this school what they meant to the inspired writers of the Holy Scriptures. According to "Unity," sin is ignorance. Redemption is accomplished by the recognition of one's own divinity. Atonement is the result of this—the at-one-ness with God that enables a man to say, "I am that I am. I am infinite love, infinite power, infinite goodness. I deny all evil and all that makes for poverty and illness or other evils."

The devotees are taught to repeat over and over certain formulas such as, "I am that I am. I am Spirit. I am Life. I am the Christ. I know no evil. I deny all sin and sickness. I have all power. I am God manifest in the flesh." The constant reiteration of these blasphemies until they become an obsession gives a sense of superiority to the ordinary ills that flesh is heir to which makes for cheerfulness and peace of mind—albeit a false peace—that enables one to triumph to a great extent over an inferiority complex or a depressed state of mind, which is readily mistaken for miraculous or divine healing.

But, needless to say, all this is the very antithesis to the scriptural teaching which insists that there can be no unity between a holy God and sinful men till regeneration and justification by grace. And even then the saved man does not become part of God, but is a partaker of the divine nature imparted only when he believes the gospel, so that he becomes a child of God by a second birth and a son of God by faith in Christ Jesus.

A more careful examination of the Unity cult shows it to be a conglomeration of ancient errors presented to modern seekers after truth as a new and attractive discovery. In addition to its gnostic ideas as to Christ and Jesus, it is theosophical in that it teaches the Hindu doctrine of reincarnation. Through many earth lives the soul is supposed to be struggling upward to attain eternal rest. How different this is to the glorious truth of the gospel that through the one offering of our Lord Jesus Christ the believer is justified from all things and perfected forever in the sight of God because "He hath made us accepted in the Beloved." Contrast with this the frank statement of the author of a little tract sent out from the Unity headquarters, entitled, "The Origin and Growth of the Unity Movement:" "Unity has been called Theosophy because it admits the necessity of reincarnation to the end that every soul may have opportunity to overcome its weaknesses and finally attain the Christ standard for man."

This is a complete denial of the gospel of the grace of God. It is salvation by enlightenment and by human merit, and leaves no place for the true propitiatory work of our Lord Jesus Christ.

APPENDICES

I. Inspiration, the False and the True.

II. What Should be the Attitude of Christian Missionaries towards other Religions?

III. Credulity of Unbelief Concerning the Inspiration of the Scriptures.

IV. How to be Saved.

APPENDIX I

INSPIRATION, THE FALSE AND THE TRUE

By W. E. Vine, M.A.

There are some who consider that the term "inspiration" as applied to Scripture is to be understood in the same way as in its ordinary application to any human genius. In other words, that Isaiah, Jeremiah and the Apostle Paul, for instance, were inspired just as any great secular writers were inspired. According to this view the inspiration claimed by, and exhibited in, the Scriptures is nothing more than the lofty elevation of mind which produces the work of any outstanding literature such as Shakespeare, Macaulay or Carlyle.

Now in the first place the term "inspiration" is nowhere in Scripture applied to the writers of its contents. Inspiration is predicated of the Scriptures themselves. The actual term which the Apostle Paul uses to declare the fact is *theopneustos,* which signifies "God-breathed" (2 Tim. 3: 16).

The absence, then, of any statement that the writers were inspired, precludes any appeal to Scripture as the basis of a comparison between them and other authors in this respect.

We will next consider what is said of the men who wrote, and whether this affords a justification of the comparison. The Apostle Peter states that, "No prophecy of Scripture is of private interpretation (the word rendered 'prophecy' does not denote prediction of future events, it signifies the telling forth of the mind of God, and applies, therefore, to all that which constitutes the Word of God), for no prophecy ever came by the will of man: but holy men spake from God, being moved (lit. 'borne along'), by the Holy Ghost" (2 Peter 1: 21). Obviously, upon this testimony, an absolute distinction must be maintained between such writers and mere human geniuses; such statements could not be predicated of the latter.

But the question still remains whether the evidences of the writings of Scripture themselves forbid the comparison. It is a simple matter to put this to the test.

A very large proportion of the Bible is, for instance, prefaced in one place or another by "Thus saith the Lord," "Hear the word of the Lord," and similar phrases, and the contents which follow vindicate the validity of the declaration. Jeremiah alone says nearly a hundred times, "The Word of the Lord came unto me." Some sixty times Ezekiel says his writings are "the words of God." In the small compass of the four brief chapters of the last book of the Old Testament, "Thus saith the Lord," occurs twenty-four times. More than 2,000 times in one way or another the Scriptures declare that they are the Word of God. Scores of other similar testimonies might be enumerated from the writers of the sacred volume. Isaiah says, *e.g.*, in reference to his message, "The Word of our God shall stand for ever" (Isa. 40: 8). Jeremiah says, "Is not My Word as fire? saith the Lord; and like a hammer that breaketh the rock in pieces?" (Jer. 23: 29). Which of the greatest writers of secular literature could have attached a "Thus saith the Lord" to their subject-matter? And in the realm of religious literature, if the greatest theologian had ventured to make such a declaration, it would have discredited the value of his writings in the eyes of his readers.

The authority displayed by the writers of Scripture is unique. The Apostle Paul after declaring the impossibility for the subjects of Divine revelation to be discoverable by natural powers, and the necessity for the operation of the Spirit of God in making them known, says "Which things also we speak, not in the words which man's wisdom teacheth, but which the Holy Spirit teacheth" (1 Cor. 2: 13). So that the apostle's writings are not merely an expression of his views, they consist of "words which the Spirit teacheth." They come, therefore, with the same Divine authority as the words of Christ Himself. And this is a fulfilment of the promise given by Christ to His disciples, "Howbeit, when He, the Spirit of truth, is come, He shall guide you into all the truth: for He shall not speak from Himself; but what things soever He shall hear, these shall He speak" (John 16: 13).

The inspiration of a human genius is simply a natural qualification. The writers of Scripture were endued with the power of God, the Spirit of God so acting that while the intelligent faculties and the character and dispositions of the writers were brought into co-operation, imparting their individual style to their writings, yet the words they used, though in a sense their own, were all God-breathed. Their language was thus fitted by Him for His own purposes. The personality of the writers was not indeed eliminated nor was the individual consciousness suspended, but all was under the control of the Holy Spirit.

Again, the inspiration of Scripture is to be distinguished from the use of the word as representing the illumination spiritually enjoyed by Christians. The Spirit of God is indeed the possession of all believers, though not all believers live so as to be Spirit-filled. There are also diversities of gifts, ministered by the Spirit (1 Cor. 12: 4-11), but this is not the same thing as inspiration in the sense of the apostle's statement that all Scripture is God-breathed. The injunctions even of the holiest men have not the same authority as those of Scripture. The former are neither given by revelation, nor are they imparted by words communicated by the Spirit. Whatever has been uttered by men of God since the completion of the Scriptures, has possessed authority only as it has been in conformity with the Scriptures themselves. No person or church has any right to claim any such authority as attaches to the Word of God. The God-breathed character of the writings of the Bible belongs to these writings alone, and in no other sense can the term "inspiration" be applied to them.

When we speak of a person having had a sudden inspiration we merely mean that the idea which has given rise to his utterance or action was exceptionally brilliant and useful. Its efficiency lay within the compass of the man's natural ability, and while such ability is the gift of the Creator, the utterances themselves could not be said to be God-breathed.

Since it is the Scriptures themselves that are God-breathed, inspiration, in that sense of the term, attaches to the very form of the statements that were given by God. In the communications of the thoughts of God the phraseology employed cannot be divorced from the sentiments expressed. With the Lord and His apostles the one court of appeal was what is written in the Scripture. Take, for instance, the first recorded utterance of the Lord in reference to it. He meets the attack of His adversary by a thrice repeated "It is written," each time quoting from the book of Deuteronomy (Matt. 4: 4, 7, 10). Both Christ and the Tempter regarded the declarations of Scripture as providing an irrefutable reply to any challenge or suggestion. There was no question on the part of either of an appeal from that authority.

The unique and God-breathed character of the inspiration of the Bible is indicated in the effect of its teachings upon the lives of those who have found life in Christ through its instrumentality, on the ground of the atoning work of His cross to which it testifies. As Professor Orr says: "The simple fact that in this sacred Volume, so marvellous in its own structure, so harmonious and complete in the view it gives of the dealings of God with man, so rich and exhaustless in its spiritual content, so filled with the manifest presence and power of the Spirit of God, we have everything we need to acquaint us fully with the mind and will of God for our salvation, and to supply us for all the ends of our spiritual life, is sufficient evidence that the revelation which God has given is, in every essential particular, purely and faithfully embodied in it. No more than the revelation from which it springs, is the Bible a product of mere human wisdom; it has God for its inspiring source! . . . The crucial expression is—Do the qualities which inspiration is expressly declared to confer on Scripture—*e.g.*, in such a classical passage as 2 Tim. 3: 15-17—really belong to it? We think it will be difficult for any candid mind to deny that they do. Who, coming to this sacred Book, with a sincere desire to know God's will for the direction of his life, will say that he cannot find it? Who, desiring to be instructed in the way of salvation 'through faith which is in Christ Jesus,' will consult its pages, and say it is not made plain to him? Who, coming to it for the equipment of his spiritual life, will say that there are still needs of that life which are left unprovided for? Who, seeking direction in the way of the life everlasting, can doubt that, if he faithfully obeys its teaching, he will reach that goal? The Scripture fulfils the ends for which it was given: no higher proof of its inspiration can be demanded."

APPENDIX II

WHAT SHOULD BE THE ATTITUDE OF CHRISTIAN MISSIONARIES TOWARDS OTHER RELIGIONS?

By Wm. Hoste, B.A.

We have been told lately this should be that of "*reverence towards all religions*, and the fullest sympathy with all the striving of the human heart toward the Unknown"* (my italics). But is there not some confusion here, between sympathy for our fellow-men, who, like ourselves, need forgiveness, comfort and deliverance, and "reverence" for the false systems which bind them? The former we emulate, the latter we deprecate. The elder brother of Luke 15 was not expected to approve of his brother's past ways, but to feel for his sad condition and to rejoice at his return. It is happily true and in a degree of which we may have little conception, that, as Paul declared to the idolators of Lystra, "God has left not Himself without witness" to or with any of His creatures, by His works of creation, by His providential dealings with man, and by the workings of His Spirit; but in the same breath the apostle went on to urge them to "turn *from these vanities* (*i.e.*, the false worship) unto the living God" (Acts 14: 15). How unlike some today, who insist much on their "apostleship," but seem to think that it is a proof of broad-mindedness to non-Christians, to profess "reverence to their religions" and ask them to contribute something from thence to the Christian Faith. From what I gather from a friend who was thirty years a District Judge in Bengal, Hindus and Moslems are not favorably impressed by this sort of thing, which they in no way look for, and would regard rather as a betrayal *of their own cause* by missionaries who act thus, and a tacit admission of the weakness of their "religion."

**N. C. Council Review* (of India), Feb. 28th, 1928, p. 78.

Certainly the Christian missionary is no mere iconoclast; he proclaims "some better thing." His attitude is not one of attack, but of blessing, if he has drunk ever so little into the spirit of his Master, who wept over Jerusalem. It may be necessary sometimes, with the Word of God in our hand (*e.g.*, Ps. 115: 3-7; Isa. 44: 9-20), to testify to the sin and folly of idolatry, but it will be in no hard, scoffing spirit, but as faithful witnesses to the Living God. We are not to give unnecessary offence; respecting the feelings of our fellow-men. Surely this is all that Paul's oft-repeated words mean: "Unto the Jew I became as a Jew, that I might gain the Jews. . . . I am made all things to all men, that I might by all means save some" (1 Cor. 9: 22). This does not imply that he Judaized; there was no greater opponent to that than he. He knew that no amalgam was possible between a heavenly thing like Christianity and an earthly system like Judaism, that they were incompatibles. But how much less can Christianity fuse with Hinduism which, unlike Judaism, has no Divine sanction. Is not the difference between the Old Testament economy and a heathen system patent? The former was instituted by God and had in it "the shadow of good things to come;" for Christ, coming from God, who is Light, cast His shadow over the whole Old Testament. He was the substance of the shadows, the Antitype of the types, the fulfilment of the prophecies and of the promises; but how could this be true of Hinduism which does not profess to reveal Christ? Christ could not cast two shadows, one the Mosaic economy, sternly hostile to all idolatry, and another the polytheistic idolatrous system of Hinduism. No doubt it is possible to extract grains of moral truth from Tukaram and other Hindu poets, but this is seriously discounted by the immoral practices inculcated by these teachers as a means of communion with God;* moral maxims only dope the soul apart from truth and holiness. Our Lord did say of the Mosaic economy, "I am not come to destroy, but to fulfil," because, as He said: "Moses spake of Me;" but to argue from this that He undertakes to fulfil Hinduism, or any other

*"Unholy deeds we should commit, if they bring the possession of God." "They enjoyed the endless one by adultery." *Tukaram,* Bhakti saint of Dehu.

idolatrous system, shows a confusion of thought, and is indeed a travesty of the truth. How could He fulfil what is confessedly neither prophetic of Himself, nor in harmony with His Holy Spirit, and that which, like the philosophy of Tukaram, was centuries *after* Him.

The direct revelation of God in the Old Testament was enshrined in His oracles committed to the care of Israel (Rom. 11: 2). Although God was also dealing with the surrounding nations, it was rather through nature and conscience, than by direct revelation; and Israel was solemnly warned against having any fellowship with their idolatrous cults (Deut. 7: 5; 12: 3).

It is a favorite phrase with some today that such and such a convert came to Christ "by way of Confucius," or "Buddha," or "Tukaram," as though these "saviours" must be allowed their share in the credit of the conversion; but "God will not give His glory to another, or His praise to graven images" (Isa. 42: 8). Paul was a Pharisee before his conversion, but he did not come to Christ "by way of Phariseeism," but in spite of it; he "counted it loss for Christ;" it was a hindrance, rather than a help.*

It will help us to a right conclusion if we are quite clear as to the *origin* of idolatry. Was it the fruit of "the strivings of the human heart *toward* God"? On the contrary, it was the fruit of men refusing to retain God in their knowledge, "Because that when they knew God, they glorified Him not as God, neither were thankful, but became vain in their imaginations . . . and changed the glory of the incorruptible God into an image made like to corruptible man, and to birds, and fourfooted beasts and creeping things," and as a consequence "God gave them over to uncleanness . . . vile affections . . . and a reprobate mind" (Rom. 1: 21, 23, 28). And are such fruits associated any less with idolatrous systems today? At what moment of the world's history idolatry became prevalent we do not precisely know; it was probably after the Flood under the leadership of Nimrod, the prototype

---

*It must be noted that the writer refers to his "Phariseeism," *not* to his knowledge of the O. T. Scriptures.

of the various heads of idolatrous systems—Bel, Tammuz, Osiris, Bacchus, etc.* We know the ancestors of Israel served idols on the other side of the Flood (Josh. 24: 14), and when Israel sojourned in Egypt idolatry was rife, for "against all the gods of Egypt judgment was executed."

Israel was definitely warned, "Thou shalt have none other gods but Me. . . . Thou shalt not make to thyself any graven image, for I the Lord thy God am a jealous God." Perhaps King Solomon in his decline carried out more than most "a reverence for all religion;" he had a specimen of all the neighboring cults round his court, but it cost him the favor of God, and his son the major part of his kingdom. How utterly foreign to the Holy Scriptures is the idea that idolatrous systems have something to contribute to the truth of God!

Idolatry is in reality the deliberate attempt of Satan to usurp divine honors, and so far he is "the god of this world." This is exemplified in 2 Kings 1: 2, 3, when the king of Israel in his sickness sent to enquire of the god of Ekron, who was in fact Baalzebub himself (Matt. 12: 24-27). Did God recognize this cult as only another form of worship to Himself or as "a striving of the human heart after the Unknown?" On the contrary, He counted it as a direct denial of Himself and it called down His severe displeasure. This harmonizes perfectly with Paul's estimate of heathenism. "The things which the Gentiles sacrifice, they sacrifice to demons, and not to God, and I would not that ye should have fellowship with demons." Even at Athens the altar to "the unknown god" hardly proves that there was an element of truth in their religion, for it was distinct from it. They were "wholly given to idolatry," and Paul was grieved to see it. The Athenians professed to know Zeus, Athene, Ares, etc., for in them their religion consisted. But lest there might be some god whom they had overlooked, because unknown, and who might call them to account, they built one more altar to this hypothetical deity, and Paul with a human touch uses this incident as a starting point for his address, but none the less he argues strongly against all idolatry.

---

*See Hislop's *Two Babylons*.

The case of Cornelius is no less striking. A heathen by upbringing, he had given heed to the strivings of the Spirit and had seen the emptiness of idolatry. We do not read that God took note of his idolatrous zeal for Jupiter, etc., but of his prayers and alms, or in other words his fear of Him and His righteous way to men. So far he was accepted, and Peter was sent to preach Christ to him. He on his part showed his sincerity, not by haggling for some sort of recognition for his national creed, but by at once believing on the Lord Jesus Christ. What would Peter have thought had some professed Christian teachers arrived at Cæsarea deprecating his style of preaching as narrow and old-fashioned, and pleading for the recognition of Cornelius' previous heathenism? We may be sure he would have taken a firm stand against them.

In conclusion, we do not come to men of other creeds, Hindus, Moslems, Buddhists, seeking to impose upon them a "Western religion," but in the spirit of the apostle, "I have delivered unto you that which I also received, how that Christ died for our sins, that He was buried, and that He rose again the third day, according to the Scriptures." God sent us this gospel by missionaries from Asia, we have received Christ as our own Saviour, and now God has sent us back to Asia, with the same gospel; not on some aeroplane of fancied superiority, boasting of our civilization, inventions or national "bigness," but as humble pilgrims vending priceless pearls from celestial seas.

I entirely agree with Canon Western's quotation from Dr. Westcott* but suggest he has misread him: "Can we doubt that India, the living epitome of the races, the revolutions and the creeds of the East, is capable of adding some new element *to the complete apprehension of the faith?*" (my italics). The Canon quotes this to show that "Christianity does not claim either that it possesses the full truth, or that Hinduism and Islam have none," but does he not confuse Hinduism with India, and *"complete apprehension of the faith,"* with "the Faith?" The Holy Scriptures are the Truth (John 17: 17), and they speak of Him who is the Truth. They are "able to make wise unto salvation through faith

**N. C. Council Review,* Feb. 28, 1928, p. 80.

that is in Christ Jesus," and so to instruct in all things necessary for spiritual life and conduct, "that the man of God may be *perfect, thoroughly furnished* unto *all* good works." It is not possible therefore for Hinduism or any other Eastern or Western cult to add to the Christian faith, but we can look to Christian Indians so to preach and expound the Scriptures by the Holy Spirit as to "add some new element to the complete *apprehension of the faith.**

---

*See article on Freemasonry, which the writer believes, throws a sinister light on present-day movements. We specially draw our readers' attention to the last sentence of the above article.

APPENDIX III

CREDULITY OF UNBELIEF CONCERNING THE INSPIRATION OF THE SCRIPTURES

By Wm. C. Irvine

That there are some things hard to explain by those who believe in the plenary inspiration of the Scriptures, we are quite prepared to concede—at the same time any honest person must acknowledge that many of the difficulties of a generation ago have vanished, having been satisfactorily met by the spade and pick of the archæologist, and the research of the scientist and scholar.

But what about the difficulties of unbelief? They are far greater than those of belief! Let us just suggest a few. Those who question the inspiration of the Scriptures, rejecting the orthodox view, must explain:—

1. How it is that the Old Testament, one of the most ancient of books, is always marvellously accurate when it touches scientific questions; whereas all other books a hundred years old,* whenever touching such questions are full of glaring, and often foolish, mistakes.

2. How it is that of the Bible, and the Bible alone, it can truly be said: "It has . . . *truth without any mixture of error* for its matter" (*Locke*). How it is that no single virtue or standard of righteousness taught elsewhere eclipses that taught in the Scriptures.

3. How it is that no references to historical events, historical characters, ancient customs, geographical and astronomical records abounding in the Bible have been proved incorrect.

---

*"Theory succeeds theory so rapidly that apologizing to the British Association for not having his paper printed, one scientist said that 'anything printed is *ipso facto* out of date.'" —*Seeing the Future*, p. 81.

4. They must explain how Christ could be "in the beginning with God," one with the Father, and at the same time err in teaching and believing that the Scriptures were verbally inspired, as He most certainly did (Matt. 5: 18).

5. How it is that hundreds of its prophecies have been fulfilled to the letter, centuries after they were recorded. In this also the Bible is *unique.*

6. How it is that a book written by some 40 individuals whose writings ranged over about 1,600 years, could, when bound together, present *one unique whole,* whose unity of thoughts in doctrine and plan is evident to the most casual of readers, and is a matter of increasing wonder and admiration to the student. How it is that this unity has never been found in any other collection of literature. Contrast the Hindu Shastras.

7. How it is that writers such as Moses, David, Isaiah, John, Paul, Peter and many others, men of integrity and spiritual acumen, could claim that many of the words they used were God's words, and all were written by inspiration, if in truth they had written them themselves apart from the control of the Spirit. The former claim is made by the writers between 3,000 and 4,000 times.

8. How it is that fishermen and others were enabled to succeed in portraying a perfect character (in the four Gospels), which accomplishment so many talented writers have attempted, only to fail.

9. How it is that the Law given to Israel millenniums ago, worked successfully for centuries *without amendment or repeal* (Deut. 4: 2); and finally was used as a basis for British Law. During the reign of Victoria 650 Acts of Parliament were repealed, to say nothing of amendments!

10. Moreover they must explain how it is that God honors all the promises in His Word when conditions are fulfilled, and when presented by those to whom they have

been given. If they are not *His* promises, why does He honor them?

11. How it is that the words of Scripture have, in numerous cases, unaided by man's influence, completely transformed the reader, turning him from the ways of sin to a holy, clean and upright life. Has any other book done this?

12. How it is that its spiritual treasures are inexhaustible. Every year produces scores of volumes, thousands of sermons, and tens of thousands of articles—all of which seek to exploit the unsearchable riches of Christ, and the precious truths and teaching found in the Bible. Can this be said of any other book?

13. How it is that apart from the enlightenment of the Holy Spirit much of the contents of the Bible are hidden from the wisest.

14. How it is that the Scriptures are uniquely adaptable for translation into any tongue. All other books lose greatly by being translated and the value of many would be practically lost. There are over 800 tongues and dialects in which some portion of God's Word is now obtainable in print. Many of these add freshness and beauty to a multitude of passages.

APPENDIX IV

HOW TO BE SAVED

"For by grace are ye *saved* through *faith*: and that ***not*** of *yourselves*: it is the *gift* of *God*: *not of works* lest any man should boast" (Eph. 2: 8).

This passage of Scripture declares the utter inability of any other religion to save a man; for all except Christianity declare that salvation is *by good works, religious observances* and such like, which the man himself must do or observe, in order to be saved.

One of the grandest hymns ever written truly says:—

"Not the labor of my hands
Can fulfil Thy law's demands;
Could my zeal no respite know,
Could my tears for ever flow,
All for sin could not atone;
Thou must save, and Thou alone."

If then I cannot save myself, if I canot be saved by anything I can do, how *can* I be saved?

First, note, God says it is by *grace* we are saved. Until I take the position of a lost sinner, unworthy and undone, a proper subject for *grace,* there is no hope for my soul. When I humbly take that position, the *grace* of God which has supplied a Saviour steps in: the gracious words of the Lord Jesus fall on my ears—"Him that cometh unto Me I will in no wise cast out:" and God's gracious promise reaches me in all my sins—"Whosoever believeth on Him (the Lord Jesus Christ) shall not perish, but have everlasting life." Oh, the *grace* of God in giving His only Son! Oh, the *grace* of the Son of God, who "though He was rich, yet for our sakes . . . became poor, that we through His poverty might be made rich!" Truly, *"by grace* are ye saved."

But the Word of God says also, "Ye are saved through *faith.*" *Faith* is the hand that reaches out and takes salvation which is the *gift* of God. *Faith* is taking God at His word. *Faith* lays hold of God's promise and says, "I believe it."

And what does God's Word say about us? God's Word says—"All we like sheep have gone astray;" *faith* says, "That's true of *me*: I've wandered far from God." God's Word continues to say of us—"We have turned every one to his own way;" *faith* replies, "Alas, that is also true of *me!* God be merciful to me the sinner." It is *then* that God's Word meets us in our need and adds—"The LORD hath laid on HIM (Christ) the iniquity of us all;" hearing this good news *faith* cries out, "Praise be to God, that is also true. Christ Himself bare *my* sins in His own body on the tree, *my* sins though many are all atoned for. I believe it. I now accept Christ as *my* SAVIOUR, I'm saved by the *grace* of God through *faith.* Hallelujah!"

Dear reader, *salvation* is the *gift of God.* Delay no longer. Now as you read these lines, stretch out the hand of faith and grasp the gift of God, then humbly falling on your knees give thanks to God for His marvellous grace in saving a poor sinner like you.

"Upon a life I did not live,
Upon a death I did not die,
Another's life, Another's death,
I stake my whole eternity."